THE SANE SOCIETY IDEAL IN MODERN UTOPIANISM

Kerry S. Walters

Problems in Contemporary Philosophy
Volume 7

The Edwin Mellen Press
Lewiston/Queenston
Lampeter

Library of Congress Cataloging-in-Publication Data

Walters, Kerry S.
 The sane society ideal in modern utopianism.

 (Problems in contemporary philosophy ; v. 7)
  Bibliography: p.
 Includes index.
  1. Utopias. 2. Utopias in literature. 3. Ideology.
I. Title. II. Series.
HX806.W24 **1988**   335'.02   87-28126
ISBN 0-88946-331-X

This is volume 7 in the continuing series
Problems in Contemporary Philosophy
Volume 7 ISBN 0-88946-331-X
PCP Series ISBN 0-88946-325-5

The Edwin Mellen Press   The Edwin Mellen Press
Box 450   Box 67
Lewiston, New York   Queenston, Ontario
USA 14092   L0S 1L0 CANADA

Mellen House
Lampeter, Dyfed, Wales
UNITED KINGDOM SA48 7DY

Printed in the United States of America

For Fred

CONTENTS

We find your soft Utopias as white
As new-cut bread, and dull as life in cells,
O scribes who dare forget how wild we are,
How human breasts adore alarum bells.
You house us in a hive of prigs and saints
Communal, frugal, clean and chaste by law.
I'd rather brood in bloody Elsinore
Or be Lear's fool, straw-crowned amid the straw.
Promise us all our share in Agincourt
Say that our clerks shall venture scorns and death,
That future ant-hills will not be too good
For Henry Fifth, or Hotspur, or Macbeth.
Promise that through tomorrow's spirit-war
Man's deathless soul will hack and hew its way,
Each flaunting Caesar climbing to his fate
Scorning the utmost steps of yesterday.
Never a shallow jester any more!
Let not Jack Falstaff spill the ale in vain.
Let Touchstone set the fashions for the wise
And Ariel wreak his fancies through the rain.

Vachel Lindsay, *An Argument:*
The Voice of the Man Impatient
with Visions and Utopias

ACKNOWLEDGEMENTS

Many individuals have helped to make this study possible. I would like to express my sincere gratitude to John McEvoy, Harvey Mullane, Thomas Long and Leo Rauch for their careful (and sometimes merciless!) reviews of early drafts. Their contributions have made this a much better book than it otherwise would have been. Special thanks are also due to Tim Allen and Kenneth Ray, each of whom patiently allowed me to use them as sounding-boards upon which to sort out my ideas on the nature of utopianism and ideology in the modern era. My colleagues in the Philosophy Department at Gettysburg College, Chan Coulter and Lisa Portmess, have likewise generously provided me with support and inspiration. I would also like to render my thanks to Ike and June Phipps, Patt and Ronnie Wood and Kim Hayday for their contributions during the two years in which this book was written. A special debt of gratitude is owed to my philosophy students at Xavier University, the University of Cincinnati and Gettysburg College for the stimulating class discussions on the topic of utopianism in which they enthusiastically participated. Cathy Hancock and Joyce Sprague cheerfully and expertly typed various drafts of this work and in the process convinced me of how completely helpless we academics would be without departmental secretaries. Finally, I owe the greatest debt to Suzanne Seger, who not only helped me to express my ideas clearly, but also kept me from taking myself too seriously.

INTRODUCTION

> The history of ideas was the creation
> of an "idea-struck" age, which
> involuntarily re-interpreted the past
> in the light of its own central
> experiences.
>
> Karl Mannheim,
> Ideology and Utopia

I

This is a study of the birth and maturation of a modern ideological form: that of the "sane society." The notion was given its first systematic expression by Francis Bacon in the early seventeenth century, and came of age in the nineteenth century through the medium of the so-called "utopian" novel. The barbarisms produced by the present century--two world wars, recurrent international economic crises, the Nazi and Stalinist holocausts, ecological destruction and, of course, the nuclear bomb--have done much to shatter the earlier optimism surrounding the sane society exemplar. But it is still very much a part of the contemporary worldview, despite the fact that it is more moderate in tone. The concluding chapter of this work will argue, in fact, that a lingering emotional allegiance to the sane society prototype is itself largely responsible for the irrationalities that seem to permeate present day theoretical and socio-economic structures.

What is the "sane society" which serves as the main character of this study? Simply put, it is that putatively ideal vision of a society in which individual and collective dissent and economic irregularities have been eradicated by applying to social structures the same methods and experimental techniques which the physical sciences apply to the natural realm. The

underlying assumption is that human, social nature and nonhuman,
physical nature share identical characteristics and hence are
subordinate to, explicable by, the same set of natural laws.
Natural forces can be reduced to a set of rational laws and bent
to human will through an adequate scientific methodology.
Likewise, human   relations can be   translated   into purely
scientific, quantifiable terms, thereby rendering them equally
controllable. The sane society, then, is one which has carried
over its ideal of objective analysis and domination of natural
phenomena into the human realm.   It seeks to   reduce all
subjective elements in social structures to strictly quantifiable
relations.   The goal is to attain such technological and
managerial sophistication as to successfully eliminate crime,
scarcity and "irrational" dissent in society in the same way as
the physical sciences overcome nature's recalcitrant hold upon
minerals, energy sources, and foodstuffs.   Both types of
phenomena--the physical and the social alike--are reduced to
quantifiable analyses and hence "rational" control by virtue of
their possession of identical natures.

    What the sane society understands to be "rational" is,
primarily, that which is utility-laden.   As I shall argue in
later chapters, the ideal sane society has very little use for or
patience with what it takes to be merely "abstract" reason. It
is not concerned so much with the production of valid syllogisms
or airtight but inutile arguments as it is with what I have in
this study called "instrumental reason."   The latter is a
"scientific" method whose fundamental aim is the enrichment of
the mechanical sciences and, consequently, the domination of
nature and the control of man.

    It must not be supposed, however, that the champions of the
sane society vision were power-hungry groups of individuals who

valued physical and social domination only because it furthered
their own interests. The situation is far more complicated than
that. The proponents of a rationalized, sane society defended
their model because, as far as they were concerned, it was the
one best suited to usher in the good life for all men. Their
intentions were by and large reformist. They sincerely believed
that the strict control of both natural and social
irrationalities was the only viable route to the realization of
the good life--or "utopia."

     Although there have been various attempts throughout the
history of the race to map out blueprints of the ideal
society--Plato's Republic, of course, being one of the earliest
and best known--the particular type of ideal society which is the
subject matter of this study (or, again, what I choose to call
the "sane society") is a relatively recent phenomenon. As I
indicated earlier, its first systematic expression was made by
Bacon, and the exemplar itself really only hit its heyday in the
nineteenth century. The material causes for the proliferation of
the specific values and worldview of the sane society as well as
for its initial appearance in the seventeenth century can, I
believe, be traced back to one and the same foundation: the rise
of capitalism as the dominant Western economic model. The sane
society of both Bacon and the nineteenth century utopias
mirrored and reinforced the increasingly hegemonic world of the
bourgeoisie. Middle class values, religions, taboos, forms of
government, theories of commerce, class and gender relations and
the apotheosis of instrumental reason and the mechanical arts
were all fundamental ingredients of both the sane society's
worldview and the capitalist mode of production which grew to
maturity in the seventeenth through the nineteenth centuries.
The sane society motif gave expression to the conceptual and
normative models of those years. In doing so, it provided an

intellectual legitimation of them which grew in popularity and influence as the capitalist economic model itself grew in material and political power.

II

Few individuals have been as successful in capturing the modern imagination as Francis Bacon. The conceptual flaws in his new logic were recognized by even some of his own contemporaries--an awareness which continued to grow among savants who followed him. But his vision of a scientific methodology that promised continual advances in the mechanical sciences, increasing dominion over nature and the ultimate scientization of social relations, served as an inspiration for the seventeenth, eighteenth and nineteenth centuries' almost obsessive faith in the inevitability of progress. There were, of course, hundreds of influential thinkers after Bacon who likewise defended the notion that social and physical reality were equally reducible to mechanical analysis. The idea was one of the recurring themes of the period. But Bacon was the first to systematically defend the notion that both natural and social structures could and should be manipulated by scientific analysis. Even more significantly, he provided a "new" method--instrumental reason, in place of the earlier "abstract" syllogistic logic--which claimed to do so.

Writing in a period when the European capitalist class was beginning to exert that economic and intellectual hegemony which it would enjoy almost unchallenged until the eruption of the first world war, Bacon ably served as the leading spokesman for the ascending bourgeoisie. From a methodological perspective, his system proved compatible to the new ruling class because of its insistence that the only good science was that which led to an improvement in the mechanical arts, which in turn stimulated

industry and commerce. From a sociological perspective, his
fear of the laboring classes and eloquent defense of strict
legislation to promote the political, economic and normative
interests of the rising industrialists, likewise earned him and
his system the enthusiastic support of the middle class. And as
the bourgeois hegemony consolidated its command in the centuries
after Bacon, his dual role as the first luminary of modern
science and the earliest prophet of the sane society became even
more secure.

The extent to which Bacon's influence grew after his death
can be gauged by an examination of what might be described as the
most extreme expression of the bourgeois vision of the sane
society--the nineteenth century utopian novel. The nineteenth
century was the period in which the European and American middle
class made its greatest strides. Industrial technology, the
medical arts, and the physical and biological sciences made
dramatic advances, reinforcing the by then entrenched adulation
of the Baconian system, as well as an optimistic assurance that
the inauguration of the ultimately rationalized society was
inevitably just around the corner. An entire literary genre, the
nineteenth century utopian novel, arose to give expression to
this primarily classbound self-confidence. These novels
purported to be blueprints of the future perfect society that
was, to the nineteenth century eye, obviously already in the
process of gestation, a society in which all human needs would be
met and the last vestiges of irrationality eradicated. Moreover,
each of the novels' programmes claimed to be revolutionary.
True, they accepted as absolute the century's "progress" in
science and commerce as well as its basic normative and
theoretical assumptions. But they also acknowledged that the era
had not yet eliminated all social ills, and hence stood in some
need of second-order reform. With very few exceptions, however,

the nineteenth century utopian novels drew a picture of the
future sane society as one which was fully automated by
industrial technology, which had finally subdued natural laws and
bent them to its own use, and which strictly regulated economic
and social relations. All of them, notwithstanding their
revolutionary claims, wholeheartedly accepted the same values to
which the seventeenth century Baconian vision had first given
systematic expression. As such, each of them served as powerful
influences in cementing the ascendent class's hegemony. The
future sane society of the nineteenth century fictional utopias,
like the earlier Baconian model, was irretrievably classbound,
directly mirroring and furthering the interests of the
economically dominant bourgeoisie.

III

Although both Bacon and the nineteenth century utopias
claimed that their sane society motif was revolutionary,
representing a fundamental rupture with traditional normative and
societal models, I have suggested that the sane society exemplar
is ideological. This is not to say that it is a totally false
representation of reality; as we shall see in the following
chapter, one of the characteristic features of an ideological
form is that it is a subtle mixture of appearance and reality,
fact and fiction. Rather, I shall argue, following the analysis
of Karl Mannheim, that the sane society vision is ideological on
three different counts.

First, it is self-deceived as to both its origins and its
latitude. Instead of recognizing that its methodological
assumptions and ethical values arose out of a specific
socio-historical context, a context which was molded by the
changing material conditions of post-feudal Europe, the
proponents of the sane society thought its values to be

absolute, directly reflecting the objective nature of both the physical and the human realms. The assumption was that the worldview of the sane society enjoyed metaphysical (and, according to Bacon, theological) guarantee. Sensibly enough, given their denial of its contextual character, the proponents of both capitalism and the sane society likewise saw the values they defended as universal, equally applicable to and felicitous for all classes of persons. Bacon, for instance, insisted that a steady improvement in the mechanical arts was an absolute good for all members of British society, as was a concomitant growth in private property, and made both key features in the New Atlantis, his own sketch of the sane society. Even before his time, however, there was strong empirical evidence to the contrary. Improved technological modes of production, for instance, certainly appeared to produce beneficial consequences for both the national revenue of Britain as a whole and, more obviously, for the class which controlled those new modes of technique. But in retrospect it is clear that the silver lining concealed a much darker cloud. British emphasis upon competition in the international wool trade, in addition to the concentration of early industrial centers in urban areas, dispossessed thousands of agricultural laborers and artisans whose sources of livelihood were preempted by the new technology. Likewise, it is obvious that the eighteenth century industrial revolution, which so impressed the nineteenth century utopias, served as a necessary condition for a dramatic increase in mechanical inventions and technological expertise. This explosion in new technique, then, led to an increasing enrichment of the dominant middle class, which enjoyed ownership of the means of production, and a relative impoverishment of the laboring class. The sane society exemplar, in short, was more an ideal middle class society than a society whose beneficence was equally bestowed upon all segments of its citizenry. It is

precisely because the sane society image so adequately captured
and reinforced the values and aspirations of the increasingly
empowered middle class, in fact, that it proved so enduring in
the long run. Thus the sane society's normative and theoretical
structure, far from being "objectively" absolute and universal,
in reality was a vehicle for the expression and dissemination of
the values and interests of but one historical class. As such,
it was self-deceived as to its true nature, and hence championed
an illusory--i.e., ideological--picture of reality.

    The ideological character of the sane society model also
reveals itself in its ultimate inability to inaugurate the social
agenda that arose from its network of theoretical and normative
ideals. Keep in mind that the sane society's goal was to so
"rationalize" human relations as to not only make them
mathematically expressible (hence controllable), but also
maximally conducive to the well-being of all segments of the
population. But in order for such ideals to be truly felicitous
for all classes, they must be universally applicable to all
social strata. As I have pointed out, however, the very fact
that the sane society image became such a strong metaphor for
the capitalist mode of production in the seventeenth, eighteenth
and nineteenth centuries points to the fact that it directly
mirrored and hence furthered the interests of the dominant
class--the bourgeoisie--at the expense of economically
subordinate classes. The very nature of the sane society vision
created a blindspot that prevented its proponents from seeing
that its social programme of universal betterment was
incompatible with the classbound values it espoused. As we shall
see in Chapter One, Mannheim isolates as one of the fundamental
characteristics of ideological forms the inability to concretize
their social agendas because of the unperceived incompatibility
between their rhetorical aspirations and their material

interests.

Finally, the ideals of the sane society prove to be ideological because in intellectually legitimating the values and worldview of the contextually empowered class, they perpetuate the socio-economic status quo by insisting upon the need for a rigidly supervised hierarchy in scientific research, economic production and social relations. These authoritarian structures, needless to say, augmented the interests of the ascendent class and served, in the long run, to bolster its hegemony--not the overall good of society at large.

In summary: the seventeenth century, largely through the influence of Francis Bacon's scientific and social vision, gave birth to an ideological model of society which I have called the "sane society." Its goals were to mathematize and hence control first nature, then social relations themselves, in order to usher in the good life for all humans. Moreover, this Baconian model was given its most extreme expression by the rash of nineteenth century utopian novels, which likewise claimed to paint the picture of a future society in which all classes were equally benefitted. In point of fact, however, this exemplar of the sane society, as expressed by both Bacon and the nineteenth century utopias, was nothing more than an intellectual reification of the class relations, interests and values definitive of the increasingly empowered bourgeoisie. Instead of inaugurating a new society informed by universal values, it legitimated conventional society's power-laden structures and encouraged the perpetuation of classbound and hence dominant social forms. Furthermore, failing as it did to recognize the merely contextual character of its vision, it doomed its reformist social agenda, based upon the instantiation of putative absolute values, to ultimate failure.

It will be one of the major purposes of this study to analyze the historical connection between the sane society motif and the material and normative structures of the capitalist mode of production of which it was an ideological expression. In showing how both the Baconian and the nineteenth century utopian worldviews served as legitimations of a particular classbound hegemony, I hope to demonstrate the historical continuity of a vision that has strongly influenced the character of the modern era.

IV

This study of the sane society vision has another goal. It seeks to clarify the functional criteria which serve as the basis for differentiating ideological from utopian forms in general.

The distinction between ideological and utopian models is one that either has or should have occupied sociologists of knowledge since at least the appearance of Marx's The German Ideology. Ideological forms, as we have seen, can be described as distortions of reality. Instead of being objective representations of the "true" nature of things (social, scientific, normative or economic) they are theory- and value-laden structures whose content has been intimately influenced by socio-historical factors. They are not totally false descriptions because they do mirror, even if only in an oblique way, the material conditions existing in the particular context from which they spring. Their illusory character is due to the fact that they fail to recognize their contextual natures. They purport instead to be objective representations.

But utopian forms are likewise distortions of reality. They attempt to map out the social relations, economic conditions, technological expertise, value structures, and so on, of societies which, quite simply, do not exist. They in no way directly mirror "objective reality," except insofar as the necessary starting point for any utopia will, of course, be conditioned by the socio-historical context in which it arises. Plato's _Republic_, for example, ignores technological questions and concentrates upon the relationships between the individual and the polis because of the historical milieu in which Plato was situated. Similarly, Campanella's _City of the Sun_ or More's _Utopia_ are heavily informed by the imagery and value assumptions of both Catholic Christianity and Renaissance humanism, again because of the limits of each man's respective ethos. But such examples in no fundamental way support the assumption that putative utopias are objective reflections of either their historical periods or of reality "in itself." They simply reinforce the already commonsensical realization that literary utopias are not written in a vacuum.

The problem arises, then, as to whether any meaningful distinction can be made between ideological and utopian forms. Both are, to a greater or lesser extent, colored by the historical context from which they emerge. Likewise, both are distortions of reality. These similarities have prompted some critics to suppose that there really is no significant difference between the two, that utopias can be reduced to ideologies. Such seems, for instance, to have been the opinion of Marx and Engels. Other critics have been reluctant to make an identity between utopian and ideological forms, but have argued that, precisely because both distort reality (i.e., do not objectively describe it), they are equally deleterious forms of expression, and should be eliminated as at best deceptive and at worst dangerous structures.

Notwithstanding this tendency on the part of some to either identify ideology and utopia or to dismiss both as infelicitous expressions, there is the intuition, shared by utopian writers over the last two thousand years, that their productions are both different from what we today call ideological forms and that they are somehow valuable. The acknowledgement is made that utopias are not accurate depictions of reality, but it is qualified with the insistence that such distortions enrich rather than impoverish human sensibility. Furthermore, this intuition on the part of utopian authors is obviously shared by their readers. Utopian images have always captured the imagination of the reading and listening public. The unfortunate thing about such claims, however, is that they have never been supported by convincing arguments. Utopias may strike a sympathetic chord in the human heart, but this in no necessary way establishes them as either nonideological or valuable expressions. One suspects it is this failure to clearly argue for the intuition that the utopian imagination somehow enriches the human condition which so exasperated Marx and Engels, prompting them to contemptuously dismiss utopian forms as "unscientific" and socially regressive.

It is my contention, however, that ideological and utopian forms <u>are</u> distinct and, furthermore, that the latter possess a value which the former do not. Following Mannheim's suggestions in <u>Ideology and Utopia</u>, I shall argue that the distinction can best be demonstrated if one approaches the problem from a functional perspective. Granted, ideologies and utopias share a similar verbal definition, but analysis will show that they can be differentiated through an examination of the particular functions they perform in any socio-historical matrix. Both distort reality. Ideologies do so, however, unintentionally, while utopias do so deliberately. The lack of self-transparency which characterizes ideological forms functionally serves to

legitimate and hence strengthen the conventional socio-economic
relations and subsequent theoretical and normative assumptions of
an historical period.   As such, ideological distortions tend to
produce   social   stagnation,   if   not   retrogression,   by
institutionally discouraging social or conceptual innovation.
After all, change is not only unnecessary but actually represents
distortion from the perspective of ideological reification.
Utopias, on the other hand, deliberately call into question the
reified social, conceptual and normative assumptions of an
historical period by presenting imaginary alternatives to them.
In showing, if only in literary form, that there is no necessity
to current social structures, they pave the way for innovation
and change.   Thus the social functions of ideological and utopian
forms   are   quite   different and   serve   as   criteria for
distinguishing between the two. The one form impedes social
innovation and encourages a static subservience to the status
quo; the other loosens the hegemonic power of the status quo,
thus   opening the   possibility for   change, by   presenting
alternatives to it.

    This functional analysis of the utopian imagination, which
I discuss at some length in Chapter One, has convinced me that
the putative utopian novels of the nineteenth century are, in
fact, disguised ideologies. I have already suggested that the
future societies which they blueprint exhibit a great deal of
continuity with the   ideological sane society first   given
expression to by Francis Bacon. As such, they in effect mirror
and reinforce the hegemonic purview of nineteenth-century
capitalism.   In fact, the very subtlety of their ideological
defense of the status quo--expressed, as it is, in
"revolutionary" terms--makes them even more effective as vehicles
for the dissemination of bourgeois interests. If I am correct in
my designation of nineteenth century utopian novels as disguised

ideologies, we have at our fingertips one of the most startling examples of the pervasiveness of ideological forms yet encountered: ideological structures solidifying their hegemony through the auspices of a mode of expression whose fundamental claim is to be anti-ideological. This analysis of nineteenth century utopias as "sane societies"--i.e., disguised ideological forms--will be elaborated in Chapters Three and Four of this study.

V

At this point, let me explicitly state the plan of action in the chapters to come.

In Chapter One I will discuss Mannheim's distinction between the ideological mentality and utopian mentality, indicating both his reliance upon Marx's earlier analysis of ideological forms and his attempt to redress the weaknesses of that analysis with his pivotal distinction between "particular" and "total" ideologies. I will also, borrowing from Mannheim, argue my case for a functional definition of utopian forms. The purpose of this chapter is to provide the analytical criteria for the examination of the Baconian and nineteenth-century utopian sane society motif in particular, and the relationship between social knowledge and socio-historical conditions in general.

Chapter Two is devoted to an analysis of Bacon's "new" system. The central question of the chapter is why Bacon's vision was so influential in the formation of the modern era's scientific and social sensibility, notwithstanding the crippling philosophical flaws from which it suffered. I argue that the influence of the new canon is a result of its apotheosis of instrumental reason as the only viable scientific method, and its normative defense of a socio-economic structure which stresses the predominant role of the merchant and industrialist. Both

notions owe their original enthusiastic acceptance and subsequent
long life to the fact that they directly reflected the interests
of the rising middle class, thereby providing the nascent
capitalist mode of production with a pseudo-intellectual and
scientific respectability. But because Bacon failed to recognize
the classbound nature of his model, insisting instead that it
offered absolute normative standards and "objective" descriptions
of reality, it fulfills Mannheim's ideological function. Far
from presenting innovative interpretations of the world, the
Baconian system merely reified already existing class-based
assumptions. I will attempt to spell out the ideological
character of Bacon's new science by examining in some detail the
social implications derived from it and given expression to in
his fragmentary New Atlantis.

Chapter Three will be devoted to an elucidation of the
deceptive nature of the nineteenth-century utopian novel--that
nature, once again, being that although the productions of this
genre call themselves "utopian," and have been accepted as such,
they in fact are subtle ideological forms, reflective of the
worldview of the empowered bourgeoisie. To emphasize the
contextual nature of the genre, I will spend some time in
analyzing the historical conditions present in the nineteenth
century which served as the immediate basis for the optimism
which in turn expressed itself in the eruption of literary
visions of the sane society. Then I will outline the
similarities between the sets of theoretical and normative
assumptions definitive of both the actual nineteenth-century
worldview and the "revolutionary" imaginary sane societies of the
nineteenth century utopia. I hope to thereby indicate that a
tension does indeed exist between the putatively utopian
character of these novels and the conventional values they
espouse. If the functional definition of utopias which I argue

for in the first chapter is sound, the general description of
nineteenth century utopias in the third will suggest that there
is reason for calling into question the presumed utopian
character of these novels.

In Chapter Four, I more closely analyze the themes and
values which personified mainstream nineteenth-century utopian
novels by examining three of the most representative of them:
Hovorre's Milltillionaire, Bellamy's Looking Backward and
Bogdanov's Red Star. Two points will, I believe, become obvious.
First, these nineteenth century utopias explicitly accept the
Baconian vision of the sane society. As such, they illustrate
the continuum in theoretical and normative models that
personified the modern era. Second, these latter-day
counterparts to Bacon's sane society are ideological forms,
directly reflective of the interests of the industrially-based
bourgeoisie of the nineteenth century. Far from representing
innovative breaks with the normative status quo, then, these
putative utopias in effect bolstered conventional social and
normative structures in a most effective fashion.

In Chapter Five, I summarize the argument of the entire
study and allow myself a little space to speculate about the
influence of the ideological metaphor of the sane society in
twentieth-century culture. I argue, briefly, that although the
dream of ultimately scientizing society has lost a great deal of
its earlier naivete and popularity, its effects are still very
present today. A brief examination of the criticisms leveled by
Max Horkheimer and C. Wright Mills against contemporary
Anglo-American sociology especially reveals the still
influential currency of the sane society ideal. Finally, I shall
suggest that the lingering hold of this ideological form upon the
contemporary imagination is at least partially responsible for

some of the social irrationalities and normative confusions
existing today.

VI

Before concluding my introductory remarks, I should like to
say a few words regarding the overall character of this study. A
few years ago a project like this one would have been called, I
suppose, an exercise in the "history of ideas." Perhaps, in
fact, most persons would still call it that today. I have no
major problems with the label so long as one carefully indicates
what is designated by it. Let me spell out first what I don't,
and secondly what I do, mean by the term "history of ideas."
Doing so will, I think, help to explain the general
historiographical assumptions which lie behind this study of the
sane society motif. (Chapter One will discuss the entire matter
in greater detail.)

What I most emphatically do <u>not</u> mean by the history of ideas
is any exercise which suggests that the "intellectual" realm
somehow has a life of its own, enjoys an existence fundamentally
independent from material conditions operative in any
socio-historical context, and accepts as its primary working
assumption the thesis that the history of the race is best mapped
by showing how the philosophical and religious ideas of one
generation affect the ideas of the next. My objection to such a
definition of the history of ideas is twofold. First, such an
exercise all but ignores the relationship between what a
particular culture <u>thinks</u> and how it concretely <u>lives</u>. It
discounts the increasingly apparent fact that social knowledge is
a reflection of material conditions. Second, the very assumption
that the fundamental "motor" of history is a set of reified,
absolute and transhistorical ideas is itself, as Mannheim so
nicely says in the epigramme which opens this Introduction, the

creation of a recent historical tendency among savants to become
so "idea-struck" as to project into the historical process
itself their own intoxication with ideas. We too often, as
Mannheim puts it, reinterpret the past in the light of our own
central experiences. We forget, or are blinded because of the
fact that we dwell in an ideological medium, that the very
character of our own central experiences are themselves the
result of a long historical process, not the absolute standards
we often take them to be. In short, we are often deceived about
the origins of our knowledge. Traditional history of ideas,
because of its almost Platonic deprecation of material
conditions, unwittingly perpetuates that deception.

What I do mean by the history of ideas is any exercise
which attempts to trace the connections between the intellectual
inventory and the material conditions of a particular period,
thereby indicating how the forms of knowledge are fashioned by
domestic economic relations, international trade, class
divisions, political structures, and so on. This is not to say
that I am assuming a crude deterministic model of history, in
which material conditions somehow give rise to ideas which are
merely epiphenomenal. Rather, what I mean to suggest is that
knowledge is social, not abstract. It changes its character,
relocates its perspective, and arranges its values in
synchronicity with changing socio-historical conditions. The
"history of ideas," then, is really better described as the
"history of social knowledge." Consequently, the "historian of
ideas" will rest content only when he has, to invert Mannheim's
epigramme, reinterpreted the central experiences of the present
in light of the past--i.e., when he explains the ethos of his
own period through a consideration of the material conditions
and economic relations which underlie it. The present study is a
modest attempt at just such a reconstruction.

CHAPTER 1

THE FUNCION OF UTOPIAN THOUGHT

Dogmatization in science, religion,
social life, or art is the entropy of
thought. What has become dogma no
longer burns; it only gives off
warmth--it is tepid, it is cool.
Instead of the Sermon on the Mount,
under the scorching sun, to up-raised
arms and sobbing people, there is
drowsy prayer in a magnificent abbey.
Instead of Galileo's "But still, it
turns!" there are dispassionate
computations in a well-heated room in
an observatory. On the Galileos, the
epigones build their own structures,
slowly, bit by bit, like corals.
This is the path of evolution--until
a new heresy explodes the crush of
dogma and all edifices of the most
enduring stone have been raised upon
it.

> Yevgeny Zamyatin, "On
> Literature, Revolution,
> Entropy, and Other
> Matters"

Only those orientations transcending
reality will be referred to by us as
utopian which, when they pass over
into conduct, tend to shatter, either
partially or wholly, the order of
things prevailing at the time.

> Karl Mannheim, Ideology
> and Utopia

I

Utopian visions of the ideal society are at least as old as
Plato.[1] Indeed, certain anthropological studies suggest that
stories of "blessed isles and paradises are a part of the

dream-world of savages [sic] everywhere,"[2] the   implication being
that   utopian   fantasies   are   a   fundamental   ingredient   in   the
formation of   any ethos.   Furthermore,   it can   hardly   be denied
that two   of the most   influential worldviews of   the "civilized"
West,   Judeo-Christianity and   secular collectivism,   share as   a
common   exemplar   the   millennarian vision   of   a   future, perfect
society.

The utopian paradigm--that imaginary society in   which human
beings   have   overcome   problems   such   as   economic   scarcity,
political   disorder, crime   and illness--appears,   then, to   be a
culturally ubiquitous one.   It resurfaces   continually, sometimes
as   the   explicitly   formulated   construction   of   an   imaginary
perfect society, but more often as a general millennarian longing
for a better world.   Classical Greece's legends of a   Golden Age,
the Christian City   of God, the Citta   Felice of   the Renaissance
humanists, Rabelais'   Land of Cocaigne,   Rousseau's   monde ideal,
Marx's   classless   society: all   of   these   (and   many   more)
illustrate the historically recurrent quest for utopia.

The constancy of the utopian mentality is certain; that much
is obvious from the historical and literary record.   What   is not
so straightforward is the value   we are to place upon it.   There
are   two general   schools of   interpretation.   The   first--and, I
believe, the more popular--argues that utopianism, inasmuch as it
represents a willful distortion of reality, encourages   humans to
retreat   into   a   dreamworld   of   fantasy   and   imagination.   The
utopian mentality, according to this interpretation, is at best a
naive, self-indulgent form of escapism.   It represents   a refusal
to deal with real problems arising from real   material conditions
in   the   world,   and   as   such   is   an   obstacle   to   concrete
problem-solving.   The   very   label   "utopian,"   as   far   as this
hard-headed school   is concerned,   is   one   of   opprobrium.   To

characterize a project as "utopian" is to condemn it as
"nonrealistic," "frivolous," "impractical."

The second, less influential school of interpretation,
while admitting that utopianism is a distortion of reality,
claims that it is a nevertheless valuable one. Inasmuch as the
utopian imagination seeks to create a societal model which,
compared to the actually existent one, has eradicated traditional
evils such as war, economic inequality, superstition and illness,
it serves a twofold function. On the one hand, it provides an at
least implicit critique of conventional normative and cultural
standards; on the other, it acts as an exemplar and catalyst for
innovative activity. By offering an image of what the future
ideal society might be, utopias encourage dissatisfaction with
the status quo while at the same time serving as inspirations for
moving beyond it. Lewis Mumford, for instance, sees the function
of utopian visions as providing a means of harmless escape from
present societal ills in addition to acting as imaginative agents
for social reformation.[3] Arthur Morgan sees utopianism as an
important source of social innovation, and claims that utopian
models serve as remedial exemplars to existing disorders.[4]
David Riesman argues that the utopian imagination functions as a
valuable and necessary complement to "over-literal" and
uninspired socioanalysis.[5] Ernst Bloch agrees that utopia is an
"incomparable instrument of thought because it [allows] a
systematic exploration of a variety of specific possibilities."[6]
And commentators as diverse as Harvey Cox, Josef Pieper, Johan
Huizinga, Friedrich Nietzsche and Simone de Beauvoir claim that
utopian images foster the faculties of festivity and fantasy,
both of which they view as necessary (although not sufficient)
conditions for transformations of values and the social order.[7]

The most systematic attempt to date to defend the

proposition that utopianism serves the valuable function of introducing normative and conceptual novelty into otherwise rigidly orthodox cultural milieux is Karl Mannheim's Ideology and Utopia.[8] Mannheim argues that the utopian imagination serves as a catalyst for social and political change because it injects into a culture's conceptual framework heterodox ways of thinking which tend to call into question and hence erode the very foundation of that culture's intellectual self-justification. Utopianism, argues Mannheim, opens the way for alternative worldviews that affect concrete human relations by calling into question a society's conventional assumptions about the nature of reality. It thereby serves the function of stimulating both conceptual and political innovation, a stimulation that any currently reigning orthodox worldview--or what Mannheim calls an "ideology"--by nature cannot provide. For Mannheim, a society that discourages utopianism is a stagnant society, a rigified edifice of orthodoxy which has denied itself the possibility of healthy growth. Without the utopian mentality serving as a necessary counterweight to ossified social ideology, "man would lose his will to shape history and therewith his ability to understand it."[9]

In this chapter, I should like to examine in some detail Mannheim's analysis of the functional relationship between ideology and utopia. The value of Mannheim's argument in the context of the present study is twofold. First, it provides a persuasive response to the claim that utopianism is a self-indulgent distortion of reality which is at best a waste of time, at worst a retreat into fantasy. As I have already indicated, Mannheim argues instead that the utopian mentality is a necessary condition for cultural change. Second, Mannheim's analysis provides us with a functional definition of utopia which is formal enough to enable us to identify true utopianism from

merely apparent utopianism—a yardstick which is central to the
project of this study—while at the same time flexible enough to
accommodate a wide diversity of historically specific content.

II
Overview of Mannheim's Project

Mannheim's concern in Ideology and Utopia is with the
sociology of knowledge—i.e., that discipline which attempts to
understand conceptual and normative models by analyzing their
relationship to historically contextual material conditions.
According to Mannheim, the particular worldview that
characterizes any cultural ethos, far from being an "objective"
description of reality, is in fact a reflection of the "social
habitat" whence it arises. "Social habitat" is the generic label
that Mannheim uses to refer to the material conditions and
socio-economic structures of a given society. It corresponds
rather roughly to what Marx calls a society's "material base."
This material base, influencing as it does all aspects of human
existence, necessarily colors a society's image of both the
world and itself. Conceptual boundaries, be they philosophical,
religious, scientific, jurisprudential or political, are all
ultimately circumscribed by the character of their social
habitat. As such, the normative and conceptual apparatus of any
society roughly corresponds to Marx's notion of superstructure.
It is no mere coincidence that Mannheim's historicist description
of the nature of social knowledge so closely parallels Marx's;
Mannheim readily acknowledges an indebtedness to the latter's
socioanalysis.

The entire conceptual and normative apparatus which arises
from a social habitat—or what both Marx and Mannheim rather
broadly call an "ideology"—is characterized by its lack of

transparency. In general terms, an ideology is an opaque representation of reality, neither totally true nor totally false, but instead an intricate mesh of fact and fiction. An ideology is not a total distortion of reality because it is an inadvertent though reliable reflection of the nature of the material base upon which it rests--a reflection which, within the context of its own circumspect boundaries, tends to be quite coherent and systematic. But neither is an ideology a reliably "objective" mirror of reality. This is because it is self-deceived about both its origins and its latitude. Ideologies characteristically deny their contextual natures, insisting instead upon an abstract universality to which they simply have no legitimate claim. It is this pervasive absence of insight into its own nature which accounts for ideology's distortion of reality, for its inability to see things as they really are. Thus an ideology is an illusion, but an illusion which possesses a certain amount of verisimilitude. As Henri Lefebvre says, ideologies "are something more and else than mere illusions. Such appearances are the modes in which human activities manifest themselves within the whole they constitute at any given moment--call them modalities of consciousness. They have far greater consistency, let alone coherence, than mere illusions or ordinary lies. Appearances have reality, and reality involves appearances."[10]

Because ideological structures claim an historical universality for themselves, they characteristically lack flexibility. They are, consequently, normatively opposed to and structurally incapable of easily accommodating themselves to social or conceptual innovation. This fidelity to the status quo, in addition to perpetuating a distorted image of reality, tends to lead to a kind of societal sclerosis in which the capacity for innovative malleability atrophies through

institutionalized discouragement. The conceptual and normative
models defended by an ideology thus inevitably tend towards
increasing levels of rigidity, hostility to change, insistence
upon orthodoxy and an inability to effectively confront new
problems that arise.

    Now it might be supposed, given Mannheim's insistence that
ideologies are harmful distortions of reality, that the form of
social consciousness which he champions in place of them
involves an objective, self-transparent correspondence of idea to
reality. But in fact Mannheim is not very sanguine about the
possibility of ever achieving this empiricist ideal.   His
epistemological starting point is far removed from the assumption
that the _percipiens_ is merely a passive receptacle for the
absorption of sense data. For Mannheim, knowledge involves
praxis rather than passivity. He assumes that the subject comes
to know by doing, which necessarily means that a reciprocity of
influence transpires.   The subject comes to know X by actively
engaging himself with X; but the process of engagement changes
the character of X as well as the character of the subject.
There is, then, no independent set of completely detached objects
that serves as the unchanging basis of our individual and
collective knowledge.   Inasmuch as the subject is always an
active, creative participant in the act of knowing, "objective"
knowledge, at least as defined in traditional empiricist terms,
is impossible.

    This does not mean that Mannheim considers the ideological
mentality inevitable. Fundamentally juxtaposed to the ossifying
orthodoxy of ideology is another type of social mentality which
Mannheim calls "utopian." The utopian mentality is no more an
"objective" reflection of reality than is an ideology.   It too
is a distortion, an illusion, an appearance.   But there is a

crucial difference between distortion _qua_ ideology and distortion _qua_ utopia. Ideological structures are distortions because they fail to recognize their own contextual natures; they are distorted because they are deceived. Utopian structures, however, are _deliberate_ distortions of reality. They are self-conscious misrepresentations of reality that deliberately reject and (hopefully) go beyond conventional, orthodox models, both social and conceptual. Inasmuch as the conscious distortions offered by utopian thinking strive to present alternative perspectives to the ideological apparatus, it is quite possible for them to serve as catalysts for the breakdown of ideological constraints. The utopian mentality, then, tends to encourage the conceptual and normative flexibility which a society requires in order to effectively respond to collective needs and to grow.

This, in brief, is Mannheim's position. His entire sociology of knowledge might be reduced, without fear of over-simplification, to an examination of the dynamic relationship between ideological and utopian forms of social consciousness. In what follows, I will focus more systematically upon the functional role of utopian thought, first by examining Mannheim's analysis of ideology, then by investigating its relationship to utopia.

The Ideological Mentality

Marx's Concept of Ideology

Although the concept of ideology did not originate with Marx and Engels (the word itself was coined, with a nonpejorative connotation, at the end of the eighteenth century by the French savant Destutt de Tracy),[11] their nineteenth-century analysis of the notion has dramatically influenced the character of contemporary socioanalysis. Furthermore, Mannehim himself takes great pains to acknowledge his indebtedness to the Marxian analysis of ideology, even though he eventually criticizes it for what he sees as an ultimate lack of coherence. Mannheim's discussion of the ideological mentality, consequently, is best appreciated if compared to the Marxist theory of ideology which serves as its starting point.

Marx and Engels agree that ideologies are opaque representations of reality, neither totally false nor totally reflective of the actual nature of things, but instead a complicated collage of fact and fiction. For them, ideological constructs, claiming as they do to consist of sets of universal claims about the nature of reality, have as one of their primary characteristics the tendency towards totalization. There exists a sort of conceptual trickle-down effect in ideology: basic propositions which constitute the heart of an ideological model in turn determine the character of any secondary constructs which might arise. Thus fundamental descriptions of reality, along

with all of the disciplines which claim them as starting points,
take on an ideological tint. Indeed, it can be argued that even
certain putatively objective, value-free "sciences"--such as, for
instance, the nineteenth century's doctrine of Social
Darwinism--are ideological contrivances. This web-like character
of ideology is expressed by Engels in a passage from his Ludwig
Feuerbach: "once it has arisen...every ideology develops in
conjunction with the given conceptual material [i.e., the
ideology's set of basic universal claims] and elaborates on it;
otherwise if would not be an ideology."[12]

     Marx and Engels are confident about their general
representation of ideology as a totalizing mesh of fact and
fiction. They are much more ambivalent, however, in their
efforts to provide a detailed analysis of the phenomenon. At
times they imply that the appearance of any given ideology is
adequately explained in psychological terms which remind one of
the later Freudian notion of rationalization. At other times,
however, ideology is portrayed as a network of conceptual and
normative beliefs which directly arises from, reflects, and
promulgates the vested interests of the dominant socio-economic
class of any historical period. Embedded within this second
sociological explanation lies a further ambiguity. Sometimes
Marx and Engels speak as if ideology is a deliberate, conscious
strategy on the part of the ascendent class to solidify its
position, while at other times they imply that ideology is an
automatic, nondeliberate reflex of a society's class structure
which deceives all groups equally. To complicate matters even
further, the two explanations often appear almost side by side in
the same treatise.

     In The German Ideology, for instance, Marx and Engels
introduced their well-known metaphor of ideology as a camera

obscura. An ideology is seen as arising from the misguided
assumption that the ideational realm enjoys an existence of its
own, an existence which in turn serves as the ultimate foundation
for the character of material conditions in any given society.
This abstraction of conceptual and normative models from the
activity of humans in the world bestows upon the conceptual realm
the semblance of a life of its own, suggesting as it does that
consciousness is in no way dependent upon concrete social
processes. Thus the causal relationship between the conceptual
realm and the material realm is "inverted" and "men and their
circumstances appear upside down as in a camera obscura."[13]
Instead of correctly seeing ideas as arising from a foundation
of actually existing material and social conditions, the latter
are believed to be unilaterally dependent upon the former.

This assumed independence of conceptual models from
material conditions, sometimes referred to as the "Great
Man/Great Idea" tradition, is often associated with the
presupposition that theoretical models are exclusively the
products of solitary, detached geniuses who, unsullied by
commerce with the everyday world, create or discover pure mental
forms. Furthermore, although the genesis of these "great ideas"
is in no way reliant upon the social realm, they themselves, once
released from the brow of the Great Man, exert colossal influence
upon the character of political and social structures. Engels
suggested that this delusion was encouraged by the assumption,
based upon unreflective experience, that inasmuch as "all action
is produced through the medium of thought, it appears to [the
thinker] to be also ultimately based upon thought."[14] Marx
lampoons this "inverted" position as both epistemologically
unsound and pragmatically absurd: "Once upon a time an honest
fellow had the idea that men were drowned in water only because
they were possessed with the idea of gravity. If they were to

knock this idea out of their heads, say by stating it to be a
superstition, a religious idea, they would be sublimely proof
against any danger from water."[15]

The implication here is that abstracted thought which
denies any original relationship with the material world is
ideological--i.e., an opaque representation of the nature of
reality--because of its mistaken assumption about its own
character. As an alternative to this abstracted inversion, Marx
and Engels suggest a new methodological programme:

> We do not set out from what men say, imagine, conceive
> nor from men as narrated, thought of, imagined,
> conceived, in order to arrive at men in the flesh. We
> set out from real, active men, and on the basis of
> their real life-process we demonstrate the development
> of the ideological reflexes and echoes of this
> life-process. The phantoms formed in human brains are
> also, necessarily, sublimates of their material
> life-process, which is empirically verifiable and bound
> to material premises. Morality, religion, meta-
> physics, all the rest of ideology and their
> corresponding forms of consciousness, thus no longer
> retain the semblance of independence.[16]

The rather crude model of mechanistic materialism implied in
this passage, with its simplistic language of "reflexes,"
"echoes" and "phantoms," seems to be a departure from Marx's
earlier argument in the 1844 Manuscripts that the relation
between the realm of ideas and the material-social world is a
dialectical, reciprocal one. Furthermore, his later analyses of
praxis, as in, for instance, the Grundrisse,[17] appear to reject
The German Ideology's crude mechanism in favor of a return to the
earlier dialectical approach. Nevertheless, the rather narrow
characterization of ideology as speculative abstraction was never
entirely dropped by either Marx or Engels--as evidenced in
Engels's Ludwig Feuerbach, in which ideology is seen as an

"occupation with thoughts as with independent entities, developing independently and subject only to their own laws,"[18] or in a letter which he wrote to Franz Mehring in 1893, in which he describes ideology as "a process accomplished by the so-called thinker, consciously indeed but with a false consciousness. The real motives impelling him remain unknown to him, otherwise it would not be an ideological process at all. Hence he imagines false or apparent motives. Because it is a process of thought he derives both its form and its content from pure thought, either his own or that of his predecessors."[19]

Thus far Marx and Engels' psychological account of ideology differs very little from later non-Marxist ones. Further on in The German Ideology, however, we find a somewhat different account of the appearance and nature of ideology, the sociological one which carries the distinctively Marxian trademark. Here ideology is described not simply as an abstracted body of beliefs, but rather as an illusory network of knowledge-claims whose specific character is a direct result of the division of mental and manual labor typical of a class-structured society.

According to Marx and Engels, a social distinction between manual and mental labor arises at that historical stage in a society's development when its specific mode of production is sophisticated enough to create the requisite amount of material surplus needed to free a sector of the population from the unhappy necessity of physically laboring in order to survive. This sector, by virtue of its _physical_ emancipation from productive activity, soon supposes itself likewise _conceptually_ emancipated from material conditions. Consciousness looks upon itself as self-sufficient, and both it and its constructs acquire a double aura of independence and necessity (necessary, of

course, because of their independence from the merely accidental
world of appearance).   As Marx and Engels say, "division of
labour only becomes truly such from the moment when a division of
material and mental labour appears.   From this moment onward
consciousness can really flatter itself that it is something
other than consciousness of existing practice, that it really
represents something without representing something real; from
now on consciousness is in a position to emancipate itself from
the world and to proceed to the formation of pure theory,
theology, philosophy, ethics, etc."[20] The ideological inversion
of reality is obvious once again. The class of mental laborers
convinces itself that it is conceptually independent of material
influences, when in point of fact it is precisely the material
mode of production characteristic of the society in which it
finds itself which serves as the necessary condition for its very
existence.

     This division between manual and mental labor in early
surplus societies does much more than merely encourage the
illusion of abstracted consciousness and knowledge. Even more to
the point from a Marxian perspective, it creates a class of
primarily mental laborers who, because they are the only members
in the society freed from the necessity of day-to-day physical
labor, have a virtual monopoly on the leisure time needed for the
acquisition and elaboration of that society's store of knowledge.
Not surprisingly, the normative, jurisprudential and conceptual
models promulgated by this class of already empowered and
privileged individuals, although claiming universal validity, is
in fact reflective of that class's special interests. The
worldview it creates either explicitly or implicitly supports the
status quo by providing justifications for the continuation of
the division of labor. Furthermore, the original separation of
labor into mental and manual leads to a subsequent division of

labor within the former class which serves to further consolidate its position: the "thinkers"--or ideologues--of the privileged class, whose conceptual models serve to theoretically justify its   interests,   and   the   "doers"--politicians,   magistrates, military leaders and so on--of the privileged class whose concrete activity in society solidify their class's legal, economic, and material dominance. As Marx and Engels explain,

> The division of labour...mainfests itself also in the
> ruling class as the division of mental and material
> labour, so that inside this class one part appears as
> the thinkers of the class (its active, conceptive
> ideologists, who make the perfecting of the illusion of
> the   class about   itself their   chief source   of
> livelihood) while the other's attitude to these ideas
> and illusions is more passive and receptive, because
> they are in reality the active members of this class
> and have less time to make up illusions and ideas
> about themselves.[21]

Thus the   forms of ideological justification promulgated by the privileged class, according to Marx and Engels, permeate the entire ideational and administrative apparatus of any given society--the   legal,   political,   economic,   religious   and philosophical models by which the society defines itself and its relationships to "reality."

> The ideas of the ruling class are in every epoch the
> ruling   ideas: i.e.,   the class   which   is   the ruling
> material force of society is at the same time its
> ruling intellectual force.   The class   which has   the
> means   of material   production   at   its disposal,
> consequently   also   controls   the   means   of mental
> production, so that the ideas of those who lack the
> means of mental production are on the whole subject to
> it. The ruling ideas are nothing more than the ideal
> expression of the dominant material relations,   the
> dominant material relations grasped as ideas; hence of
> the relations which make the one class the ruling one,
> therefore, the ideas of its dominance.[22]

It is at this point that the earlier psychological definition of

ideology as a network of illusory, abstracted belief shifts to a
sociological one. Ideology becomes a network of illusory,
abstracted belief founded upon the interests of a certain social
class.

As indicated earlier, a final ambiguity is embedded within
this sociological account of the nature of ideology. Sometimes
Marx and Engels speak as if ideology's claim to universal
validity is a deliberate falsification promulgated by the
ascendent class's ideologues in the furtherance of their own
class interests. Thus in the previously quoted passage dealing
with the division between "thinkers" and "doers" in the
privileged class, the former are those who earn a livelihood by
"making up illusions and ideas about themselves," by
"perfecting...the illusion of the class" to which they belong.
The implication seems to be that the ascendent class's ideologues
are quite aware of the nonobjective character of their
justifications of the status quo. According to this
interpretation, ideological structures acquire a peculiar kind of
self-transparency. Seen from within, they are recognized by
their authors as conscious deceptions. It is only when seen from
without, as it were, from the perspective of the nonascendent
class, that their illusory quality holds. At other times,
however, Marx and Engels speak of classbound ideology as "false
consciousness" (although only Engels actually uses this
particular locution)--i.e., as a system of illusory beliefs whose
claim to universality deceives all classes in society equally.
In this case, ideology is not at all self-transparent. The
ideologues as well as the nonideologues accept the "objective"
basis and "universal" validity of their own constructs. Thus in
Capital, Marx says that "the label on a system of ideas is
distinguished from that on other articles, amongst other things,
by the fact that it deceives not only the buyer, but often the

seller   as   well."[23]   And,   in   speaking   of   petit-bourgeois
democracy, Marx elaborates upon the point:

> One must not make the narrow minded assumption that the
> petty bourgeoisie wills to promote in principle an
> egoistic class interest. Rather, it believes that the
> particular conditions of its emancipation are universal
> conditions within which alone modern society can be
> saved... Just as little must one assume that its
> democratic representatives are all shopkeepers or their
> enthusiasts. According to their education and
> individual situation they may be heavens apart. What
> makes them representatives of the petty bourgeoisie is
> that in their heads they have not gotten beyond the
> limits which the latter haven't gotten beyond in life,
> that they are driven theoretically to the same tasks
> and solutions that the latter are driven to practically
> by their material interests and social situation. This
> is in general the relation of the political and
> literary representatives to the class they
> represent.[24]

To exacerbate the situation even more, when Marx and Engels
do not so clearly opt for one or the other of the two senses of
classbound ideology, they often speak in exasperatingly ambiguous
terms, as in this passage from The German Ideology: "each new
class is compelled...to represent its interest as the common
interest of all the members of society, but in an ideal form; it
will give its ideas the form of universality, and represent them
as the only rational, universally valid ones."[25]

How   are   we   to   understand   the   "is   compelled"   in   this
passage? Should we take it to mean that the ascendent class in a
society is forced to consciously deceive the nonascendent class
in order to further its own interests, or should we read it as
implying that the ascendent class "is compelled" by the internal
logic of its own process of value- and concept-formation to
likewise believe in the illusory network of beliefs supportive of
its social privilege? It is not at all clear from the context of

this and many other passages which interpretation is intended.

Marx and Engels' description of ideology, then, is ambiguous--an ambiguity which Mannheim will use as the critical point of departure for his own discussion of ideology. Although Marxist socioanalysis claims as its unique contribution the definition of ideology as a classbound network of illusory belief, I have tried to show that there are in fact several different accounts of the notion in the Marxist canon. Neither Marx nor Engels appear to have ever quite reconciled the tension between ideology as primarily a psychological mechanism and ideology as a sociological reflection of class division. Furthermore, within the latter category, there exists the problem of whether classbound ideology is most appropriately understood as false--i.e., deceived--representation, or as falsifying--i.e., deceptive--representation. Although generalization is risky, it is probably safe to characterize the subsequent course of neo-Marxist analyses of ideology as torn between this deceived-deceptive ambivalence.

The issue is not merely a textual one. Issues in epistemology and the sociology of knowledge are also at stake. If one opts for the interpretation of classbound ideology as deceptive, one assumes that a society's stock of knowledge and values are simple epiphenomenal eruptions from the material conditions and relations of productions characteristic of its particular class structure. In addition to having to defend a rather simple account of the mechanistic genesis of theoretical models, in which religions, philosophies and sciences are reduced to totally dependent "echoes" of material conditions, this interpretation is also forced to assume the equally problematic thesis that the ideational apparatus of a given society is the result of a conspiratorial and finely orchestrated powerplay on

the part of its ascendent class. Notwithstanding what seems to
be the apparent naivete of this position, it has been championed
by several Marxist theorecticians, most notably Nikolai
Bukharin.[26]

If, on the other hand, one opts for the interpretation of
classbound ideology as ubiquitously deceived representation, the
epistemological implication is that a society's ideational
apparatus tends to take on a life of its own, wresting a curious
kind of independence for itself, and equally deceives all
segments of a class society with its disguised classbound
theoretical and normative models. The problem then arises as to
how any single segment of society can ever escape from ideology's
influence long enough to recognize its illusory character. If
all of society is contained within the ideological medium, it is
a mystery as to how an "objective" perspective is to be gained.
Indeed, in such a scenario, it seems to be a bit strange to speak
of ideological "falsification" at all, since the latter
accusation appears to presuppose a break in the illusory
ideological web--an occurrence which the thesis of ideology as
deceived representation apparently prohibits. The epistemological and sociological perplexities suggested by this second
model of ideology have been focused upon in the twentieth century
by the members of the so-called Frankfurt School (with Marcuse,
perhaps, being the best known representative). But they have
also been a source of concern for other Marxists such as Gramsci
and Althusser--and, at times, even for Marx himself.

Mannheim's Concept of Ideology

The ambiguities embedded within Marx and Engels' general
notion of ideology serve as the starting point for Mannheim's

analysis.   His goal,   as he   says, is   "to   disentangle   all the
different   shades   of meaning which   are blended"   in   the earlier
Marxist analysis, thereby providing "a more precise   statement of
the variations in the meanings of the concept"[27] of ideology.

Mannheim   disentangles   ideology's   "different   shades   of
meaning" by claiming that   "there are two distinct and   separable
meanings of the term 'ideology'"--what he calls   the "particular"
and the "total."[28]   This distinction represents, for   Mannheim, a
significant   improvement   upon   Marx   and   Engels'   earlier and
somewhat confused analysis.   The notion of particular   ideology,
he says, "is implied when the term denotes that we   are sceptical
of   the   ideas   and   representations   advanced"   by   an opponent,
whereas the concept of total ideology refers "to the   ideology of
an   age or   of   a   concrete historico-social   group, e.g.,   of   a
class."[29] The   former may be regarded as a more or less conscious
distortion   of   a   specific   situation's   reality   by   either   an
individual or a small   interest group.   The latter, on   the other
hand,   is an   unwitting distortion   held in   common by   an entire
cultural milieu.   It is, according to Mannheim, a "composition of
the   total   structure   of the   mind   of   this epoch   or   of   this
group."[30]

Particular and total ideologies perform   different functions
within a societal matrix.   But   they also share a set of   general
characteristics.   Each   of   them, for   instance,   is   a partial,
fragmented   and distorted   representation of   the subject's   life
situation (in one case, of course, the subject is   an individual;
in the   other the subject   is an entire   culture).   Each of   them
attempts   to provide   abstract, theoretical   justifications which
both   defend   and   reinforce the   subject's   specific   lifestyle,
values and general orientation to reality.   Neither of them has a
purely   intellectual   basis,   notwithstanding   their   claim   to

objectivity. As forms of ideology, they both rest at least in
part upon emotional commitment and perceived self-interest. In
addition, particular as well as total ideologies are
characterized by a tendency towards totalization. The subject,
whether an individual or society, attempts to filter all
conceptual and normative models through the same ideological
prism. Finally, and most importantly for Mannheim, both forms of
ideology can be best understood by examining their separate
functions within a cultural milieu. It is this emphasis upon
functional explanations, in fact, which is most characteristic
of Mannheim's approach to the ideological and utopian
mentalities.

An ideology, according to Mannheim, be it particular or
total, is a function of the subject that holds it as well as of
the worldview appropriate to the socio-historical context in
which the subject is situated. The ostensible set of theoretical
constructs that comprises an ideological model, although of
course interesting and important in and of itself, is not the key
to understanding the nature of the ideological mentality. It
serves only as an indicator, as a pointer, to the life-situation
or "social habitat" which lies behind it and which serves as its
ultimate foundation. This insistence upon a functional
definition of ideology highlights Mannheim's assumption that
ideological constructs are not disinterested, "objective"
portrayals of reality, but rather are perspectives determined by
the subject's social and historical setting.

> The common element in these two conceptions [i.e.,
> particular and total ideologies] seems to consist in
> the fact that neither relies solely on what is actually
> said by the opponent in order to reach an understanding
> of his real meaning and intention. Both fall back on
> the subject, whether individual or group, proceeding to
> an understanding of what is said by the indirect method
> of analyzing the social conditions of the individual or

his group. The ideas expressed by the subject are thus
regarded as functions of his existence. This means
that opinions, statements, propositions, and systems of
ideas are not taken at their face value but are
interpreted in the light of the life-situation of the
one who expresses them. It signifies further that the
specific character and life-situations of the subject
influence his opinions, perceptions, and interpretations.[31]

A functional definition of ideology provides us, then, with
both a general account of the nature of ideological constructs
and a methodological principle to use in the understanding of
them. The nature of an ideology is to be a function of the
socio-historical milieu in which it appears. It is not a
discrete, independent body of knowledge which stands on its own
two feet, but rather is an outgrowth of a discernible social
habitat. Methodologically, an ideology is appropriately analyzed
not by an exclusive examination of the body of theoretical
beliefs which constitute it, but rather by a generic tracing-back
of the socio-historical conditions for its appearance. An
ideological construct should not be taken at "face value," as if
it possessed an internal logic independent of concrete
life-situations which, when finally mapped out, provide a
complete understanding of the model under investigation. In
fact, to abstract an ideological model from its social habitat,
even for the purpose of analysis, is to abort one's project from
the very beginning. Inasmuch as an ideology is a function of its
subject (individual or group) it cannot be understood in
abstracto.

Before moving on to a discussion of the differences in the
meanings of total and particular ideologies, I think it best to
pause a moment here to anticipate without discussing a caveat
which this functional definition of ideology may have prompted in
the reader's mind. The objection might be expressed like this.

Mannheim's sociology of knowledge precludes the possibility of a
traditional percipiens-percipiet act of knowing, if such an act
is understood to mean that knowledge consists of the "pure"
intuition of an "objective" realm on the part of a passive
subject. As I explained earlier, Mannheim argues that thought is
never disinterested. Mental objects are always informed by the
subject's activity-in-the-world, an activity which in turn is
circumscribed by the social habitat in which he finds himself.
If such is the case, it would appear that all ideas necessarily
become a function of "the life-situation of the one who expresses
them." Consequently all thought can be described as
ideological--which, to say the least, tends to deflate both the
importance and philosophical interest which Mannheim claims for
the concept.

I must reserve a complete discussion of this objection for
the latter part of this section. Let me simply say at this point
that Mannheim is quite aware that if ideology is exclusively
defined in terms of its functional reliance upon the social
habitat, the distinction between it and non-ideological knowledge
collapses. But ideological constructs have additional
characteristics which set them apart from other descriptions of
reality in general and from utopian descriptions in particular.
As Mannheim says, they "fail to take account of the new realities
applying to a situation,"[32] and thus tend to be either opposed to
social innovation or downright regressive. But more of this
later.

Notwithstanding the similarities between the particular and
the total meanings of ideology, there are significant
differences between the two. As mentioned earlier, it is
precisely in the elucidation of these distinctions that Mannheim
feels he has cleaned up the ambiguous treatment of the concept in

the writings of Marx and Engels.

The particular conception of ideology argues that only parts
of a subject's total worldview are ideological in
character--i.e., that even though some of the content in his
theoretical apparatus is consciously or semi-consciously opaque,
the overall structure of that apparatus is such that it
incorporates certain "objective" canons of validity which are
acceptable to both him and his opponent. As Mannheim describes
the situation, even if

> it is claimed...that a [particularist ideologue] is
> lying, or that he is concealing or distorting a given
> factual situation, it is still nevertheless assumed
> that both parties share common criteria of validity--it
> is still assumed that it is possible to refute lies
> and eradicate sources of error by referring to accepted
> criteria of objective validity common to both parties.
> The suspicion that one's opponent is the victim of an
> ideology does not go so far as to exclude him from
> discussion on the basis of a common theoretical frame
> of reference.[33]

The content which the particularist ideologue distorts
acquires its ideological character by virtue of the subject's
need to protect what he perceives to be his interests. It is not
the subject's total outlook that is distorted. Rather, it is
specific content--details, as it were--within that outlook which
acquire an ideological character, simply because the subject
feels he has a vested interest in defending certain specific
perspectives rather than others. These distortions are sometimes
self-conscious attempts to protect one's position. They can
acquire, for example, the status of what we most commonly refer
to as "lies." But usually the mechanism at work is not as
one-dimensional as deliberate deception. More commonly, the
particularist ideologue has convinced himself, to one degree or
another, that the specific content which he has distorted

possesses verisimilitude. As such, particular ideology usually manifests itself as a type of psychological rationalization. The subject believes his distortions because he <u>has</u> to believe them in order to defend his perceived interests. Indeed, what might have originally started out as a deliberately deceitful interpretation on the part of a subject can quite often subtly metamorphose into a sincere belief in his conceptual and normative apparatus. "The particular conception of ideology therefore signifies a phenomenon intermediate between a simple lie at one pole, and an error, which is the result of a distorted and faulty apparatus, at the other. It refers to a sphere of errors, psychological in nature, which, unlike deliberate deception, are not intentional, but follow inevitably and unwittingly from certain causal determinants."[34]

    This particular meaning of ideology, based as it is upon a consideration of the psychology of interests and motivation as well as the influence of specific socio-economic conditions, helps to make sense of the different intuitions about ideology which Marx and Engels tended to piece together into a rather confusing patchwork. Recall that sometimes the two characterized ideology as primarily psychological in nature, arising out of a rationalized inversion of reality ultimately traceable to the need to protect what the subject perceived as the demands of self-interest. Also recall that they tended to be ambiguous on the question of whether this inversion was consciously promulgated by the subject or was a phenomenon characterized as much by self-deceit as by deception. Mannheim's notion of particular ideology can accommodate this psychological interpretation. Some forms of ideology <u>are</u> semi-lucid, hovering between conscious deception and unwitting self-deceit. Specific content in one's conceptual and normative apparatus can be distorted because of the subject's need to protect his position in the social habitat, regardless of whether that deceit takes the form of opaque abstraction (as in the case, for instance, of the "Great Man/Great Idea" tradition) or a more uneasy--yet still psychologically "necessary"--rationalization of economic, political or racist behavior, such as one sees in certain antebellum justifications of American slavery which based themselves upon the "white man's burden" thesis.[35]

The primary characteristic of the particular conception of ideology, then, is that it distorts discrete content on the basis of psychological motivation. The total conception of ideology, on the other hand, is, as Mannheim says, "noological" in nature rather than psychological.[36] It is not so much the reflection of an individual's perceived interests as it is a function of the structure of a given socio-economic group's worldview. The notion of total ideology is thus more comprehensive than particular ideology. In the case of the former, the entire form of a society's conceptual and normative worldview is under consideration, not simply isolated bits of content. As Mannheim says, the total concept of ideology, working as it does on a noological rather than a psychological level, deals with "not merely the content but also the form, and even the conceptual framework of a mode of thought as a function of the life-situation of a thinker."[37]

Particular ideologies, arising as they do from the subject's attempt to justify to himself the content of particular beliefs which he holds, can, as we saw earlier, be semi-transparent. They possess the character, sometimes simplistically and sometimes quite elaborately, of the psychological mechanism of rationalization. Total ideologies, however, by virtue of being functions not merely of an individual's life-situation but rather of the entire Zeitgeist of a particular historical period, do not allow an analogous degree of transparency. The illusory purview of a total ideology does not pertain simply to what an individual thinks about certain propositions. Rather, it colors the very basis of how an entire culture comes to think about propositions with the latter's nature being itself, of course, circumscribed by the ideologically conditioned methodological and ontological assumptions which the culture accepts as it primitives. We see here the "trickle-down" effect characteristic of ideological constructs pointed out by Marx and Engels. Inasmuch as total ideologies are a function of an historical worldview's theoretical and normative structure, the content of those structures must be, to one degree or another, likewise ideological in nature. Hence the comprehensiveness of a total ideology.

In a peculiar way, total ideologies take on a life of their own, at least in the sense that their structural nature is in no significant way dependent upon the individual instances of particular ideology which are embedded within them. Particular ideologies, on the other hand, are necessarily colored by the nature of the total ideological worldview in which they are located. Conceptual and normative assumptions, when examined on an individual-by-individual basis, admit a certain amount of variability arising from the subject's unique psychological needs and material situation within the society as a whole. But the boundaries of this individual variation have been determined by the theoretical apparatus of the culture's total ideology. Thus particular and total ideologies are, as Mannheim tells us, "in reality...always intertwined."[38] One must not infer from this interpenetration that a total ideology is nothing more than the sum of a society's particular ideologies. Rather, the total ideology serves as the medium which shapes the character of the particular ideologies it contains. As Mannheim puts it, "as soon as the total conception of ideology is used, we attempt to reconstruct the whole outlook of a social group, and neither the concrete individuals nor the abstract sum of them can legitimately be considered as bearers of this ideological thought-system as a whole."[39]

It is because of total ideology's independence from the psychologisms which lie behind instances of particular ideology that Mannheim often refers to the former as "objective" or "ontological" or "noological." Of course he does not mean to imply by these labels that a total ideology is an "objective" (in the traditional sense of the word) reflection of the "real" nature of things. Such an ascription would, after all, violate not only his basic epistemological starting point but also the very meaning of the word "ideology." Rather, his point is that a total ideology, as a function of the overall material structure of any socio-historical context, can be examined as a more or less stable phenomenon which is not subject to the whims of individual, subjective caprice. Consequently, it is possible for the sociologist of knowledge to identify, in an ex post facto way, the total ideologies which have been associated in the past with specific socio-historical periods, notwithstanding the inevitable but still circumscribed amount of conceptual and normative flexibility produced by those same periods' particular ideologies. It is this "objective" quality of total ideologies which allows for the possibility of a "science" of ideological forms in general. As Mannheim insists, "when we attribute to one historical epoch one intellectual world and to ourselves another one, or if a certain historically determined social stratum thinks in categories other than our own, [it is only because] we refer not to the isolated cases of thought-content, but to fundamentally divergent thought-systems and to widely differing modes of experience and interpretation."[40]

How does Mannheim account for the genesis of a specific socio-historical milieu's total ideology in the first place? It is here that his indebtedness to Marxist socioanalysis is most evident. He accepts Marx and Engels' thesis that total ideologies arise as the result of the division between mental and manual labor in early surplus-producing economies. The leisured and propertied class of mental laborers systematizes a set of conceptual and normative assertions which, although claiming universality, in fact are reflective of the interests of their particular class. Although this interested worldview may in the beginning have involved a certain degree of self-awareness and conscious manipulation, it soon acquires the nature of a genuine total ideology. The ascendent class, just as much as the subordinate classes, eventually comes to believe the model's claims of objectivity and universal validity. It consequently acquires the illusory character of unassailable orthodoxy, and institutionally discourages, sometimes dramatically but more often subtly, nonconventional perspectives. As Mannheim says, "...representatives of a given order have not in all cases taken a hostile attitude towards orientations transcending the existing order. Rather they have always aimed to control those situationally transcendent ideas and interests which are not realizable within the bounds of the present order, and thereby to render them socially impotent, so that such ideas would be confined to a world beyond history and society, where they could not affect the status quo."[41] One of the established order's most effective strategies for pulling the teeth of nonconventional perspectives--or "situationally transcendent ideas"--is to relegate them to an arena beyond "history and society" by lampooning them as "idealistic" or "unrealistic" or "utopian." As Mannheim says, "The representatives of a given

order will label as utopian all conceptions of existence which
<u>from their point</u> of view can in principle never be realized."[42]

The assumption, of course, is that these situationally
transcendent ideas are "unrealistic" simply because they do not
conform to the total ideology of the empowered order. But,
again, it is crucial to keep in mind that this institutionalized
discouragement of nonconventional ideas is not a deliberate
machination on the part of the ascendent class. The total
ideological structure has blinded it as much as the rest of
society. Indeed, as we have seen, once a total ideology is set
in motion, it has very little need for the active participation
of ideologues. It runs on its own steam, as it were, with a set
of inbuilt mechanisms for self-extension as well as an almost
automatic safety-net of checks and balances which discourages the
very possibility of the appearance of nonideological thought.
The total ideology of a specific socio-economic milieu is not a
perpetual-motion machine. An examination of the historical
record clearly indicates periodic shifts in the character of
stuctures of total ideologies, shifts which are ultimately
dependent upon the fluctuations of the material and economic
conditions that serve as social habitats. But within the
contexts of discrete historical periods, total ideologies do
acquire a kind of bulldozer effect, moving of their own accord
within a circumscribed arena. Thus the nature of a total
ideology is to be opaque to all segments of a particular
socio-historical milieu, notwithstanding the fact that it
originally arose from and continues to solidify the interests of
that society's ascendent class. In discussing total ideology's
lack of self-transparency, Mannheim claims that

> The concept "ideology" reflects the one discovery which
> emerged from political conflict, namely, that ruling
> groups can in their thinking become so intensively

interest-bound to a situation that they are simply no
longer able to see certain facts which would undermine
their sense of domination. There is implicit in the
word "ideology" the insight that in certain situations
the collective unconscious of certain groups obscures
the real condition of society both to itself and to
others and thereby stabilizes it.[43]

We saw earlier that Mannheim's notion of particular ideology
was able to accommodate Marx and Engels' occasional references to
ideology as a psychological, semi-deliberate system of illusory
beliefs. Now, with his discussion of the concept of total
ideology, he has done justice to their intuitions that ideology
can also manifest itself as a sociological phenomenon that arises
from the class structure of a given socio-historical setting.
This distinction between particular and total forms of ideology,
considered by many to be Mannheim's most significant contribution
to the sociology of knowledge, goes a long way in cleaning up the
traditional Marxist analysis of ideology while still doing
justice to the richness of its original insights. Mannheim's
typology enables us to see that Marx and Engels' discussions of
ideology really do not contain the incoherencies often attributed
to them. All their descriptions have weight. The ambiguity is a
consequence of their failure to realize that they were, in
effect, talking about two different kinds of ideological
structures.

As we have seen, Mannheim prefers to think of ideology, in
both its particular and its total modes, in functional terms.
An ideological construct is a function of the specific
socio-historical setting with which it is associated and can be
understood only with reference to the social habitat which gives
rise to it. Earlier in this section, however, I suggested the
reader might object that all conceptual models, given Mannheim's
epistemological assumptions about the nature of social knowledge,

could be described as a function of their socio-historical
milieux, thus rendering any attempted distinction between
ideological and nonideological knowledge somewhat specious. And,
indeed, if Mannheim's analysis of the ideological mentality had
ended at the point to which I have thus far taken it, that
objection clearly would be justified. But Mannheim pushes his
treatment one step further, and in so doing absolves himself by
providing a criterion for the discrimination of ideological
functions from nonideological ones.

It is unquestionably true that all social knowledge for
Mannheim is a function of socio-historical settings. But
ideological functions can be differentiated from nonideological
ones on the basis of what Mannheim calls their "concrete
effectiveness." An ideological model leads to certain practical
results which are unique to it alone and which thereby serve as
markers to distinguish it from other models. I will conclude
this section on Mannheim's analysis of the ideological mentality
by discussing this point.

Recall the two primary characteristics of the total
conception of ideology. In the first place, its nature is a
reflection of the interests of a specific class of empowered
individuals within the context of a discrete socio-economic
setting. Insofar as it is supportive of this set of class
interests, it is necessarily hostile to change, on either the
theoretical or the concrete levels. What fluidity it does allow
must be capable of being subsumed within its own circumscribed
boundaries. Thus total ideologies may often display a semblance
of openness to "transcendent" content and even show a certain
flexibility in the theoretical assumptions which define their
worldviews. In point of fact, however, such fluidity is
illusory, because transcendent ideas are easily absorbed and

hence controlled by the ideological structure as a whole.
Putatively transcendent ideas, in other words, have no
innovative, concrete effect on material, classbound conditions.
In fact, they indirectly support the ideological status quo by
serving as impotent outlets for societal dissent. As Mannheim
puts it,

> every period in history has contained ideas
> transcending the existing order, but these did not
> function as [nonideological ideas]; they were rather
> the appropriate ideologies of this stage of existence
> as long as they were "organically" and harmoniously
> integrated into the worldview characteristic of the
> period (i.e., did not offer revolutionary
> possibilities). As long [for instance] as the
> clerically and feudally organized medieval order was
> able to locate its paradise outside of society, in some
> other-worldly sphere which transcended history and
> dulled its revolutionary edge, the idea of paradise was
> still an integral part of [the classbound ideology of]
> medieval society.[44]

Another point must be kept in mind. Total ideology is also
characterized by its lack of self-transparency. As an
ideological mode, it is deceived about its own real nature.
Although in fact a ubiquitously extended reflection of the
interests of a discrete class, it claims universal validity.
This general deception leads to two results. First, as indicated
earlier, total ideology tends to obstruct new developments in
conceptual and concrete arenas which are antithetical to the
absolutistic worldview it sustains. This leads to an incremental
stagnation of the society in question which aborts the
open-endedness necessary for the very possibility of growth.
Second--and more interestingly--it prevents the ideological
structure from ever successfully realizing its specific social
programme. Ideologically determined conduct--and, ultimately,
theoretical or normative justifications of that conduct--will

always fall short of its intended meaning precisely because it
mistakenly believes what is in reality a set of relativistic
standards which appropriately "fit" only one segment of the class
structure to be a set of universal propositions applicable to all
classes.   Inasmuch as each discrete social class can be
identified by a set of interests unique to it and it alone, a
forced totalization of class interests such as ideology attempts
is doomed to failure. It can never succeed--and necessarily
so--in transforming the existing social habitat into one more in
accord with its own conceptions. Let's examine these two points
in more detail.

Ideological ideas are in their own way situationally
transcendent. They do not faithfully reflect the total nexus of
actual material conditions and economic relationships which
comprise the social habitat of their historical setting. True,
they do mirror the character of a segment of the social
habitat--the ascendent, empowered class--but, as we have seen,
the nature of a total ideology is to mistakenly claim to
represent values which are reflective of the entire social
apparatus. The conceptual and normative aspects of a total
ideology, then, do not enjoy an isomorphic relationship to
concrete reality. They unwittingly transcend--i.e., do not
faithfully reflect--the actual situation. This is simply another
way of expressing the fact that ideologies, by definition, are
distorted systems of belief.

Now a situationally transcendent idea, according to
Mannheim, may or may not be capable of concrete realization.
Indeed, as we shall see later, the distinctive characteristic of
utopian transcendent ideas is that they are realizable and really
do change the existing social order. Regardless of whether or
not a set of situationally transcendent beliefs can be realized,

however, each adopts a social agenda which is in keeping with
the theoretical assumptions about reality that serves as its
basis. It attempts to concretize those assumptions by setting
into motion political and magisterial institutions which it
perceives as being reflective of the natural order of things.
These institutions naturally come to be seen as vehicles towards
the realization of ideals, of the attainment of those ultimate
goals which the set of transcendent ideas has accepted as its
desiderata. In the case of total ideologies, these institutions
also take on the semblance of absolute necessity. They have so
totalized their worldview--so frozen it, so to speak--that the
social agenda and consequent structural institutions espoused by
them are seen as the only possible means to the attainment of the
set of ultimate goals. It follows that a total ideology can have
very little patience with alternative ideals or institutional
models. Because the ideals and models which it accepts are
absolute, any deviation from them represents not merely an
obstacle but also a threat to the final actualization of the
"perfect" order.

This absolutization of its situationally transcendent
ideals accounts for the first characteristic of total ideology
mentioned earlier--namely, its hostility to innovation. This
championing of orthodoxy, however, is in the long run
self-defeating. It leads to increasing levels of rigidity,
sterility and ultimate stagnation by systematically discouraging
nonconventional theoretical exploration and concrete activity.
In convincing itself that its worldview is the only possible one,
it lessens its ability to accommodate itself to changing material
conditions; in Mannheim's words, "it obstructs comprehension of a
reality which is the outcome of constant reorganization of the
mental processes which make up our worlds."[45] Total ideology's
inability to see through its own illusions creates for itself "an

ontology handed down through tradition [which] obstructs new
developments, especially in the basic modes of thinking. ...As
long as...the conventional theoretical framework remains
unquestioned we will remain in the toils of a static mode of
thought which is inadequate to our present stage of historical
and intellectual development."[46] Furthermore, the incapacity of
a total ideology to maintain its institutional integrity
escalates as the conditions become more apparent. As the
reigning ideology senses the slow eradication of its hegemonic
hold on a socio-historical setting, it tenaciously retrenches and
adopts an even more absolutistic hostility towards innovation--a
strategy which may enjoy short-term success, but which in the
long run only serves to speed up the process of dissolution.

This brings us to the characteristic failure of ideological
models to transform the existing material reality of which they
are a function into one that is more in accord with their own
conceptions. The preceding analysis points to one of the reasons
for this failure: total ideology's insistence upon absolutism
depletes its institutions of adaptability, which inevitably leads
to a chronic inability on its part to respond to changing
material conditions. But there is another reason for total
ideology's de facto failure, and it too is based upon the
ideological model's mistaken vision of itself as universally
valid.

Because total ideology mistakenly attributes the same
conceptual and normative standards to all classes within a
particular socio-historical setting, standards which in fact are
reflective of the character of only one of those classes, its
social agendas, theoretical models and values are assumed to be
representative of the human predicament in general. This
blindness to its own classbound nature leads it to presume that

the social agenda which is most conducive to the perpetuation of
the ruling class is also in the best interests of all the other
classes. This absolutization of what is essentially a set of
classbound   categories   prevents   the   total   ideology   from
successfully consummating its social agenda because, concretely,
it demands the forcing of conceptual and normative assumptions
upon segments of the social setting which they simply will not
fit. Consequently, the ideals espoused by a total ideology
cannot be actualized throughout the society as a whole. They are
properly applicable to only one segment of the social setting,
and cannot comfortably take root, as it were, outside of that
circumscribed   context.   As   such,   "ideologies   are   the
situationally transcendent ideas which never succeed de facto in
the realization of their projected contents."[47]

      An example will help to make the point clearer. As I will
show more fully in Chapter Three, one of the ideals of the sane
society espoused by Francis Bacon in the seventeenth century was
unlimited industrial growth.   According to Bacon, the primary
role of "correct" science was to facilitate improvement in the
technological sciences. These improvements were valuable, Bacon
argued, because they produced the industrial capacity necessary
for the material betterment of all classes within society. In
point of fact, however, the gradual industrialization of Britain
led to only a relative improvement in laboring class income. On
the other hand, an absolute increase in income was created for
the mercantile and industrial bourgeoisie, in whose hands rested
the capital necessary to pay for improved means of production.
The social programme of industrialization, in fact, increasingly
concentrated both wealth and political power in the hands of the
middle class, while simultaneously impoverishing both the
laboring class and, to a lesser extent, the entrenched
aristocracy. The upshot was the creation of huge

disproportionalities   in   the   distribution   of   the   economic
advantages which resulted from the new emphasis upon centralized
production.   In   effect,   then,   the   Baconian   vision   of
industrialization as an absolute good was the expression of a
classbound value which, far from benefiting all members of
society, actually enriched one segment at the   expense of most
others. As such, the ideal was illusory in that it proved to be
tied to relative class interests instead of the interests of
society as a whole. It ultimately failed to instantiate its
totalizing agenda for   overall social improvement because it was
unable to see that neither its stated aims nor its programme for
achieving them gave equal expression to the interests of all
classes.

      In   summary,   then,   Mannheim's   functional   analysis   of
ideology   accomplishes several purposes. First, it serves to
clear up   the ambiguities which weakened the Marxist   account of
ideology   by distinguishing between two different   types   of
meanings of ideology--the particular and the total.   Second, it
provides an   explanation for the   origins of ideologies   which is
based upon   material, socio-historical conditions.   Finally, and
most importantly in the context of the present study, it outlines
functional characteristics of ideological transcendent ideas
from non-ideological ones.   Those characteristics are twofold.
First, ideological forms, because of their tendency towards
totalization, are directly linked to the material interests of
any given society's ascendent class and hence are supremely
protective of the economic, conceptual and political status
quo--an attitude which encourages stagnation (if not downright
regression), and discourages innovation. Second, ideological
forms are incapable of ultimately actualizing the social agenda
based upon their totalized worldview because they fail to see
that such agendas are relative in nature, not universal.

Consequently, as Mannheim says, they do not succeed in
"transforming the existing historical reality into one more in
accord with their own conceptions."[48]   Even more to the point,
they are not even aware of the distance between their putatively
absolute ideals and actual classbound programmes of action until
the resultant social tensions become so great as to result first,
in increasing societal dissent and then, possibly, actual
revolution.

The Utopian Mentality

We are finally in a position to examine Mannheim's
functional analysis of the utopian form of social knowledge.
Given the large amount of space spent thus far in discussing the
ideological mentality, it might appear as if we have lost the
forest for the trees, inasmuch as this chapter, after all,
purports to deal with the function of utopian thought. But I
believe it will become clear that the digression was necessary.
The dynamic of the utopian function can be fully appreciated only
if it is juxtaposed to its ideological counterpart in the
sociology of knowledge. The importance of the comparison will
become even more apparent in later chapters, where I shall argue
that the ideological model which I call the "sane society" has
historically taken on the deceptive form of a bona fide utopia.

What, according to Mannheim, is a utopian model? As I
indicated in the Introduction, the utopian mentality, just as
much as the ideological mentality, is a distortion of reality.
As Mannheim says, a "state of mind is utopian when it is
incongruous with the state of reality within which it occurs."[49]
This awareness of the equally illusory character of ideologies
and utopias has prompted some critics to assume either that they
are identical, or that the latter are somehow merely a subset of
the former. But Mannheim disagrees. Just as he insists that

ideological forms can be adequately identified only by an appeal
to their concrete consequences, so he adopts an identical
criterion for the recognition of utopian functions. A genuine
utopian form is recognized not merely by an awareness of its
"transcendent" character, since, after all, ideologies are
likewise "transcendent." Rather, a utopian is differentiated
from an ideological model by virtue of what it does. And the
functions of the two forms are quite distinct.

    Mannheim's distinction between   the two models is   as
follows:

        [a utopian] state of mind in experience, in thought,
        and in practice, is oriented towards objects which do
        not exist in the actual situation. However, we should
        not   regard as utopian every state of mind which is
        incongruous with and transcends the immediate situation
        (and in this sense, "departs from reality").   Only
        those   orientations transcending   reality will   be
        referred to by us as utopian which, when they pass over
        into conduct, tend to shatter, either partially or
        wholly, the order of things prevailing at the time.

        In limiting the meaning of the term "utopia" to that
        type of orientation which transcends reality and which
        at the same time breaks the bonds of the existing
        order, a distinction is set between the utopian and the
        ideological states of mind.[50]

This distinction between utopias and ideologies, then, is based
upon   the difference   in the   "concrete effectiveness"   or
"realization" of each. Ideologies, as we saw in the previous
section, are networks of transcendent ideas which de facto fail
to instantiate their appropriate social agendas, a failure which
is directly linked to the totalizing nature of their worldviews.
As Mannheim says,

        their contents can never be realized in the societies
        in which they exist...because one could not live and
        act according to them within the limits of the existing

social order.[51]

Utopias, on the other hand, are sets of transcendent ideas which
de facto succeed in the realization of their projected ideals.
They not only call into question the established conceptual,
normative and social structures of the historical context whence
they arise, but also serve to erode the strength of those
structures' authority, thereby preparing the way for genuine
theoretical and social innovation. In short, utopias "succeed
through counteractivity in transforming the existing historical
reality into one more in accord with their own conceptions."[52]

But how is it that utopian forms succeed in breaking through
the ideological continuum which defines the context from which
they emerge? Furthermore, if the purview of a total ideology is
as pervasive as Mannheim claims, how do dissenting, utopian
elements arise in the first place? It would seem that a
necessary condition for going beyond the orthodox structures of a
totalizing ideological medium is the ability to "separate"
oneself from the very milieu in which one lives, a milieu
moreover which circumscribes the boundaries of not only what one
thinks but also how one thinks (i.e., both content and
methodology). But how is such a leap possible? How is it that a
socially-determined mentality can ever distance itself from its
socio-historical situation long enough to call it into question?
The value of Mannheim's analysis ultimately rests upon how
satisfactorily he can answer these fundamental questions.
Inasmuch as the latter problem is the logically prior of the two,
I will address it first.

Necessary Conditions for the
Emergence of the Utopian Mentality

One of the primary characteristics of total ideologies, as
indicated earlier, is the inability to successfully instantiate
the "ideal" social agendas which arise from their absolutization
of what are essentially classbound values. Although the
disrupting concrete consequences of this tension at first may be
easily absorbed by the overall ideological structure, the
incommensurability of the ideology's classbound goals with its
milieu's actual material conditions becomes increasingly evident.
As classical Marxism would describe the situation, the
ideologically shaped relations of production gradually come into
conflict with changing material modes of production. The
steadily growing social awareness of this conflict of interests
forces an ideological structure in turn to inaugurate steps by
which to reinforce its hegemony. As we have seen, these
strategies of retrenchment normally assume one of two guises.
Either the established ideology digs in its heels and attempts to
secure its totalization by means of the rigorous suppression of
dissenting models, or it creates "safe" avenues for social
dissent which release levels of popular dissatisfaction without
doing permanent damage to the total ideological character of
society as a whole (a strategy, by the way, which Marcuse later
called "ideological containment" in his One-Dimensional Man).
Both attempts to protect the ideological hegemony, however
effective they might prove to be in the short run, are ultimately
problematic. The first alternative only serves to exacerbate the
conceptual and social tension which was precisely the reason for
dissent in the first place. The second alternative, which is
more often employed than the first, also slowly erodes the
stability of the hegemonic orthodoxy by allowing a steadily

growing number of nonideological ideals to bore through the foundation of the total ideology. So long as the total ideology can maintain its hegemonic stability, this official toleration of dissent will in all likelihood prove effective. As Mannheim says, in a "well stabilized society the mere infiltration of the modes of thought of the lower strata"--i.e., of the increasingly dissatisfied classes--"into the higher would not mean much since the bare perception by the dominant group of possible variations in thinking would not result in their being intellectually shaken."[53] But it is unlikely that a total ideology can maintain its stability for an extended period of time after it begins a policy of controlling dissent by allowing it "safe" forms of expression. Even seemingly innocuous gestures expressive of divergent worldviews tend to chip away incrementally at the monolithic hegemony which a total ideology must sustain in order to survive.

For example, one of the ways in which an ideological structure might attempt to deflate dissent by allowing it "harmless" outlets is through loosening (without, of course, eliminating) the traditional constraints upon social mobility. Dangerously dissatisfied elements of the society are "bought off," as it were, by being allowed to rise, up to a certain point, in the social and economic hierarchy. But this strategy of containment only contributes to the erosion of the dominant hegemony, precisely because it highlights the point that the "absolute" hierarchial structure of society is not, in fact, necessary. This rupture in the stasis which hitherto defined the social form has far-reaching consequences. It encourages the subordinate class elements to push even harder for their own social agenda, based upon a counter-ideological theoretical foundation, while at the same time forcing the hegemonic class to uneasily call into question the absolutism of its beliefs. The normative and conceptual confusion which arises from the effects of increased social mobility, then, creates a gap in the ideological continuum that serves as the condition for the appearance of widespread nonideological thought-forms. As Mannheim argues,

> ...the multiplicity of ways of thinking cannot become a problem in periods when social stability underlies and guarantees the internal unity of a world-view. As long as the same meanings of words, the same way of deducing ideas, are inculcated from childhood on into every member of the group, divergent thought-processes cannot exist in that society. Even a gradual modification in ways of thinking (when it should happen to arise), does not become perceptible to the members of a group who live in a stable situation as long as the tempo in the adaptations of ways of thinking to new problems is so slow that it extends over several generations.[54]

The catalyst which changes the hitherto innocent "multiplicity of ways of thinking" into an effective weapon against a total ideology's authority, however, is precisely the "intensification of social mobility which destroys the earlier illusion, prevalent in a static society, that all things can change, but thought remains eternally the same."[55]

It is important to realize that Mannheim is not claiming new thought forms themselves serve to break the ideological containment. He in no way espouses an abstract, idealist theory of historical change. Rather, he insists that the new values and theoretical models which call into question the hitherto "absolute" total ideology of a culture arise only because changing material conditions—as represented, for instance, by an increase in social and economic mobility between class strata—encourage the emergence of worldviews which clash with the established one.

In short, then, the increasingly apparent contradictions which arise between the material conditions definitive of a particular socio-historical context and its total ideological apparatus create a vacuum in which new normative and theoretical models which better express the ideals and ways of thinking of the subordinate classes can take root. When an historical ethos finds itself confronted with divergent worldviews, the supposedly unassailable ideological edifice begins to crumble. As Mannheim says, "it is with this clashing of modes of thought, each of which has the same claims to representational validity, that for the first time there is rendered possible the emergence of the question which is so fateful, but also so fundamental in the history of thought, namely, how it is possible that identical human thought-processes concerned with the same world produce divergent conceptions of that world."[56]

One of the more specific ways in which social mobility facilitates the appearance of divergent worldviews within the fabric of an existing total ideology is through the creation of a "radical" intelligentsia which expresses the interests and values of the dissenting subordinate social classes.[57] In a society in which a total ideology is secure (and in which, as a result, innovation is at a minimum), the established intelligentsia tends to give expression to the interests of the dominant class, thereby acquiring "a well-defined status or the position of a caste in that society."[58] It enjoys a "monopolistic control over the molding of that society's world-view, and over either the reconstruction or the reconciliation of the differences in the naively formed world-views of the other strata."[59] This ideologically-bound intellectual stratum reinforces the reigning hegemony by dogmatically reasserting a litany of traditional normative and theoretical models which claim to be absolute but in fact are classbound. Moreover, it increasingly loses its

capacity to think nonideologically because it encloses itself
within an ivory tower of abstraction that blinds it to "the open
conflicts of everyday life."[60] Thus the worldview of the
established intelligentsia "does not arise primarily from the
struggle with concrete problems of life nor from trial and error,
nor from experiences in mastering nature and society but rather
much more from its own need for systematization"[61]--a need which
is present because of the intelligentsia's fidelity to the
totalizing project of the ideology which it serves.

The authority of this caste of dogmatic and
ideologically-bound intellectuals is weakened through the earlier
discussed mechanism of social mobility. As contradictions within
the ideological milieu become more apparent, the hitherto vague
aspirations of the subordinate classes are given voice by a
rising group of "new" intellectuals, who come from and express
the interests of those classes. The emergence of this "free"
intelligentsia, as Mannheim calls it, inaugurates the appearance
of counter-ideological worldviews which compete with the dogmatic
models of the traditional epigones. This clash of worldviews
leads to two results. First, it gives both systematic expression
and intellectual legitimation to the nonideological values and
theoretical assumptions within the social structure. Second, it
tends to break down the absolute faith in the traditional
ideological model defended by the entrenched intelligentsia.
According to Mannheim, in "this process the intellectual's
illusion that there is only one way of thinking disappears. The
intellectual is now no longer, as formerly, a member of a caste
or rank whose [dogmatic] manner of thought represents for him
thought as such... With the liberation of the intellectuals from
the rigorous organization of [a total ideological structure],
other ways of interpreting the world [are] increasingly
recognized."[62]

It can be seen, then, that the results of increased levels
of social mobility for the "free" intelligentsia coincide quite
closely with the results of a general increase in social mobility
for nonintellectual members of the subordinate classes. The
effects of mobility upon the latter group tend to materially
reinforce its vague intuitions of the illusory character of
ideological authority, while the effects of mobility upon the new
intelligentsia provides the opportunity for those intuitions to
be systematized and disseminated. The general result in both
cases is the same: an increase in skepticism which prepares the
way for nonideological models more representative of the
interests of the entire society than are the ideological models.
And because the "free" worldviews which carry the new values are
more expressive of the actual material conditions within that
society, their consequent social agendas are more likely to
achieve concrete instantiation--which is, of course, the
functional criterion characteristic of utopian models.

The necessary condition for the appearance of the utopian
mentality, then, is a gradual breakdown in the ubiquitous
hegemony of a society's total ideological structure. This
breakdown is a direct result of the increasing awareness on the
part of members of the subordinate classes that fundamental
conflicts exist between the putatively absolute values of the
ideology and actual material, economic and social conditions.
The growth in skepticism which this awareness produces is only
exasperated by the ideological authority's attempts to retrench.
Harsh supression of dissent tends to increase the tension, while
more subtle attempts at containment, such as the
institutionalized tolerance of social mobility, indirectly
encourage the proliferation of nonideological worldviews. The
consequent clash of opposing conceptual and normative models, one

representing the interests of the subordinate classes,   creates a
gap in the ideological   continuum in which the utopian   mentality
can flourish.

The Non-totalizing Character
of the Utopian Mentality

We can   now turn to   a consideration of   the   other question
which   Mannheim must   answer in   order to   adequately defend   his
notion of the   utopian mentality: how is   it that   utopian forms
succeed in replacing their ideological predecessors?   Or,   to put
it another way, how do   we know that a putative utopian   model is
not   itself   simply   another   ideology,   just   as   illusory   and
classbound as the   structure it replaces?

Recall that utopian   forms, just like ideological   ones, are
not accurate   portrayals of "objective"   reality.   Instead, they
are   intricate   sets   of   "transcendent   ideas"   which,   although
arising from a   discrete material context, do   not isomorphically
mirror it.   This failure to   objectively represent reality   does
not   make   them   illusory, however;   it   simply   points to   their
partially imaginary character.

The   distinction is   a crucial   one.   Ideological   forms are
illusory, not   so much because   they fail   to   adequately portray
reality, but because they falsely   claim to do so.   They fail   to
recognize   that the   set of   normative   and   conceptual standards
which   they defend   are contextual.   Instead,   they   assume that
these structures enjoy   an absolute, metaphysical guarantee.   It
is this   blindness to their   own natures   that   makes ideological
forms illusory.

Utopias, on the other hand, are deliberate attempts to "transcend" both "objective" reality and currently existent ideological structures. They make no claim to either metaphysical privilege or universal validity. They are imaginary speculations about what the character of a nonideological social matrix might be. In separating themselves from the total ideological structure, they both criticize its shortcomings and offer for consideration alternative models, but do so with full knowledge that these alternative models do not exist, are not representative of a "real" state of affairs. They are not illusory in the same way that ideologies are, because they are not deceived about their own characters. They are imaginary and claim only to serve as inspirational vehicles for the construction of a new society. They are "self-conscious" transcendent ideas, whereas ideological structures might be described as "blind" or "unconscious" ones.

In addition to their freedom from the self-deception which characterizes ideological forms, utopias can also be said to more adequately capture the general interests of a given socio-economic context than ideological totalizations. Keep in mind that the utopian mentality first arises as a result of the increasing awareness on the part of a society's subordinate classes of the inability of ideological structures to adequately represent either their interests or their values. Ideologies, insofar as they tend to mirror the worldview of the economically dominant segment of a population, are really quite limited in their appropriateness. True, they claim absolute validity for themselves, and certainly do, for circumscribed periods of time at any rate, define the general worldview for the context over which they have hegemonic jurisdiction. But the direct beneficiaries of such worldviews--the economically empowered class and its small group of supportive intellectual apologists--numerically constitute but a small fraction of the total population. The normative and conceptual standards which arise from the classbound worldview in no significant way represent the interests of the rest of society's strata.

It is precisely because utopian forms are attempts on the part of the dissenting segments of society to give expression to their real dissatisfaction that they are more representative than ideologies. This is not to deny the earlier assertion that utopias are "transcendent ideas," that they are deliberately imaginary scenarios of the good society rather than objective mirrors of existent society. But the interests, normative standards and conceptual assumptions which serve as the occasion for the elaboration of utopian visions do exist, even if somewhat inchoately, for a much larger section of a society's population than the one represented by ideologies. Consequently, the nascent utopian worldview of subordinate classes, reflecting as it does their material and economic situations, is built upon a foundation much broader in applicability than the worldview of an ideology. As such, it is more representative--without, of course, being absolute--than its ideological counterpart. It is thus more reflective of the real interests of society, notwithstanding the fact that it is, nevertheless, "transcendent."

The broader representationality of bona fide utopian models is an important facet which is often overlooked by commentators upon the utopian project. All too often, the assumption is that utopian visions are primarily solitary, isolated productions which in no fundamental way enjoy the support of large segments of the population until after their initial appearance (if, of course, even then). Mannheim argues that this is an inversion of the real situation. Those forms of social knowledge which he

designates   as   utopian   depend for   their   very   appearance upon
widespread   dissatisfaction with   existent ideological   forms, in
addition to a common intuition about the character of alternative
models.   Utopian thought forms, in short, are social products, as
is   all   knowledge   for   Mannheim.   That   they   can   serve   as
competitors   and   eventual replacements of   ideological structures
points to the fact that they are perceived by   increasingly large
segments   of   a   given   society's   population   to   be   more
representative of their interests than ideological thought forms.
Mannheim clearly spells out   the social character of the   utopian
mentality in the following passage:

> In   the sense   of our   definition, an   effective utopia
> cannot in the   long run be the   work of   an individual,
> since the individual cannot by himself tear asunder the
> historical-social   situation.   Only   when   the   utopian
> conception   of   the   individual   seizes   upon   currents
> already   present in   society   and   gives expression to
> them, when in this form it flows back into   the outlook
> of the   whole group, and   is translated into   action by
> it, only then can   the existing order be challenged   by
> the striving for another order of existence.[63]

So far   we have seen   that utopian forms   which arise in   a
socio-historical context   lack the ideological   characteristic of
self-deception.   Moreover,   they are more   representative   of the
interests of the greater   part of society than their   ideological
counterparts.   But there is still another feature of   the utopian
mentality   which   clearly   indicates that   it   is   not simply   an
ideological replacement of the older ideological structure.   That
quality is its nontotalizing character.

The proponents of   a utopian model, given   its nondeceptive,
self-transparent quality, are aware   of the fact that the   values
which they   espouse are classbound   or   nonabsolutistic.   Indeed,
it is precisely the realization on the part of the   proponents of

a utopian structure that the worldview they defend is in
fundamental competition with the entrenched ideological worldview
which prevents them from assuming that its socio-economic ideals
are universal in applicability. They recognize both the
existence and claims of ideological values, but correctly insist
that the latitude of those claims is much more circumscribed than
normally assumed. This is simply another way of expressing the
fact that defenders of utopian models realize the incompatability
of ideological values to the interests of the subordinate classes
in a discrete socio-economic setting, notwithstanding the fact
that those former values reflect quite adequately the hegemonic
interests of the entrenched dominant class. At the same time,
defenders of the utopian model are also cognizant of the fact
that the alternative worldview it defends is more supportive of
their own interests than those of the dominant class. They do
assume that their worldview is more representative of the
majority of individuals in the socio-economic setting than is the
worldview of the incumbent ideology, but they do not suppose,
given the class structure of the society in which it arises, that
it represents the immediate interests of the entire spectrum of
social strata. They do not, in short, attempt to totalize the
utopian form's set of normative and conceptual models, because
they are aware that different socio-economic classes have
different values and fundamentally divergent ways of interpreting
the world.

In a word, then, bona fide utopias do not totalize--and
hence are not simply subtle ideological forms--because they do
not insist that either their worldview or consequent social
programmes are applicable to all classes within a given context.
Rather than forcing their agendas upon inappropriate
socio-economic groups, as ideologies do, utopias argue that a
more realistic approach is to change the hierarchical class

structure of the society from which they spring. They seek to ameliorate the radical differences in socio-economic privilege which served as the necessary material condition for the emergence of classbound ideology in the first place. As such, utopian social programmes, unlike their ideological counterparts, are innovative and revolutionary in character. They call for a radical reorientation of not only the conceptual and normative worldview definitive of a particular culture, but also of the socio-economic material relations which that worldview mirrors.

In addition to escaping totalization through their awareness of the nonuniversal applicability of their alternative worldview, utopian forms also remain free from ideological tendencies by virtue of their postulation of an open-ended and flexible future. Unlike ideologies, which suppose that their models enjoy metaphysical guarantee and hence are nonmalleable, utopian structures recognize the contextual origins of their normative and theoretical assumptions. The awareness that it has risen from a growing discontent with entrenched ideological values, and that it in turn better reflects current material conditions, provides the utopian worldview with the knowledge that its ideals and social programme are subject to continual future revision, revision which changes in material conditions will call for. As Mannheim says, "the utopian element in our consciousness is subject to changes in content and form. The situation that exists at any given moment is constantly being shattered by different situationally transcendent factors... [Furthermore,] this change in substance and form of the utopia does not take place in a realm which is independent of social life."[64] This utopian sensitivity to the need for a continual re-examination of normative ideals and social agenda in the light of changing material conditions is one which ideological forms by definition are incapable of, given the inability on the part of

their proponents to imagine the very possibility of viable
alternatives to the reigning status quo. As Mannheim insists,

> From the [ideological] position, it is practically
> impossible to transcend the limits of the status quo.
> This reluctance to transcend the status quo tends
> towards the view of regarding something that is
> unrealizble merely in the given order, so that by
> obscuring these distinctions one can suppress the
> validity of the claims of the...utopia. By calling
> everything utopian that goes beyond the present
> existing order, one sets at rest the anxiety that might
> arise from...utopias that are realizable in another
> order.[65]

III

We have seen, following Mannheim, that utopian thought forms
can be distinguished from ideological ones on the basis of a
difference in their social functions. Ideologies tend to support
the conventional, normative and conceptual models operative in a
given socio-economic context. As such, they tend towards
totalization, which in turn discourages social and conceptual
innovation and leads to a stagnation which eventually gives rise
to alternative utopian models. Utopias sense the tension between
the putatively absolute standards of ideological structures and
actually existent socio-material conditions and strive to
alleviate it by introducing alternative worldviews and social
agenda. In doing so, they chip away at the ideological
continuum, thereby acting as vehicles for social and theoretical
innovation.

We have also examined two of the ways in which new utopian
structures separate themselves from their ideological

predecessors. First, they are more clearly representative of the interests of the major segment of population in the societies where they appear. True, they can be said to be classbound, but the latitude of this contexuality is wider than that possessed by ideological models. Moreover, utopias are not self-deceived about the extent of their applicability. They recognize the existence of alternative worldviews (namely, ideological ones), and furthermore acknowledge the fact that their own utopian values do not mirror the interests of their society's dominant class or classes. This self-transparency prevents them from falling into the project of totalization which is characteristic of ideological worldviews. It also enables them to retain the fluidity necessary to accommodate future changes in the economic and material conditions which define their historical setting.

Mannheim's analysis of the functional roles of ideological and utopian forms of social knowledge provides us, then, with a set of methodological standards by which to test any putatively utopian model. Granted, the barometer must be applied _ex post facto_, as Mannheim readily admits. We can conclusively determine whether or not a particular historical worldview is utopian or ideological only by examining the social and conceptual consequences to which it gives rise. But in the absence of any other systematic litmus test, even one which can be applied only after the fact is welcome.

The importance of Mannheim's analysis will become obvious, I believe, throughout the subsequent chapters of this study. As indicated in the Introduction, one of the most pervasive ideals in the modern era is what I have called the "sane society." The conceptual and normative standards of this worldview, from its first systematic expression by Francis Bacon in the seventeenth century to the apogee of its popularity in the nineteenth

century, have claimed to be "utopian"--i.e., revolutionary,
innovative and progressive. But I shall argue that this claim
is false. Far from exhibiting any of the functional
characteristics of utopian thought forms, the sane society is in
fact a classic example of what Mannheim would call a total
ideology. The interests which it represents are classbound,
reflecting the values of the modern era's dominant bourgeois
class. Furthermore, the sane society worldview has been one of
the most effective champions of the capitalist hegemony to arise
in the last three centuries. Finally, as I shall indicate, the
social programme of this worldview has failed. Its putatively
universal ideals, while claiming to benefit all segments of the
population, in fact have tended to further the interests of the
dominant class at the expense of subordinate ones. The
implication of all this for the sociology of knowledge in general
and the understanding of the modern era in particular is
shocking--namely, that it is possible for an ideological form to
both cement its hegemony and safely channel societal dissent by
masquerading as a bona fide revolutionary vehicle. The careful
examination of just how this charade has been played out in the
modern era is the subject of the rest of this study.[66]

CHAPTER 2

BACON'S GREAT INSTAURATION

For the end which this science of mine proposes is the invention not of arguments but of arts; not of things in accordance with principles themselves; not of probable reasons, but of designations and directions for works. And as the intention is different, so accordingly is the effect: the effect of one being to overcome an opponent in argument, of the other to command nature in action.

Francis Bacon,
The Great Instauration

Nature becomes...purely an object for men, something merely useful, and is no longer recognized as a power for itself. The theoretical cognition of its autonomous laws appears only as the cunning by which men subject nature to the requirements of their needs...

Karl Marx,
Grundrisse

I

The reputation of Francis Bacon (1561-1626) as a philosophical luminary has dimmed in recent years. He has been severely criticized by contemporary thinkers such as Alexandre Koyre, E.J. Dijksterhuis and Sir Karl Popper, all of whom argue that his historical influence is disproportionate to his actual philosophical contributions. Each of them claims that his "new

logic" not only failed to incisively condemn the older
Aristotelian method, but also achieved no new results in science.
Furthermore, this twentieth century devaluation of Bacon's
methodology was anticipated in the nineteeth century.   Although
even then Bacon had a few notable champions--including John
Stuart Mill and John Herschel[1]--most methodologists and
philosophers of science agreed that the justifications for his
inductive method were woefully inadequate. As William Leiss puts
it, "according to his [nineteenth-century] critics, Bacon's heart
was in the right place, but unfortunately his actual
perscriptions for a new scientific approach were a hopeless
muddle."[2]

Notwithstanding reservations about the ultimate coherency of
his methodology and epistemology, it is clear that Bacon's
influence has been enormous, both during his lifetime and
afterwards. His own contemporaries dubbed him the "secretary of
nature."[3] His campaign for organized and collaborative
scientific research served as the primary inspiration for the
founding in 1662 of the British Royal Society and, soon
thereafter, the French Academie des Sciences. During the latter
half of the seventeenth century his reputation in England was
unmatched, with both Robert Hooke and Robert Boyle competing
against one another in their praises of him. (Of course there
were exceptions. Thomas Hobbes is, perhaps, the most outstanding
example.) The Continental philosophes of the next century
likewise accepted Bacon as one of their chief inspirations.
D'Alembert lauded his "sublime genius" in the Preliminary
Discourse to the Encyclopedia, and no less a celebrity than
Diderot claimed that the Encyclopedia's "principle debt" was to
the vision of Bacon.[4] Interestingly enough, the veneration in
which the philosophes held Bacon was inspired not so much by his
epistemology, which they tended to ignore, as by his eloquent

defense of the inevitability of progress in the mechanical and physical sciences.[5] This curious coupling of regard for the Baconian project with the (sometimes contemptuous) rejection of his method continued into the nineteenth and twentieth centuries. Macaulay almost embarrassingly praised Bacon as a prophet of positivism and utility, but rather harshly criticized his inductive procedure. Macaulay's philosophical reasons for dismissing Baconian induction are unclear at certain points and downright wrongminded at others. Regardless of the sloppiness of his thinking, however, his rather schizoid appraisal of Bacon is representative. The vastly superior philosopher C.S. Peirce agreed with Macaulay's remarks (although Peirce's reasons for rejecting Bacon's inductive technique have nothing in common with Macaulay's save a common use of the English language). Peirce admired Bacon's overall schema, but was unpleasantly struck by what he took to be the inadequacy of its analysis of scientific procedure. And even E.J. Dijksterhuis who, as noted above, is not overly sanguine about the logical merits of Bacon's philosophy, willingly acknowledges the remarkable influence which Bacon's project exerted upon the modern imagination:

> Nothing is easier than to enlarge on his defects, his unfair judgement of the achievements of others, his undervaluation of mathematics and the fact that he did so little to further science. But the note he struck at the beginning of the seventeenth century is not silenced and his inspiring influence not destroyed by this.
>
> The Athenians, when obliged to support Sparta in war, instead sent the lame poet Tyrtaeus. His fighting value was nil, but with his war-songs he inspired the Spartans so greatly that they were victorious. Bacon was--to speak in his style--the Tyrtaeus of seventeenth century science. Without personally enriching it with concrete discoveries, he inspired numerous others to further it.[6]

Bacon's role in the history of ideas, then, is a perplexing

one. On the one hand, most subsequent philosophers have tended
to discount the coherency of his system and deny that it led to a
concrete enrichment of science. At best, they allow that if
Bacon has any legitimate claim to philosophical originality, it
is because of his revamping of the inductive process. But even
here there is no clear consensus, as I shall discuss later, that
the Novum Organum was in fact as "new" as Bacon claimed. On the
other hand, there is almost unanimous agreement that Bacon's
"project," his "vision" of a new science, is one of the chief
inspirations of the modern imagination, from Bacon's own time
right down to the present day. The implication of these two
evaluations is startling. It is that the character of the modern
era's "correct" scientific mentality has been shaped by a man
whose philosophy of science is muddled. Even more amazing is
the fact that the very individuals who recognize the flawed
character of Bacon's philosophy are also among those who praise
it for the liberating breadth of its vision.

The bizarre nature of this state of affairs is so striking
that it demands an explanation. If the acknowledged influence of
Bacon is not due to the correctness of his philosophy, how is it
to be understood? How is it that an age which so prides itself
upon a fidelity to "logical" thinking and "objective" criteria of
verification could nevertheless be so utterly permeated by a
vision which, according to most critics, falls short of both
standards? What is Bacon's vision? Why has it proven to be so
influential, notwithstanding its lack of coherence and concrete
efficacy? In short, what is the nature of the siren song with
which this seventeenth-century Tyrtaeus so beguiled the modern
imagination?

I shall try to shed some light on this puzzling question in
the present chapter. In brief, it is my contention that Bacon's

vision was a new logic--what might be called "instrumental
reason"--which claimed to provide the necessary tools for the
systematic conquest of nature and, by implication, the ultimate
rationalization of societal and interpersonal relationships.
This "new organon" claimed to be objective and value-free. In
point of fact, however, I shall argue that it directly reflected
the interests of the rising middle class, which began to come
into its own in Bacon's generation, achieved maturity in the
eighteenth century and blossomed in the nineteenth. The
pseudo-philosophical justifications for the ideals of systematic
utilitarian science and of inevitable scientific and social
progress, which Bacon's "new logic" claimed to provide, helped to
legitimate the increasing hegemony of both a Christian capitalist
economy and its attendent class structure. Bacon's putatively
objective vision, then, served as a foundation for the
construction of a conceptual and normative worldview which both
mirrored the interests of and intellectually legitimated the
socio-economic structure of the modern era. Herein, I submit,
lies the secret of its appeal. It provided a theoretical and,
despite Bacon's denial, a normative justification for the actions
and values of an increasingly empowered economic and political
class. As such, its force as a "scientific" justification for
the hegemonic worldview it helped solidify continued long after
its claims of philosophical coherence fell into disrepute.

     In support of this thesis, my plan of action for this
chapter is as follows. First, I will indicate Bacon's criticism
of the "old logic," as personified, for him, in the writings of
the Greeks, the Scholastics and the alchemists, and discuss the
nature of the proposed "new logic" which he introduced as the
saving alternative. Second, I will show why Bacon thought his
new methodology superior to the old, and in so doing demonstrate
how closely his justifications mirrored the interests of and

hence appealed to the ascendent capitalist class of the
seventeenth century. Finally, I will show how Bacon's new
scientific vision served as not only an incentive to early
capitalist industry, but also as a blueprint for the structure of
an ultimately "sane society" in which class hierarchy and gender
relations are rigidly controlled--or, as the later
nineteenth-century utopias will prefer, "rationalized."

A few words need to be said here about those works of
Bacon's to which I refer in this chapter. As Benjamin Farrington
convincingly argues,[7] there is a remarkable degree of continuity
between Bacon's earliest manuscripts and his later ones. Bacon
seems to have had the germinal idea for his "new logic" as early
as his university days at Cambridge, and all his subsequent
philosophical writings are attempts to give expression to it. As
a result, his oeuvres tend to be quite repetitious in regards to
their subject matter; individual differences in the manuscripts
are primarily stylistic. In the early Temporis Partus Masculus
(1603), for example, his criticism of Greek and Scholastic logic
are substantially identical to those found in the Novum Organum
(1620). The main difference is that the earlier critique is much
harsher, more polemical, than the later one. Similarly, Bacon's
descriptions of his new method in the Advancement of Learning
(1605) are both repeated and, to a certain extent, enlarged upon
in the later Novum Organum, as is his analysis of the four
idola.

Given Bacon's habit of re-working the same basic ideas in
each of his manuscripts, my strategy in this chapter has been to
focus upon the later manuscripts (primarily the Novum Organum)
rather than earlier ones (most notably, the Advancement of
Learning), since the former represent Bacon's thought at its
maturest stage. I have not hesitated to cite from the

pre-Organum manuscripts, however, when it seems that they
substantially disagree with the Organum, express in a clearer way
points that are rather cryptically dealt with in the Organum, or
discuss topics that are missing from but in keeping with the
philosophical tenor of the Organum.

II

Bacon on His Predecessors

Like other "modern spirited" thinkers, Bacon felt that the
immediate obstacle to an appreciation of the need for a new
scientific and logical methodology was the sterile, rigid hold
which traditional canons of learning had on the scientific and
popular imagination of his time. His discussion of the four
idola in the Novum Organum[8] is an attempt to clearly spell out
the ways in which men are confused about both the nature of
reality and the method most appropriate to an understanding of
that nature. The erosion of the intellectual purview of these
illusory idola constitutes a necessary condition, so far as Bacon
is concerned, for the instauration of a correct appraisal of the
nature of physical and social reality.

Of the four types of idola, clearly the most fundamental are
the so-called "Idols of the Theatre"--i.e., the traditional
philosophical interpretations of nature that not only serve as
the foundation for the construction of worldviews but also
provide a "logic of discovery" which, according to Bacon, is
incapable of enriching scientific knowledge. The illusory models
based upon the Idols of the Theatre subsume the other three
idola: the Idols of the Tribe, which encourage the already
present human propensity to project values and anthropological
predicates upon nature; the Idols of the Cave, which incorporate

mistaken interpretations that arise from the contextual education
of individuals; and the Idols of the Marketplace, which so
distort human understanding of the meanings of words as to
impede reliable conceptualization. It is obvious, so far as
Bacon is concerned, that the received dogmas and methodologies of
traditional philosophies--the Idols of the Theatre--create the
general medium which gives rise to and color the character of the
other three idola.[9] Consequently, the destruction of the more
encompassing of the four types will go a long way towards pulling
the teeth of the others.

It is no accident, then, that Bacon prefaces most of his
discussions of his new method with polemics against his confused
philosophical predecessors--the various "priests" of the Idols
of the Theatre. His denunciations are usually directed against
the three groups of intellectuals whom he considers to be the
most dangerously influential: Aristotelians/Platonists,
Scholastics and alchemists. The members of each of these groups
are "sham philosophers" whose teachings "debauch our minds. They
substitute a false coinage for the true." Even more contemptible
than the original luminaries of each confused tradition, who at
least enjoyed occasional moments of insight, are the "satellites
and parasites of the great ones, the whole mob of professional
teachers," who mindlessly memorize and mouth the bookish precepts
of their masters without ever turning to the more reliable book
of nature for verification.[10] So far as Bacon is concerned, a
blind fidelity to written tradition, as displayed by the savants
of his time, is the nucleus around which conventional learning
has revolved. "But," he warns, "generally speaking science is to
be sought from the light of nature, not from the darkness of
antiquity. It matters not what has been done; our business is
to see what can be done."[11]

The disinclination on the part of his contemporaries--the "professional teachers"--to test hypotheses in the light of experience rests, then, upon what Bacon sees as a long tradition of methodological precedent. Both Aristotle and Plato set the ball in motion by refusing, to one degree or another, to apply themselves to "the study of things."[12] Aristotle, "that worst of sophists stupified by his own unprofitable subtlety, the cheap dupe of words,"[13] was more concerned with "dialectics" than with the examination of nature. His syllogistic logic concentrated upon the perfection of arguments which resulted only in the production of necessary conclusions deduced from abstract premises. It did not provide new and useful knowledge about the world; instead, it formulated a strategy for deriving logically necessary conclusions from a priori propositions. As such, in both Aristotle's physics and metaphysics one hears "the voice of dialectics more often than the voice of nature. What solidity of structure can be expected from a man who constructs a world from categories?"[14] Plato, "that mocking wit, that swelling poet, that deluded theologian,"[15] likewise encouraged men to ignore empirical data, advising them to turn instead to the contemplation of "theological" constructs such as the Forms. Speaking rhetorically to the spirit of Plato, Bacon not only subjects both the ancient philosopher and, by implication, the scientists of his own time to a damning indictment; he also implies the outlines of his "new" empirical method:

> When...you gave out the falsehood that truth is, as it were, the native inhabitant of the human mind and need not come in from outside to take up its abode there; when you turned our minds away from observation, away from things, to which it is impossible we should ever be sufficiently respectful and attentive; when you taught us to turn our mind's eye inward and grovel before our own blind and confused idols under the name of contemplative philosophy; then truly you dealt us a mortal blow. [16]

The direct descendents of Aristotelian dialectics and
Platonic theology, the Scholastics and the alchemists, are no
less harshly condemned by Bacon. The former, "ingenious
contrivers of eccentrics and epicycles,"[17] represent the logical
conclusion of an intoxication with abstract syllogistic thought.
Totally detached from the light of experience, the Scholastics
contrive elaborate logical structures which, because of their
abstractness, are utterly incestuous and hence sterile. At best,
they elicit nothing more than an aesthetic appreciation of their
intricacy. Pragmatically, the fruits of Scholastic labor are
utterly without value. They serve, consequently, as monuments
to misdirected, wasted talent. As Bacon laments, "what
acuteness, what strength of intellect, these [Scholastics] had!
Yet what spiders' webs they wove for us, wonderful for their
texture and the fineness of their thread, but useless for any
practical purpose!"[18] The alchemists, it is true, show more
loyalty to empirical observation than do the Scholastics. But
their infatuation with the search for neo-Platonic essences,
whose discovery will magically solve all of nature's riddles,
both turns their attention away from a consistent collection of
natural data and forces them to account for the phenomena they do
observe in terms of the fantastical a priori Forms they accept,
thereby rendering their hypotheses ridiculous and their
experiments sterile. The alchemist, anxious as he is to force
nature into an elaborate network of mysterious categories,
fabricates "a complete system out of a limited range of
experiments to which he has become accustomed." He is like the
vain, spoiled boy "who found a plank on the strand and dreamed of
building himself a ship...[He is] in love with [his] art,
possessed with the ambition to base a whole philosophy on a few
experiments made in [his] furnaces."[19]

In short, then, Bacon rejects as useless a great deal of

what passed itself off as scientific and philosophical knowledge
in his time.   True, he does admit that   his predecessors
occasionally chanced upon a felicitous discovery or   insight, but
such an event is a happy accident rather   than the result of a
rational methodology.   In one of his most delightful images,
Bacon grants that a "pig might print the letter A with   its snout
in the mud, but you would not on that account expect it to go on
to compose a tragedy."   Similarly, the "kind of knowledge which
is deduced from scientific analogy is very different from a mere
coincidence between experience and some baseless hypothesis.
Genuine truth is uniform and self-reproducing. Lucky hits are
contradictory and solitary."[20] Consequently, the fidelity which
the Scholastics and alchemists show to traditional   lore is
indefensible. In the words of one of the Biblical passages Bacon
was so fond of sprinkling throughout his   writings, such
strategies truly involved building houses upon sand. As Bacon
himself succinctly remarks, "To think of the whole process of
discovery and invention being left to the obscurity of tradition,
the giddy whirl of argument, the bellows of chance, and the
devious course of mere experience! To think that nobody succeeded
in opening up a middle way between practical experience and
unsupported theorizing!"[21]

This passage nicely captures, in very   general terms,
Bacon's primary reasons for rejecting the old organum defended by
the ancients. First, he accuses them of either adopting no
consistent methodology at all (the "bellows of chance") or of
laboring under a methodology which is so abstract, resting as it
does upon the acceptance of a priori principles, as to be
ultimately more concerned with demonstrating   the necessary
connections between propositions than with understanding nature
(the "giddy whirl of argument").   Moreover, even the primitive
methodology that his predecessors did employ was incapable of

"opening up a middle way" between observable phenomena and
hypothetical generalization. So far as Bacon was concerned,
neither Plato nor Aristotle (and certainly not their intellectual
heirs) were able to link up in any meaningful way their
"theological" or "dialectical" a priori categories with the realm
of experience. Consequently, they were reduced to the
straitjackets of either overblown theoretical flight or hasty
generalization from the immediate observation of experience.

Entertaining as Bacon's ad hominem polemics against his
predecessors are—and it can scarcely be denied that few
philosophers have been more adroit at this sort of thing than
he—they really don't provide us with more than a very general
impression of precisely why he rejects traditional methodological
assumptions. In order to gain a better idea of why Bacon
repudiates the old organon, it is necessary to focus upon his
specific criticisms of Aristotle's logic (or at least what Bacon
understood to be the Aristotelian method). Regardless of how
broad his criticisms of tradition are, it is clear that Bacon
considered the Aristotelian method to be the primary Idol of the
Theatre operative in his day. The very fact that he styled his
system the "Novum" Organum indicates that he threw his
philosophical gauntlet directly at Aristotle. Seeing why Bacon
considers this methodology inadequate, then, will help to flesh
out his general condemnation of his scientific and philosophical
predecessors. It will also serve as a convenient prolegomenon to
a discussion of his proposed "improved" logic.

The "Old" Logic and the "New" Logic

Bacon's Critique of Aristotelian Logic

In the polemical caveats against his predecessors, Bacon's primary critical point is that the old logic of discovery in no consistent way leads to practical results in the sciences. As he says time after time, the old methodology is more concerned with the creation of deductively necessary propositions than with the discovery of new knowledge capable of enriching human "arts" or "inventions." For Bacon, the very fact that the traditional logic has contributed so little utility to the mechanical sciences is an indication of its conceptual muddiness. His working assumption is that correct science will result in pragmatic consequences only insofar as it explains the way nature works. If, therefore, a putative scientific methodology leads to no enrichment of the applied sciences, one has good _prima facie_ reasons for suspecting the existence of a radical flaw in it. "Correct logic," then, is much more than merely a conceptual device for understanding reality. It is also an instrumental calculus which leads, directly or circuitously, to good works. As such, a proper scientific methodology will ground itself ultimately upon a careful observation of and experimentation from empirical data. It will concentrate its attention upon the realm of experience, using as primitives correlations of observed phenomena rather than sets of _a priori_, universal propositions. It will, in short, concern itself with "facts," not with logical relations between abstract premises.

In the "Preface" to his unfinished The Great Instauration, Bacon provides us with as nice an encapsulation of what he takes

to be the primary differences between the old logic and the new
logic as we find anywhere in his corpus.   It is a rather long
passage, but it serves as an excellent preliminary to the more
detailed discussion which follows.

> ...all those before me who have applied themselves to
> the invention of arts have but cast a glance or two
> upon facts and examples and experience, and straightway
> proceeded, as if invention were nothing more than an
> exercise of thought, to invoke their own spirits to
> give them oracles. I, on the contrary, dwelling purely
> and constantly among the facts of nature, withdraw my
> intellect from them no further than may suffice to let
> the images and rays of natural objects meet in a point,
> as they do in the sense of vision; whence it follows
> that the strength and excellence of the wit has but
> little to do in the matter. And the same humility
> which I use in inventing I employ likewise in teaching.
> For   I   do   not   endeavor   either   by   triumphs   of
> confutation, or pleadings of antiquity, or assumptions
> of authority, or even by the veil of obscurity, to
> invest these inventions of mine with any majesty; which
> might easily be done by one who sought to give lustre
> to his own name rather than light to other men's minds.
> I have not sought (I say) nor do I seek either to force
> or ensnare men's judgment, but I lead them to things
> themselves and the concordances of things, that they
> may see for themselves what they have, what they can
> dispute, what they can add and contribute to the
> common stock.[22]

What is it about the "old" logic, the Aristotelian organum,
which falls short of the general characteristics predicated of
the "new" logic in this passage? What is the nature of the old
canon's "veil of obscurity" which renders it so inutile in
Bacon's eyes?

    Surprising as it might seem, given his earlier damning
criticism of Aristotle's method, Bacon readily accepts the main
outline of his predecessor's inductive-deductive model of
scientific procedure. He agreed with Aristotle's insistence that
correct science involves a movement from the "naked" observation
of empirical phenomena to the formation of general principles,

which in turn serve as "filters" for the further observation of
experience. Bacon breaks with Aristotle's general schema,
however, in two ways. First, he denied that the latter's initial
inductive procedure was adequate, calling it "puerile" and
subject to "uncertain conclusions" and contradictions.[23] Second,
he insisted that Aristotle misused the deductive procedure built
into his model. Instead of deducing, as he should have,
practical applications from the general principles arrived at
through the earlier process of induction, Aristotle was content
to limit the scope of deduction to the elaboration of "specious
meditations" and "speculations,"[24] abstract propositions which,
although flowing necessarily from the original generalizations
(arrived at, keep in mind, by an already "puerile" inductive
process), possess no instrumental value. The handicaps of the
old logic, then, are its inability to rationally collect data,
and its subsequent failure to connect the realm of fact with the
realm of speculation.

More specifically, Bacon's criticism of Aristotle's
understanding of the inductive stage in the inductive-deductive
model breaks down into three interrelated parts.[25] First, Bacon
accuses Aristotle and his followers of indulging in a too
uncritical and haphazard collection of data. Most significantly,
there is little if any attempt to acquire data through systematic
experimentation or the use of mechanical, precision instruments.
The phenomena observed and catalogued are almost exclusively
merely those which the senses stumble across, as it were, in
their contact with the world. As such, the Aristotelian method
of collecting data is completely passive, involving no more than
immediate sensual contact with nature. The absence of any
experimental interaction between the speculative observer and
natural phenomena both mirrors and reinforces the difficulty
which the old logic has in linking theory with reality.

Secondly, the Aristotelian method of induction is based upon the fallacy of hasty generalization. Traditional methodologists leaped too quickly from a handful of detached observations to the postulation of general principles. Because only a few initial observations served as the material basis of these hypothetical principles, philosophers were forced to tack onto them an increasingly elaborate and artificial network of theoretical provisos to accommodate later conflicting observations. The Ptolemic astronomical model, with its painful system of interpenetrating epicycles, is an obvious instance of how a too hastily formulated general principle is forced to proliferate in order to explain data which it neglected to originally consider.

Finally, Aristotelian induction is inadequate because it rests content with simple enumeration, in which apparent similarities of properties found to hold for several particulars of a given kind are affirmed to hold for all particulars of that kind. The problem with simple enumeration (as William of Ockham and Roger Grosseteste before Bacon, and J.S. Mill and William Stanley Jevons after him argued) is that it can lead to false conclusions by failing to take negative instances into consideration. It is not enough simply to enumerate correlations of observed properties. One must also possess some sort of calculus which is capable of differentiating between real and merely apparent similarities while at the same time accounting for the existence of genuine counter-examples.[26]

Bacon's general criticism of the deductive stage of traditional Aristotelian methodology can also be broken down into more precise terms. There are two specific caveats. To begin with, the first principles which the Aristotelians claimed to infer from their faulty inductive processes, and which they in turn used as major premises to deduce general conclusions, possessed predicates which in themselves were so ambiguous--if not downright mystifying--as to render useless the syllogistic arguments in which they appeared. It was all very well to construct syllogisms enjoying valid forms whose predicates included, for example, "attraction," "repulsion," "form" and "matter." But if the predicates themselves had no decisive meaning, the entire deductive enterprise ultimately reduced itself to nothing more than an abstract logical game whose only concern was a fidelity to the rules of identity and excluded middle. As Bacon remarks,

> The syllogism consists of propositions, propositions of words; words are the signs of notions. If, therefore, the notions (which form the basis of the whole) be confused and carelessly abstracted from things, there is no solidity in the superstructure.

> ...We have no sound notions in logic or physics; substance, quality, action, passion, and existence are not clear notions; much less weight, levity, density, tenuity, moisture, dryness, generation, corruption, attraction, repulsion, element, matter, form, and the like. They are all fantastical and ill-defined.[27]

The point, then, is that syllogistic entailments from first principles only possess practical merit (as opposed to exclusively "logical" merit) if the terms in the principles are well defined. But because of the inadequacy of the preliminary inductive procedure, as well as an over-reliance upon a priori categories which are nonsusceptible to meaningful empirical verification or conceptual elucidation, the traditional terms which served as the content of a syllogism were necessarily inchoate.

Bacon's second complaint against the traditional deductive technique is that its deductive procedure is overemphasized at the expense of the inductive one. Bacon's point here is twofold. First, he claims that the Aristotelian model emphasizes

deduction so much, because of its insistence that   only deductive
certainly leads to reliable   knowledge, that it ignores the   need
for   proper   safeguards   in   the   collection   and   correlation of
observed data.   But because proper inductive strategies   serve as
the   basis   for   sound   deductions   from   first   principles,   an
overemphasis on   the latter and   an underemphasis   on   the former
weakens the   entire method.   Bacon   is not at   all as hostile   to
natural deduction as some   of his commentators have argued.   But
he is clear in   his insistence that sloppy induction   negates the
possibility of utile deductions.

Moreover,   according   to   Bacon,   Aristotelian   deduction
stresses logical form at the expense of instrumental conclusions.
This point harkens   back to his criticism   that the old logic   is
concerned   exclusively with   form,   with   drawing   necessary
connections between major and minor premises and conclusions.   So
far as   he was concerned,   traditional   methodologists considered
their   task   accomplished   when   they   demonstrated   the   logical
validity of a   syllogism.   They failed to   see that   the ultimate
value   of a   deductive argument   rested upon   whether or   not its
conclusions   led   to   an enrichment   of   the   mechanical sciences
through the production of "arts" or "inventions."

Clearly, then, the bottom   line of Bacon's rejection of   the
old   logic was   its perceived   inability to   further instrumental
reason.   It failed   to formulate   a   scientific   methodology and
calculus   which   would   provide new   knowledge   about   nature, in
addition to   indicating how that   knowledge should be   translated
into concrete, mechanical terms.   This is not to imply that Bacon
denied a place   in his new methodology   for what might be   called
"abstract" knowledge, or "pure" as opposed to   "applied" science.
He   after   all   acknowledges   that   the   necessary   condition for
improvement in "inventions"   is a sound inductive   strategy which

prepares the way for the formulation of theoretical first principles. But he also clearly insists that abstract knowledge is never an end in itself. In the "Preface" to The Great Instauration, for example, he remarks that "no man can rightly and successfully investigate the nature of anything in the thing itself; let him vary his experience as laboriously as he will, he never comes to a resting place, but still finds some thing to seek beyond."[28] Rather, the value of speculation resides solely in its serving as the necessarily abstract means to an instrumental end. It is precisely the Aristotelian insistence that abstract, syllogistic knowledge is an end worth pursuing for its own sake that reduces it, according to Bacon, to a detached logical game, ultimately incapable of either describing or manipulating natural phenomena. (As he puts it, "demonstration by syllogism" lets "nature skip out of its hands."[29]) As such, it only follows that "the entire fabric of human reason which [the old logicians] employ in the acquisition of nature, is badly put together and built up, and like some magnificent structure without any foundation."[30]

The Baconian distinction between the "new" instrumental logic and the "old" syllogistic logic cannot be overemphasized. It serves as the starting point for an understanding of why Bacon felt he had radically broken with past tradition, why he thought that a correct understanding of nature would necessarily increase human dominion over it (or, as he says at the beginning of the Novum Organum, "Knowledge and human power are synonymous"[31]) and why, as we shall see later, his new method so adequately captured and reinforced the mood of his time. It is crucial to keep in mind that the new, instrumental logic is not merely distinguished from the old by virtue of methodological adjustments. It also separates itself from tradition on the basis of motivation, or intent. Its aim is different from that

of a syllogistic logic because it seeks knowledge as an
instrument, not an end. It proposes to change the human
condition, instead of merely describing it. It is instrumental
from beginning to end. This switch in emphasis is clear in the
following passage from The Great Instauration:

> The art which I introduce...is a kind of logic; though
> the difference between it and the ordinary [or
> syllogistic] logic is great; indeed immense. For the
> ordinary logic professes to contrive and prepare helps
> and guards for the understanding, as mine does; and in
> this one point they agree. But mine differs from it in
> three points especially; viz., in the end aimed at; in
> the order of demonstration; and in the starting point
> of the inquiry.
>
> For the end which this science of mine proposes is the
> invention not of arguments but of arts; not of things
> in accordance with principles, but of principles
> themselves; and not of probable reasons, but of
> designations and directions for works. And as the
> intention is different, so accordingly is the effect;
> the effect of the one being to overcome an opponent in
> argument, of the other to command nature in action.[32]

What was the nature of the new logic which Bacon claimed was
such an improvement, in both method and intent, over the
traditional syllogistic logic? What were the characteristics of
this novum organum which purported to provide, far and beyond a
mere facility in disputation, the key to the mastery of nature?
It is to a consideration of this question that we must now turn.

                          The "New" Induction

    Bacon's new instrumental logic claims to correct the
deficiencies it sees in both the inductive and deductive

procedures of the old logic. It attempts to purge scientific
method of the hazards involved in hasty generalization and simple
enumeration in the realm of induction. Moreover, it strives to
generate deductive first principles whose predicates are both
nonambiguous and conducive to the stated aims of instrumental
reason--i.e., the production of "arts" rather than mere
arguments. I shall discuss both of these points in turn.

Perhaps the best known facet of Bacon's new method is its
heavy emphasis upon the importance of proper inductive procedure
(an emphasis which, as I mentioned earlier, has led some
commentators to all but ignore the strong role which Bacon
assigned to the deduction of first principles). We saw earlier
that Bacon criticizes the old logic for its sloppy induction. We
also saw that the putative inadequacy of traditional induction
was chalked up as much to its basic presuppositions about the
nature of knowledge as to its methodological weaknesses.
Aristotle's inductive technique, in Bacon's eyes, is faulty not
simply because it relies upon haphazard observation and hasty
generalization. Its inadequacy is more fundamentally
attributable to its overemphasis upon a priori categories at the
expense of empirical data. The old logic, then, failed to arrive
at efficient rules of observation more because of its distrust of
empirical knowledge than because of observational laziness,
although it is clear that Bacon does not discount the latter as a
contributing factor.

Bacon's basic working assumption is just the reverse (or,
again, so he thought). He argues that a solid empirical
grounding is a necessary condition for the sound deduction of
first principles. Accordingly, the first aim of his new logic is
to provide rules for the reliable collection of data. His aim,
as he says, is to "sink the foundations of the sciences deeper

and firmer." This demands beginning "the inquiry nearer the source than men have done hitherto,"[33] and the source is experience:

> ...hitherto the [logical] proceeding has been to fly at once from the senses and particulars up to the most general propositions, as certain fixed poles for the argument to turn upon, and from these to derive the rest by middle terms: a short way, no doubt, but precipitate; and one which will never lead to nature, though it offers an easy and ready way to disputation. Now my plan is to proceed regularly and gradually from one axiom to another, so that the most general are not reached till the last: but then when you do come to them you find them to be not empty notions, but well defined, and such as nature would really recognise as her first principles, and such as lie at the heart and marrow of things.[34]

Bacon insists, then, that the inductive procedure in scientific method must be taken quite seriously, even if it means slowing down the process of deducing first principles. His technique is to first carefully collect simple observations and then to map out the correlations in similarities between them. The general statements which express correlations are what he calls "axioms" in the above-quoted passage. One of the most fruitful ways of collecting and correlating data is, for Bacon, the use of controlled experimentation: "for the subtlety of experiments is far greater than that of the sense itself, even when assisted by exquisite instruments; such experiments, I mean, as are skillfully and artificially devised for the express purpose of determining the point in question."[35] Even at this preliminary stage in the logic of discovery, Bacon insists upon the need for an active relationship between the observer and the observed, a departure, as we have seen, from Aristotelian logic's primarily passive acquisition of empirical data.

Notwithstanding the efficacy of experimental technique in

induction, the simple collection of data is scarcely useful
unless there exists a reliable calculus with which to weed out
merely apparent from essential similarities. Recall that the
absence of such a calculus in the old logic's simple enumeration
is, according to Bacon, one of its fundamental weaknesses. In
order to rectify simple enumeration's lack of a reliable
falsification or exclusionary criterion, Bacon introduces his
famous "Tables of Presence, Absence and Degrees."

Bacon's Tables provide a method of cross-indexing perceived
similarities in observed phenomena which he thinks will clearly
pinpoint and hence exclude from incorporation into inductive
generalizations those correlations which are merely accidental.
The system of checks which the Tables provide can be summarized
by the following rule: "any correlation for which there is an
instance in which one attribute is absent when another is
present, or instances in which one attribute decreases when the
other increases, is to be excluded"[36] from the set of "safe"
correlations. If used correctly, the procedure supplied by the
Tables eliminates all but essential correlations, which are of
course the appropriate raw material for the inductive
generalizations from which first principles are deduced. It is a
compliment to Bacon's perspicacity, however, that he realized
that even his Tables might be incapable of weeding out all
accidental correlations, if for no other reason than that their
ultimate reliability rests upon the stipulation that incredible
amounts of experimental and empirical data be fed into them. As
Bacon says, "but natural and experimental history is so varied
and diffuse, that it confounds and distracts the understanding
unless it be fixed and exhibited in due order."[37] It is in
order to provide a final filter for the nonessential correlates
which might escape the safety net of the Tables that Bacon
introduces, in the second part of the Organum, his so-called

"Prerogative Instances": "We must, therefore, form tables and
co-ordinations of instances, upon such a plan, and in such order,
that the understanding may be enabled to act upon them."[38]

A Prerogative Instance, of which Bacon judged there to be
twenty-seven types or "ranks," is, as Paolo Rossi argues,[39] a
mnemonic device which serves to facilitate the classification of
contentious interpretations based upon putative correlations of
data by referring the scientist to a wide variety of exemplary
test cases or models of adjudication. The Prerogative Instances
serve as convenient procedural loci which the researcher can
refer to in analyzing troublesome correlations. They constitute
a logbook, as it were, of paradigmatic experiments that can
(hopefully) resolve any questions concerning the essentiality of
a correlation which the Tables of Presence, Absence and Degrees
are unable to meet. The primary purpose of a Prerogative
Instance, then, is to serve as a signpost, as a procedural model,
which the scientist can use as a guide in deciding whether to
include or exclude any set of observations or second-order
explanations derived from the original Tables. As Rossi says,
"in order to supplement 'natural' memory so that it may serve as
an instrument for scientific research [the Baconian scientist]
must resort to topics (or catalogues of places of invention)
indicating the relevant instances for a given object of research
and to Tables classifying the instances so that the mind, instead
of being confronted with natural confusion, finds an ordered
sequence of data."[40]

Perhaps a concrete example--one provided by Bacon
himself--will help to make the point more clear. One of the most
important of the Prerogative Instances is the "Instance of the
Cross." An Instance of the Cross is one that decides the issue
between two competing explanations:

> When in investigating any nature the understanding is,
> as it were, balanced, and uncertain as to which of two
> or more natures the cause of the required nature should
> be assigned, on account of the frequent and usual
> concurrence of several natures, the instances of the
> cross show that the union of one nature with the
> required nature is firm and indissoluble, whilst that
> of the other is unsteady and separable; by which means
> the question is decided and the first is received as
> the cause, whilst the other is dismissed and
> rejected.[41]

Bacon suggests that this type of Instance could be invoked, for
example, to decide between two conflicting hypotheses--or
attempts to draw correlations between facts--about the movement
of tides on earth. One hypothesis defends the thesis that the
tides are the result of a periodic lifting and falling of bodies
of water. The other hypothesis argues that the tides are instead
the advance and retreat of waters, similar to the way liquid
sloshes back and forth in a rocking container. Bacon suggested
that the latter hypothesis would be falsified if it could be
demonstrated that the high tides of Spain were not matched--i.e.,
correlated--with temporally coincidental ebb tides elsewhere, for
instance along the coasts of Peru or China.[42] With this and other
paradigmatic Instances, Bacon claims to provide concrete examples
of a procedure for adjudicating between conflicting hypotheses
which in turn serves as an analogue for researchers confronted
with similar standoffs. (This Instance also illustrates, by the
way, Bacon's emphasis upon experimentation in induction.)

In summary, Bacon's new method claims to correct the
Aristotelian inductive procedure in four ways. First, it denies
that deduction from a priori categories is more important than
deductions from first principles generalized from the observation
of phenomena. Second, following from his devaluation of
abstracted thought, Bacon's new logic stresses the importance of

a progressive inductive strategy, facilitated by the judicious
employment of controlled experimentation. The scientist's proper
relationship to the world of experience is an active rather than
a passive one. To work with nature is to observe it. Third,
Bacon rejects induction by simple enumeration, which he thinks
leads to hasty generalizations because of its inability to
accommodate counterexamples, and replaces it with a calculus
whereby accidental correlations can be excluded from hypothetical
generalizations--the Tables of Presence, Absence and Degrees.
Finally, as a second safety net, he introduces his twenty-seven
ranks of Prerogative Instances, which serve as procedural models
in the adjudication of ambiguous interpretations based upon
putative correlations of observed data.

The "New" Deduction

     Bacon clearly thought that the rigorous systemization of
the inductive process was his greatest contribution to a logic
of discovery. We have seen, after all, that both the method and
intent of his new canon is instrumental. Consequently, the ideal
logic is one which serves as the basis for "invention" rather
than "argument." And for Bacon, induction fulfills that role:
"I consider induction to be that form of demonstration which
upholds the senses and closes with nature, and comes to the very
brink of operation, if it does not actually deal with it."[43] But
his emphasis upon correct induction shouldn't lead us to suppose
that his new method discounted deduction. Bacon was well aware
that the mere systematic correlation of data is incapable of
serving as the vehicle for progress in the mechanical sciences.

Sound general   principles deduced from   inductive generalizations
are just as   important to the advancement of learning as the
proper observation of phenomena. Accordingly, Bacon attempted to
revamp Aristotelian deduction in the second half of the Novum
Organum by way of his theory of "Forms."

Recall that Bacon criticized Aristotelian deduction on at
least two counts. First, it relied more upon a priori categories
than upon hypothetical generalizations drawn from observed data,
and hence stressed syllogistic form at the expense of utility.
Second, the predicates within the syllogism itself were
ill-defined, thereby rendering the entire deduction meaningless.
Bacon's retrenchment of inductive procedure claims to obviate the
first weakness in deduction. The second inadequacy is addressed
by his Form theory.

Bacon's Forms are neither Platonic essences nor Aristotelian
first causes. Rather, they are general principles which claim to
be verbal expressions of causal relationships that hold between
"simple natures." Simple natures in turn are those irreducible
qualities present in objects of perception.   In fact, Bacon
appears to have held that our objects of experience are nothing
more than the various combinations of these simple natures.

To understand how simple natures interact is to understand
the causal relationships--i.e., the relations among physical
properties that have the power of producing effects--between
them. The systematic correlation of causal relations between
simple natures enables us to inductively arrive at hypothetical
generalizations about causality between similar instances of
simple natures. These generalizations in turn make it possible
to deduce lawlike propositions concerning material and efficient
causation. It is this set of lawlike propositions which Bacon
calls "Forms." Consequently, an understanding of Forms implies a

logically prior adequate knowledge of objects of experience. The ultimate test for meaning is an instrumental one. The postulation of a Form (and, by implication, the definition of the simple natures which serve as predicates in the Form's propositional expression) is well defined if it so enables us to understand causal relations in the physical world as to control and modify the forces of nature.[44]

Forms in Bacon's sense are, then, lawlike expressions of regularity deduced from inductive generalizations. That Bacon considered them as such is clear. He often interchanges the words "law" and "Form" when speaking of them: "...when I speak of Forms, I mean nothing more than those laws and determinations of absolute actuality, which govern and constitute any simple nature, as heat, light, weight, in every kind of matter and subject that is susceptible to them. Thus the Form of Heat or the Form of Light is the same thing as the Law of Heat or the Law of Light."[45]

Bacon placed two logical constraints upon his Forms which even more clearly indicate their lawlike character. First, their propositional expressions must be true in every instance; second, the converses of these propositional expressions must likewise be true. The Form of Heat mentioned earlier, for example, identifies "heat" with "a rapid expansive motion of the small particles of bodies, which particles are restrained from escaping from the body's surface."[46] Consequently, a rapid expansive motion is always present when heat is present, and conversely.

Bacon's introduction of his notion of Forms, then, supposedly demystifies syllogistic logic's deductive technique. The predicates which make up the hypothetical generalizations, being the verbal expressions of causal relations between physical properties, are verified by an appeal to correlated experience, and hence are nonmysterious. Similarly, the lawlike statements derived from these generalizations, which themselves serve as the major premises for the deductive process, are likewise nonmysterious. Their clarity is ultimately vouchsafed, Bacon thinks , by their instrumental efficacy in the mechanical arts.

Critique of Bacon's "New" Logic

Such is the overall structure of Bacon's new, instrumental logic. In eliminating, as he supposed he did, the methodological flaws of the old syllogistic logic, Bacon claims to have established an organum which reunites the world of experience with human rational faculties--a union which is a necessary condition for the correct understanding and consequent control of nature. As he boasts in The Great Instauration, "...by these means I suppose that I have established for ever a true and lawful marriage between the empirical and the rational faculty, the unkind and ill-starred divorce and separation of which has thrown into confusion all the affairs of the human family."[47]

But is this claim ultimately justified? Put another way, is it really the case that the so-called new organum is really either as innovative or as methodologically sound as Bacon insisted? Contemporary philosophers of science, as I indicated at the beginning of this chapter, have generally answered in the negative, and their arguments for this denial have been well documented. It is not my purpose here to rehearse the various caveats against the merits of the Baconian system. I am more concerned with understanding why it was (and is) so influential

in spite of its flaws. Nevertheless, it is revealing to examine
a few of its more apparent weaknesses.

In the first place, recent historians of science have
pointed out that the "new" logic is not quite as new as Bacon
claimed. They argue that classic Aristotelian logic's canon of
procedure is more akin to Bacon's than the latter realized (or
admitted, as the case may be). Aristotle, so this line of
reasoning goes, was much more concerned with proper inductive
techniques than Bacon gave him credit for. The overemphasis upon
deduction from a priori categories is more a tendency of the
neo-Aristotelian Schools than of Aristotle himself. As John
Losee remarks,

> ...Bacon should have distinguished between Aristotle's
> theory of procedure and the way in which this theory of
> procedure had been misappropriated by some subsequent
> thinkers who called themselves 'Aristotelians'.
> Practitioners of a false Aristotelianism had
> short-circuited Aristotle's method by beginning, not
> with induction from observational evidence, but with
> Aristotle's own first principles. This false
> Aristotelianism encouraged a dogmatic theorizing by
> cutting off science from its empirical base. But
> Aristotle himself had insisted that first principles be
> induced from observational evidence. Bacon was unfair
> to condemn Aristotle for reducing science to deductive
> logic.[48]

Whether or not Losee's evaluation of the merits of Aristotelian
induction is overly generous, it certainly does appear to be the
case that Bacon's polemical rhetoric against the Greek
philosopher is usually unsupported by textual criticisms of
either the Categories or the Analytics.

Secondly, it seems rather obvious that Bacon's strategies
for injecting rigor into the inductive process had been
anticipated by several of his predecessors. His emphasis upon
the need for controlled experimentation in the collection and

correlation   of data   closely resembles   the methodological
criterion advocated three centuries earlier by Roger Bacon in his
so   called "Second   Prerogative   of   Experimental Science."
Furthermore, the Novum Organum's critique of induction by simple
enumeration,   and   its   call for   a   table of similarities and
differences as   a vehicle by which to   separate accidental from
essential correlations, had been anticipated in the Middle Ages
by both Roger Grosseteste and William of Ockham.   Finally, as
Rossi has convincingly   demonstrated,[49]   the safety net of
Prerogative Instances of which Bacon was so proud was a common
strategy of rhetoricians and logicians both preceding Bacon and
contemporary to him. The Protestant intellectual Melanchthon in
the sixteenth century and, even more obviously, Peter Ramus[50]
after him, had both argued for the usefulness of hypothetical
test cases   as   a means   of   deciding   between different
interpretations based upon sets of correlated data.

In addition to Bacon's rather dubious claim of novelty for
his method, it also suffers from several philosophical weaknesses
which strongly call into question its adequacy as a logic of
discovery. I will mention but two of these flaws, one embedded
within Bacon's "new" inductive strategy, the other within his
"new" deductive strategy.

Recall that Bacon introduced his Prerogatives of Instance as
a final test by which to discriminate between essential and
merely apparent correlations of observed data. One of the most
important of these Instances, as we saw earlier, is that of the
Cross, which supposedly maps out techniques for deciding between
competing hypothetical explanations of natural phenomena. This
particular Instance relies upon a strategy of falsification; one
set of explanatory premises is accepted if its competing set is
falsified.   Thus, to return to the earlier mentioned example

provided by Bacon himself, the hypothesis that tidal motion is caused by a periodic lifting and falling of waters will be falsified if it can be observed that high tides on the shores of Spain are temporally coincidental with ebb tides off the coast of, say, China. Bacon's claim is that since this observation falsifies the lift-fall hypothesis, the competing rocking basin thesis is verified.

Obviously, however, this conclusion is not entailed through a falsificationist strategy. The mere falsification of one hypothetical explanation does not necessarily clear up ambiguity. Strategies of this sort work only if there are no more than two competing explanations under consideration. Otherwise, it is not possible to conclusively prove a set of explanatory premises about a particular type of phenomenon by merely refuting its competitors. There may exist other explanations, as yet unintuited by the researcher, which are capable of explaining the observed phenomena. In the tidal motion case, for example, it may be that a judicious observation of tides on opposite ends of the earth would falsify the lift-fall theory. But that falsification does not at all entail the correctness of the rocking basin thesis. There may be yet another explanation for the movement of tides.

In short, then, Bacon overestimated the logical force of his Instance of the Cross and, by implication, the methodological value of all his Prerogative Instances. They simply do not constitute as final a safety net for inductive hypotheticals as he thought.

Bacon's attempts to retrench deductive procedure is just as problematic. His primary complaint against syllogistic deduction was that it relied upon mysterious, meaningless predicates, which rendered the arguments themselves, notwithstanding their

logical   validity,   nonsensical.   As   an   alternative,   Bacon
introduced his theory of "Forms," which argued that the proper
constituents of syllogisms are simple natures--i.e., the verbal
expression of relations between physical properties.   But the
very postulation of simple natures presupposes precisely the
framework of Aristotelian ontology which Bacon finds so
problematic. It assumes that reality is best explained in terms
of substances possessing properties and powers, all of which are
relational to one another. Regardless of whether or not Bacon's
Forms   eliminate   certain   meaningless   predicates   such   as
"attraction" and "repulsion," he has retained, as Locke in the
seventeenth century and the phenomenalists of the eighteenth and
nineteenth centuries readily recognized, equally mysterious
categories such as "substance" and "powers." In a word, Bacon's
metaphysics remained fundamentally Aristotelian--and, hence, on
his own grounds, somewhat inchoate.[51]

It seems   clear, whatever the   merits of   Bacon's   new logic
might be, that it is neither as innovative nor methodologically
sound as he claimed.   Although the more harsh criticisms of his
system have appeared within the last two centuries, it is
important to keep in mind that a handful of savants even in
Bacon's own time recognized its problematic character.   One
needn't put too much stock in King James' famous dismissal of the
Instauration as a work "like the peace of God, which passes all
understanding." His appraisal, witty as it is, is probably more
of a comment on James' critical abilities than on Bacon's
philosophy (or the peace of god, for that matter).   But one
should take more seriously William Harvey's equally clever
rejoinder that Bacon wrote philosophy "like a Lord Chancellor."
This bon mot was partly prompted, no doubt, by the Court
Physician's desire to amuse his sovereign.   But it is also
reasonable to suppose that behind its verbal cattiness lay an

appreciation of the inflated character of Bacon's claims.

The central question, then, remains. If Bacon's "new" logic
is neither all that new nor philosophically flawless, and if even
some of his own contemporaries recognized it as such, why was
Bacon's influence so pervasive, both during his lifetime and
afterwards? Why is it that at the founding of the Royal Society
in 1662, a full generation after Bacon's death, Abraham Cowley,
in his "Ode to the Royal Society," spoke for the entire learned
world of Europe when he wrote:

> From these and all long errors of the way,
> In which our wandering predecessors went,
> And like th'old Hebrews many years did stray
>   In deserts but of small extent,
> Bacon, like Moses, led us forth at last.
>   The barren wilderness he past,
>   Did on the very border stand
>   Of the blest promised land,
> And from the mountain top of his exalted wit,
>   Saw it himself, and shew'd us it.[52]

It is to a consideration of this puzzling question that we
must now turn.

III

One of Bacon's proudest claims was that his new instrumental
logic was value-free. Instead of basing its descriptions upon
normative assumptions about how the world ought to be--a primary
characteristic, according to Bacon, of Aristotelian syllogistic
logic--the new organon supposedly limited itself to "pure"
empirical accounts of the way the world is.   Nature is best
understood (and best manipulated) if it is scrutinized with
dispassionate, objective and detached vision. To act otherwise
is to fall into the self-deceptive trap of the Schoolmen, who
"apply themselves to philosophy and contemplations of a universal
nature," corrupting it with their "preconceived fancies" which

render their conclusions "little more than useless and disputatious."[53] The doctrine of the four idola, in fact, graphically illustrates Bacon's desire to rid scientific methodology of the a priori baggage, social, psychological, linguistic or philosophical, which he saw as the primary obstacle to the great instauration. As far as he was concerned, a necessary condition for the correct understanding of nature was the eradication of all normative and theoretical bias: "In general, he who contemplates nature should suspect whatever particularly takes and fixes his understanding, and should use so much the more caution to preserve it equable and unprejudiced."[54]

Notwithstanding Bacon's emphasis upon the necessity for bias-free objectivity in proper scientific methodology, it is clear that he justified his new logic to his contemporaries on very normative, assumption-ridden grounds. Bacon never simply defended his new canon of instrumental reason by an appeal to exclusively logical standards (such as, for instance, an increase in logical precision over the old syllogistic canon). Nor did he rely exclusively on even a broader (yet still arguably "objective") justification such as "the new logic is an improvement over School logic because it teaches us more about nature and gives rise to a greater number of concrete consequences." Although justifications of the new method based exclusively upon logical or pragmatic considerations do exist, they are not the only--nor even the most important--reasons that Bacon would give if we could, quite simply, ask him why his system is preferable to Aristotelian syllogistic reasoning. The justifications that clearly strike one as being most important for Bacon, in addition to being much more persuasive to the popular imagination than exclusively logical ones, are normative. They both reflect and reinforce a clearly circumscribed set of

values and theoretical assumptions about the nature of reality--a
set which, moreover, was particularly supportive of the interests
of Britain's rising middle class in Bacon's time.

There were two basic assumptions upon which Bacon justified
his model that struck especially sympathetic chords among both
his contemporaries and the generations which followed. First,
Bacon claimed that his instrumental reason was an improvement
over the old syllogistic logic because it re-established the
proper relationship between Christian men and nature. His
instauration is taken by him as a literal "restoration" of human
dominion over the physical world--a dominion which, although
originally a divine gift to humankind, had been lost after the
Fall from grace by Adam and Eve, the ancestors of the race.
Nature, originally created by god to serve the human race as a
vehicle by which the works of man could be multiplied, had as a
result of the Biblical Fall acquired a mysterious, adversarial
character. In fact, the Fall had reversed the proper
relationship between man and nature. Instead of correctly
understanding and bending lawlike nature to his will, man became
ignorant of and hence subservient to what was now perceived as a
whimsical, mysterious and frightening cosmos. This inability to
fathom and control nature was personified by the inadequate logic
of discovery defended by Aristotle and the Schools. The Fall
from grace severed the connection between the "rational" and the
"empirical" faculties, thereby encouraging inutile, abstract and
contrived interpretations of both the world and man's place in
it. The purpose of Bacon's great instauration is to restore this
"marriage" between the two faculties through the use of inductive
logic and instrumental reason. In Biblical terms, the new method
will reopen the gates of Eden to humankind, thus bringing it to
the divinely ordained end for which it was created. The
"rational" manipulation of nature--and, as we shall see,

ultimately the "rational" manipulation of social relations--thus
takes on the character of a pragmatically felicitous course of
action. Even more importantly from the standpoint of the
Baconian system's influence, it assumes the aura of a Christian
duty. The ultimate control of nature for the sake of individual
and social profit, in other words, is not simply a reflection of
what humans want to do. It now becomes, according to Christian
doctrine as interpreted by both Bacon and the ascendent British
middle class, what humans ought to do.

The second factor within Bacon's system which maximized its
influence, notwithstanding the fact that its weaknesses were
increasingly recognized by both British and Continental savants,
was its optimistically strident reformism. Perhaps the most
pervasive theme throughout Bacon's corpus, from beginning to end,
is the insistence that "good" science serves as a vehicle for
understanding physical nature as well as for progressively
improving the level of human existence. As we saw in the
preceding section, Bacon's fundamental criticism of syllogistic
logic was that it lacked utility. Proper scientific methodology,
however, leads inexorably to a wider and wider command of nature.
And inasmuch as man himself is a part of nature, his behavior can
be explained and manipulated according to the same laws that
apply to physical reality. The rationalization of social
relationships necessarily follows, therefore, from the
rationalization of natural law. And inasmuch as man himself is a
part of nature, his behavior can be explained and manipulated
according to the same laws that apply to physical reality.

Obviously enough, these two claims are clearly related to
yet another: in restoring god's plan on earth, human society not
only grows more rational but also wealthier, wiser, and more
ethical. It becomes god-like. Equally obvious, moreover, is the

fact that both claims violate Bacon's own insistence that
"correct" science is objective and value-free. They
surreptitiously slip in conventional Christian notions about the
nature of the world and man's place within it. Moreover, they
imply that the material fruits of the new instrumental reason are
not simply convenient, or conducive to human happiness, but are
also, more fundamentally, adequate barometers of moral progress.

What may not be as obvious, however, but which I shall try
to defend in the rest of this chapter, is that the fundamental
claims of Bacon's new system are ideological. Their ideological
character can be pinpointed in two distinct but interrelated
ways. First, they are self-deceived as to their real nature.
Bacon appears absolutely sincere in his desire to reform society,
to usher in, through a judicious use of instrumental reason, the
second Eden in which all men are free from ignorance and want.
Notwithstanding the purity of his motives, Bacon's agenda for the
improvement of science, society and morals is doomed to failure,
as are all ideologies, because of its inability to see that what
it accepts as universal values, appropriate for all individuals
in all economic classes, are in fact most directly supportive of
the interests of the particular dominant class. They are in the
long run at tension with, if not outrightly antithetical to, the
interests of all other subordinate classes. Bacon's emphasis
upon concrete good works places a high premium upon the absolute
efficacy of technological innovation, high national incomes,
accelerated international trade, streamlined modes of production
and increasing competition in the marketplace of both ideas and
commodities. While this set of ideals certainly represents a
widening of the rigidified economic and social boundaries
characteristic of feudal economic structures, thereby relatively
improving the life situations of most individuals, they tend to
absolutely serve the interests of only that collection of

individuals which has come to be known as the middle-class, or bourgeoisie. Bacon's ideological blindspot is in supposing that, for instance, streamlined modes of production or increased international competition will benefit nonbourgeois classes as much as the bourgeois class. Such does not seem to be the case. Centralized production, while increasing revenues for early capitalists, appears to have statistically lowered average wages, just as accelerated emphasis on international competition (particularly, in Britain's case, in the wool industry) led to Henry VII's enclosure of the commons (an action which Bacon later applauded). True, the enclosure of the commons revitalized Britain's wool revenue and added to the steadily growing affluence of the English middle class. But at the same time it dispossessed thousands of small agricultural landowners, precipitating both famines and social upheaval in fifteenth- and sixteenth-century England.[55] In point of fact, then, Bacon's apotheosis of instrumental reason as the key to absolute social improvement is self-deceived, and hence ideological. Instead of positing objectively universal values which led to a social agenda felicitous for all segments of the population, it defended a classbound normative model which necessarily militated against its own avowed goal of universal betterment. As such, it directly encouraged, by bestowing ethical and scientific imprimaturs, the already growing trend in sixteenth-century Britain towards disproportionate levels of income and rigid class and gender hierarchies. The ultimate "sane society," as Bacon portrays it, is one in which an entire social structure is based upon principles most conducive to the welfare of the hegemonic capitalist class. This will become even more clear when we examine his New Atlantis.

The classbound nature of the values underlying Bacon's new system leads us to the second characteristic which reveals it to be ideological. In addition to being deceived as to its putative universal applicability, the modes of presentation Bacon employs in advertizing his system were particularly appealing to the imagination of the ascendent bourgeois class. Put another way, the very metaphors he uses provided culturally acceptable props upon which the rising middle class could construct an intellectual hegemony to bolster its already obvious economic dominance. Bacon insists that his great instauration is the fruition of Biblical prophecy. As such, his vision is geared to be most sympathetic to the conventional Christian hierarchy and normative system of his day. There is doubtlessly a great deal of emotional comfort in supposing that one's interests (or the interests of one's class) are somehow guaranteed by divine will. Economic exploitation acquires the aura of manifest destiny working itself out. Social hierarchies, which are stabilized by the increasing disproportionality of incomes, become imbued with metaphysical necessity. And a "rationalized" society, in which individual or collective dissent against the established order of things is not merely a classbound rebellion but also an obstinent refusal to accept god's architectural blueprint for man, becomes a sacrosanct exemplar. In short, it can be argued that Bacon unwittingly employs language to fit the specific ears of the audience to whom he is primarily interested in communicating, an audience whose interests and lifestyles he accepts as exemplifying, if only in nascent form, the interests and lifestyles which will inform the future sane society. And that audience, that exemplar, is the middle class.

We now have at our fingertips the key to unraveling the question I introduced at the beginning of this chapter: why is it that Bacon's influence was so pervasive, notwithstanding the perceived philosophical weaknesses of his system? Although I have yet to provide the textual support for it, the form of my answer is as follows. Bacon's insistence upon instrumental reason as the most appropriate model for scientific method proved so influential because it legitimated, on intellectual, ethical and religious grounds, the interests of the rising dominant class of his day--the middle class. The system is ideological, in that it reified into universal standards what were in fact classbound ones, and in so doing employed modes of expression which were best able to consolidate bourgeois hegemony. But, as our analysis of Mannheim's sociology of knowledge in the first chapter revealed, ideological structures are remarkably influential, if for no other reason than that they provide pseudo-intellectual (i.e., emotionally sustaining) justifications of material relations already present in a given social milieu.

It is not surprising, then, that Bacon's star increased in brilliance throughout the three centuries following his own. His philosophical system neatly captured the mood of the increasingly powerful bourgeoisie. As its hegemony grew so did the Baconian justifications which so nicely supported it. We will see in Chapter Four that this relationship between capitalist growth and Baconian ideals was raised to its most extreme expression in the "utopias" of the nineteenth century--the era in which bourgeois hegemony reached its zenith.

In what remains of this chapter I shall attempt to defend my charge that Bacon's system is ideological by once again returning to the Baconian texts themselves. I will first analyze the ideological character of his appeal to Biblical "restoration." Then I will indicate how his proposed method of instrumental reason served as an intellectual justification of capitalist expansion. Finally, I will conclude with an examination of Bacon's own blueprint of the sane society--the fragmentary New Atlantis.

The Great Instauration as Biblical Fulfillment

More than any other one individual, Bacon made the idea of dominion over the natural world respectable to the modern mind. As William Leiss puts it, "Bacon's great achievement was to formulate the concept of human mastery over nature much more clearly than had been done previously and to assign it a prominent place among man's concerns."[56]   It was certainly the case that the growth of industrial technology, with its consequent escalation of the production of both commodities and revenues, already had gone a long way towards reconciling the sixteenth- and seventeenth-century entrepreneur to the increasing exploitation of nature.   It is equally true that traditional Christian doctrine about the relation of man and nature had always emphasized, to one degree or another, the former's divine right to subjugate animals, plants and minerals.   As Keith Thomas says in Man and the Natural World,

> In Tudor and Stuart England the long-established view
> was that the world had been created for man's sake and
> that other species were meant to be subordinate to his
> wishes and needs. This assumption underlay the actions
> of that vast majority of men who never paused to
> reflect upon the matter. But those theologians and
> intellectuals who felt the need to justify it could
> readily appeal to the classical philosophers and the
> Bible. Nature made nothing in vain, said Aristotle,
> and everything had a purpose. Plants were created for
> the sake of animals, and animals for the sake of men.
> Domestic animals were there to labour, wild ones to be
> hunted.   The Stoics had taught the same: nature
> existed solely to serve man's interests.[57]

But Bacon explicitly legitimated these two tendencies through his emphasis upon the methodological (and normative) "correctness" of instrumental reason. In so doing, he managed to wed the growing secular desire for profit with the traditional

religious need for a clear conscience. This reformulation, as
Leiss points out, "was crucial, for Christianity's hold on the
European consciousness remained strong even as the traditional
social basis of organized religion was being eroded by
capitalism."[58]

A common leitmotif in both sixteenth- and
seventeenth-century England was that the expulsion from Paradise
had deprived the human race of both moral innocence and its
divinely granted dominion over the entire natural world. The
theological pundits of the time argued that this dominion was
clearly established by sacred Scripture; in Genesis 1:28, for
instance, god blesses Adam and Eve after their creation, telling
them, "Be fruitful, multiply, fill the earth and conquer it. Be
masters of the fish of the sea, the birds of heaven and all
living animals on the earth." The Fall, however, deprived man of
this birthright; because of the sense of confusion and fear which
its Biblical ancestors bequeathed to the human race, the proper
relation between man and nature was sundered. Man lost the
ability to understand physical reality. As a result, he lost
the capacity to control it, to harness its forces for his own
advantage. So far as Bacon was concerned, this loss of original
innocence and knowledge was the indirect reason for the
stultification of the mechanical arts--which were, after all,
the barometer of successful domination of nature--that
characterized the Western tradition up to his own time.

But the expulsion from Paradise was not irrefragable. As
Bacon says in the Novum Organum, "...man by the fall fell at the
same time from his state of innocency and from his dominion over
creation. Both of these losses however can even in this life be
in some part repaired; the former by religion and faith, the
latter by arts and sciences."[59] The implication here is obvious:

there is an intimate connection between "arts and sciences,"
which have as their foundation the new canon of instrumental
reason, and a recovery of moral innocence, which is made possible
by a renewed understanding of the Christian man's role in the
natural order of things. Indeed, it is clear that Bacon saw the
connection between instrumental reason and Christian temperament
to be even stronger. The mechanic, the scientist, or the
capitalist, all of whom were interested in understanding and
manipulating nature, could derive both material and spiritual
profit from the new method if they only employed it in a humble,
Christian way. As Bacon warns in the Great Instauration,

> ...I would address one general admonition to all; that
> they consider what are the true ends of knowledge, and
> that they seek it not either for pleasure of the mind,
> or for contention, or for superiority to others, or for
> profit, or fame, or power, or any of these inferior
> things; but for the benefit and use of life; and that
> they perfect and govern it in charity. For it was from
> lust of power that the angels fell, from lust of
> knowledge that man fell, but of charity there can be no
> excess, neither did angel or man ever come in danger by
> it.[60]

In wedding right reason (instrumental logic) with right
spirit (Christian humility), Bacon accomplishes several purposes.
To begin with, he underlines the thesis that a correct
application of his new method will lead to the great restoration
of man's original dominant position in the natural order of
things. The inevitability of this restoration rests upon two
guarantees: first, that it is logically sound and necessarily
leads to pragmatically felicitous consequences in the mechanical
arts (consequences, moreover, which can only increase the quality
of human existence); secondly, that it is theologically sound,
because the correct application of the new method fulfills
Biblical prophecy by re-establishing the proper relationship
between man and the physical realm.

In addition, the postulation of a close tie between
instrumental reason and Christian morality bolstered the hope
that ethical innocence could be maintained in the systematic
exploitation of nature. Notwithstanding the Church's traditional
defense of human superiority over the rest of creation, there was
a tendency in Bacon's time (as there is in our own, for that
matter) for the faithful to fear that scientific research's
"interference" with the divinely established order of things
could bring down god's wrath. This dread of the consequences of
trespassing upon the divine plan must have been much stronger in
Bacon's day than our own, when the rising excitement brought
about by technological innovation and improved production methods
butted heads with an equally strong and pervasive Christian fear
of eternal damnation. Bacon sought to ameliorate this tension
with his denial of a necessary conflict between science and
theology. He took great pains to promote the moral innocence of
the scientific enterprise. At times, in fact, he suggests that
the instauration of man's dominion over nature will necessarily
result in a coincidental restoration of ethical awareness: "Only
let the human race recover that right over nature which belongs
to it by divine bequest, and let power be given it; the exercise
thereof will be governed by sound reason and true religion."[61]
At other times, in an effort to stress that the manipulation of
nature is "innocent," he argues that man's search for natural
secrets (and, by implication, the harnessing of them for material
ends) is an activity which is pleasing to the benevolent divine
parent. In Thoughts and Conclusions, for instance, one of
Bacon's earlier manuscripts, he compares the investigation of the
physical realm to a good-natured game of hide-and-seek played
between god and man,

> ...as if the divine nature enjoyed the kindly innocence
> of such hide-and-seek, hiding only in order to be
> found, and with characteristic indulgence desired the

> human mind to join Him in His sport. And indeed it is
> this glory of discovery that is the true ornament of
> mankind. In contrast with civil business it never
> harmed any man, never burdened a conscience with
> remorse. Its blessing and reward is without ruin,
> wrong or wretchedness to any. For light is in itself
> pure and innocent; it may be wrongly used, but cannot
> in its nature be defiled.[62]

Finally, the coupling of the new canon for understanding
and controlling the material world with theologically justified
speculations about man's divinely ordained raison d'etre,
indirectly led to the analogous assumption that human nature,
like physical nature, could and should be tamed. The implication
is that the behavior of human beings, looked at either
individually or collectively, obey the same natural laws (or
Forms) that determine the movements of physical bodies. After
all, both animate and inanimate things are equally parts of
creation. An increased understanding of how nature operates
necessarily improves the material quality of life by eliminating
scarcity, in addition to promoting psychological and social
health by eradicating the irrationalities within humans
themselves that lead to anti-social behavior. Moreover, as we
have already seen, such a "rationalization" of society not only
produces pragmatic utility, but also heightens ethical awareness.
A life in conformity with nature's laws, as revealed by
instrumental reason, "doth make the minds of men gentle,
generous, maniable, and pliant to government; whereas ignorance
makes them churlish, thwart, and mutinous."[63] In short, a
judicious application of instrumental reason, supported by the
imprimatur of Christian tradition, is capable of alleviating the
hitherto irrational and inutile relations of both man to nature
and man to man. As Bacon succinctly says,

> Neither is certainly that other merit of learning, in
> repressing the inconveniences which grow from man to
> man, much inferior to the former, of relieving the
> necessities which arise from nature. [For men] are

> full of savage and unreclaimed desires, of profit, of
> lust, of revenge, which as long as they give ear to
> precepts, to laws, to religion, sweetly touched with
> eloquence and persuasion of books, of sermons, of
> haranques, so long is society and peace maintained; but
> if these instruments be silent, or that sedition and
> tumult make them not audible, all things dissolve into
> anarchy and confusion.[64]

From this short discussion of Bacon's attempts to legitimate
his new method by appealing to theological and Biblical
authority, three conclusions become clear. First, part of the
reason for the pervasive influence of the new scientific ideal is
that Bacon presented it in terms which appealed to the
imaginations of his contemporary readers. Torn as the nascent
middle class of the sixteenth and seventeenth centuries was
between a growing infatuation with mechanical technique and the
increased exploitation for profit of nature on the one hand, and
Christian reservations about interfering with the divine
blueprint of the physical realm on the other, Bacon's marriage
of science and theology was a welcome legitimation. It bridged
the perceived gap between secular ambition and Christian
humility, and in so doing provided a religious justification for
the new capitalist mode of production that was beginning to
solidify in both Britain and Europe. In short, Bacon's mode of
presentation, couched as it was in Biblical language, bestowed a
stamp of approval upon the dominant authoritative structures of
his time, an imprimatur, moreover, bestowed by the highest
authority in the ethos of Tudor and Stuart England--god.

But this mode of expression reveals itself to be ideological
in two ways. In the first place, it is clearly confused about
its own character. At one and the same time Bacon argues that
his new method rests upon an objective, bias-free foundation, and
also that his method is both morally justified and consonant with
a theological metaphysics. The latter claim, whatever its

merits, is clearly not a hypothetical generalization based upon
sound inductive procedure.

It might be argued that Bacon's intent is to show that his
method is ethically neutral--hence his continual reference to
the "innocence" of instrumental reason--and that I have been
unfair in accusing him of violating his stated aim of
objectivity. I grant that the overall character of Bacon's work
does seem to indicate at times that he took "innocence" to
connote just such an objectivity. But one need only recall the
passage I have cited to see that "innocence" is a loaded term.
It points more often to ethical correctness than ethical
neutrality. A recovery of the "innocence" lost by the expulsion
from Paradise sacrifices much of its rhetorical strength if all
that is recovered is normative neutrality.

But there is another reason why Bacon's Biblical apology is
ideological. It reflects and reinforces the interests of the
increasingly dominant class of Bacon's day. This point will be
discussed at some length in the following section. Here it is
enough to say that the marriage of instrumental reason and
sacred scripture legitimates authoritarian structures in social
settings by arguing that human destiny, as revealed in Scripture,
is to subdue and manipulate wild and fearful elements in
creation--either human or physical. Rationality and utility are
promoted through the subordination of both nature and
destabilizing social behavior. Just as the goal of natural
science is to subdue physical laws with mathematical precision,
so the aim of social science is to do likewise with human
relations. Authoritarian structures within society, then,
guarantee stability. Furthermore, as pointed out earlier, the
Biblical apology bases its defense of authority on the highest of
all Authorities--the word of god as revealed through sacred

scripture. Of course Bacon advocated authoritarian structures in
social settings because he thought them to be genuinely
conducive to the good of society as a whole. But it is obvious
that any legitimation of authority in abstracto--and particularly
a legitimation based upon sacrosanct theological principles--is
to the fundamental good more of those segments in society which
exercise de facto authority than those which do not. And the
class in both Bacon's time and afterwards which wielded
increasing amounts of power was the rising mercantile and
industrial bourgeoisie. William Leiss accurately expresses this
point when he says, in referring to the Baconian marriage of
instrumental reason and Biblical authority,

> Here, in a proto-Hobbesian perspective, mastery of
> external nature is related to mastery of internal
> nature (human nature). The growth of knowledge will
> not only enlarge the bounds that determine the degree
> of satisfaction of material wants, but will also serve
> as an instrument for repressing the permanent
> instinctual threat to social peace.[65]

Capitalism, Instrumentality and
The Sane Society of "New Atlantis"

It cannot be pointed out too frequently that Bacon's goal,
from first to last, was a reformist one. His valuation of
instrumental reason was ultimately based on the perception that
it was more capable than syllogistic logic of producing utility.
The old logic, as we have seen, was contemptuously dismissed by
Bacon as a calculus good only for abstract, inutile deductions.
His new model, on the other hand, was prized because it enabled
men to understand the Forms of nature, and thereby to use them
for the improvement of technology, trade and social stability.

In a word, to quote Benjamin Farrington, "Bacon's ambition was to make a new England, not a new logic."[66] Traditional learning's weakness was that it overly concentrated on logic instead of practical affairs. As Bacon says in the Great Instauration, "...all the tradition and succession of schools is still a succession of masters and scholars, not of inventors and those who bring to further perfection the things invented."[67]

It has been argued, in fact, that Bacon only turned to philosophical composition after he had unsuccessfully labored to achieve his reformist policies through actual political administration. (The Novum Organum and the fragments of the Great Instauration, for instance, were written only after his fall from grace as Lord Chancellor.) It is undeniable that Bacon was an extremely ambitious man, and this personal ambition no doubt served as a strong incentive for his immersion in affairs of state. But it seems to be the case that he also sought high office out of a genuine desire to reform the realm's educational structure in order to encourage the growth of the mechanical sciences. To cite Farrington again, Bacon hoped "to reform educational policy by expelling scholasticism and alchemy. In their place he proposed to bring in industrious observations, grounded conclusions, and profitable inventions and discoveries. This defines the policy he pursued throughout the whole course of his life."[68]

In addition to the unrealized goal of administratively restructuring the educational curriculum of his day, Bacon also appears to have entered public life in the hopes of winning the approval of first Elizabeth and then James I for his vision of the rational society. Bacon was a lifelong advocate of both a large, economically strong and highly centralized state, and a powerful monarchy with an attendant intellectual bureaucracy (although he did not accept James' belief in the divine right of kings). He was highly distrustful of leaving the administration of a country in the unskilled hands of either an unenlightened monarch or the ignorant and superstitious hoi poloi. The former could easily fall prey to an irrational pursuit of unchecked ambition; the latter were all too ready to unreflectively accept traditional idola and despise innovation. In a revealing passage from the Great Instauration, Bacon accuses the rabble of perpetuating inutile superstition:

> Now the doctrines which find most favour with the
> populace are those which are either contentious and
> pugnacious, or specious and empty; such, I say, as
> either entangle assent or tickle it. And therefore no
> doubt the greatest wits in each successive age have
> been forced out of their own course; men of capacity
> and intellect above the vulgar having been fain, for
> reputation's sake, to bow to the judgment of the time
> and the multitude; and thus if any contemplations of a
> higher order took light anywhere, they were presently
> blown out by the winds of vulgar opinions.[69]

Unhappily for Bacon, however, James I was less than enthusiastic about his Lord Chancellor's desire to modernize the realm. As I mentioned earlier, he contemptuously dismissed the Baconian philosophical system (and, by implication, its social agenda), with the remark that it, like the peace of god, "passes all understanding." The frustration caused by James' shortsightedness, coupled with Bacon's irremediable fall from favor at the age of sixty, ended forever the philosopher-politician's ambition of administratively actualizing his vision. Henceforth he resorted to the written word.

Yet he could not turn to the "vulgar" audience of the great unwashed which he so feared and despised. Neither could he rely upon the academic savants--the "professional teachers"--of his day to listen with sympathetic ears to his defense of

instrumental reason. Their worldview not only disdained the
mechanical arts; it also appeared to Bacon to necessarily hinder
their growth:

> This philosophy, if it be carefully examined, will be
> found to advance certain points of view which are
> deliberately designed to cripple industry. Such points
> of view are the opinion that the heat of the sun is a
> different thing from the heat of fire; or that men can
> only juxtapose things while nature alone can make them
> act upon one another. The effect and intention of
> their arguments is to convince men that nothing really
> great, nothing by which nature can be commanded and
> subdued, is to be expected from human art and human
> labour. Such teachings, if they be justly appraised,
> will be found to tend to nothing less than a wicked
> effort to curtail human power over nature and to
> produce a deliberate and artificial despair. This
> despair in its turn confounds the promptings of hope,
> cuts the springs and sinews of industry, and makes men
> unwilling to put anything to the hazard of a trial.[70]

With the elimination of the Crown, the rabble, and the savants
of his day as likely supporters of his programme, Bacon turned
his efforts towards capturing the imagination of the only
audience left to him--an audience which, moreover, was both
materially able and emotionally eager to instantiate his model of
a rational society. That audience, of course, was Britain's
rising middle class.

Fortunately for Bacon, the social segment to which he
directed his attention possessed two qualities which made it
particularly receptive to his cry for improvement in the
mechanical arts through the apotheosis of instrumental reason and
the concomitant denigration of inutile learning. The nascent
middle class was the most influential audience of his time
because it was quickly becoming the most powerful socio-economic
bloc. Its growth was rapid. In the reign of the eighth Henry
(which ended in 1547), Britain was one of the most industrially

retarded powers in Europe. By the reign of Charles I (ending in 1642), she led Europe in both mining and heavy industry.[71] The swift rise in Britain's stature as an industrial nation was directly linked to at least two historical phenomena: the enclosure of the commons under the reign of Henry VII, and the defeat of the Spanish armada under Elizabeth. The enclosure of the commons stimulated the power of the middle class in three ways. First, it enabled England to re-capture her competitive edge in the international wool market, thereby assuring a steady increase in revenue from foreign trade. Second, it created a strong class of early agricultural capitalists by apportioning hitherto common acres to middle-sized husbandrymen. Third, it precipitated a large exodus from the country to urban areas of displaced agricultural workers who served as the necessary manpower for industrial expansion.[72] Elizabeth's partly lucky, partly skillful defeat of Philip's armada shattered Spain's control of the sea and precipitated Britain into the position of master of the oceans. This control of the seas assured the island of control of trade routes, which brought in additional revenue from both heightened European trade and taxes imposed on the vessels of other sea-faring nations.

The rising middle class of Bacon's day represented the audience most receptive to his apotheosis of instrumental reason precisely because it was the class in whose immediate interest an increase in the mechanical arts was most advantageous. The capacity to so adequately understand nature as to bend it to the will of the practical scientist and technician could only result in the improvement of old, and the invention of new, mechanical arts. These arts were vital to not only industrial modes of production and mining, but also to the efficient navigation of oceanic trade routes. Clearly, technical improvements in these three areas meant an increase in trade, production and revenue,

all of which served as the backbone of the middle class of
merchants, industrialists and husbandmen. When introduced to
Bacon's new system, the entrepreneur of the sixteenth and
seventeenth centuries realized, perhaps for the first time, that
"science" could be an invaluable aid in the production of wealth.
It was no longer the abstruse, sterile plaything of detached
academicians; it now became an instrument by which to generate
material utility and wealth. It provided a source of
exploitation and profit that, for the Tudor and Stuart
imagination, was literally bottomless--nature itself. When one
couples these economic reasons for the middle class's enthusiasm
for Bacon's new system with the facts that the new system also
provided an intellectual justification for capitalistic growth, a
theological legitimation of the exploitation of nature, and,
finally, the visionary promise of inevitable progress in the
mechanical arts and enrichment of men (a promise which rested
upon instrumental reason's guarantee to unleash the unlimited
bounties of nature in the service of commerce), it is little
wonder that the Baconian spirit soon permeated Europe's most
powerful class.

It must not be supposed, moreover, that Bacon did not share
the middle class's high regard for industry and commerce. There
is absolutely no evidence to suggest that Bacon turned to a
middle class, in whose interests he was uninterested or opposed,
out of mere expediency. We have seen over and over that Bacon
valued his new canon precisely because it furthered the interests
of the mechanical arts, rejuvenated stagnant economic modes and
promised to improve the material standard of living for all
segments of the population. Bacon did not simply become an
accidental spokesperson for the middle class through the detached
formulation of a philosophical methodology and social agenda
which just happened to tie in with the interests of commerce.

Rather, he was himself genuinely devoted to those same interests, seeing in the aspirations and accomplishments of the middle class concrete proof of the efficacy of his new instrumental reason. In a revealing passage from the _Novum Organum_, Bacon insists that "the introduction of great inventions appears one of the most distinguished of human actions." Furthermore, these technological improvements "are a blessing and a benefit without injuring or afflicting any." If anyone doubts the universal value of such mechanical innovations, he has only to consider but three of the most recent: the printing press, gunpowder and the navigational compass. Each of these inventions has done more to further the material interests of humankind than, for instance, the world conquests of an Alexander the Great or the musings of an Aristotle:

> ...we should notice the force, effect, and consequences of inventions, which are nowhere more conspicuous than in those three which were unknown to the ancients: namely, printing, gunpowder, and the compass. For these three have changed the appearance and the state of the whole world: first in literature, then in warfare, and lastly in navigation; and innumerable changes have been thence derived, so that no empire, sect, or star appears to have exercised a greater power and influence on human affairs than these mechanical discoveries.[73]

It seems clear, then, that Bacon and the seventeenth-century British middle class enjoyed a symbiotic relationship with one another in their valuation of utility. Bacon provided the normative and theoretical justifications through his instrumental reason. The concrete works of the mercantile and industrial middle classes served as the necessary material conditions for the actualization of the system. Both Bacon and the middle class wholeheartedly championed the assertion that the key to universal (and inevitable) happiness was the strict domination of nature. The physical realm, as Marx states in one

of the epigrammes to this chapter, became exclusively a
ready-to-hand object for the furtherance of commercial interest.
Theoretical science became a tool whose fundamental value lay in
its ability to promote utility.

As I have already indicated, physical reality was not the
only arena which both Bacon and the rising middle class sought to
tame. The analogous goal of subduing and rationalizing the
inconveniences of social reality likewise captured their
attention. Obviously enough, expertise in the mechanical arts
alone was incapable of ushering in the far-reaching reforms which
Bacon advocated. In order for technology to bear fruit, the
social structure in which it existed needed to be refashioned in
such a way as to maximize the promulgation of rationally
supervised instrumental ends.

From the perspective of the increasing hegemony of the
middle class, there were two primary threats to social stability:
the whimsical power of the autocracy, and the dangerous clamoring
of the class of agricultural and urban laborers. Notwithstanding
James I's rather inchoate defense of the divine right of kings,
the increasingly powerful middle class to a certain extent
curtailed the absolute power of the monarchy by the time of the
Stuart ascension to the throne. True, the breakdown of the
feudal structure at the end of the middle ages concentrated a
great deal of political power in the hands of the British
monarch. But the concomitant growth in power of the Parliament,
which by and large controlled the royal purse strings, tended to
subordinate the Crown in economic affairs to the British
burghers. This growing economic reliance of the monarchy upon
the Parliament and capitalist class not only reduced the danger
of social upheaval caused by a less-than-stable autocrat; it also
indirectly served the interests of the middle class at the

expense of the laboring class. With his royal budget
increasingly dependent upon the approval of the bourgeoisie, the
British monarch, from Henry VII onwards, was more than willing to
approve legislation which promoted, at one and the same time, the
power of the middle class and the subordination of the "rabble."

This anti-labor legislation began, as pointed out earlier,
with Henry VII's enclosure of the commons. His son and heir,
Henry VIII, followed suit: strict laws were passed forbidding
begging, and increasingly stiff penalties were prescribed for
violators. The short reign of Edward VI almost seems to have
specialized in this type of legislation, until one scans
Parliamentary records from the times of both Elizabeth and James
dealing with the penalties for "vagabondage." In the first
volume of _Capital_ Marx summarizes the pertinent legislation
enacted during the reign of Edward VI. His resume provides a
representative idea of the increasingly brutal measures by which
the middle class's economic and political dominance over the
nonascendent classes was enforced.

> A statute of the first year of his reign, 1547, ordains
> that if anyone refuses to work, he shall be condemned
> as a slave to the person who has denounced him as an
> idler. The master shall feed his slave on bread and
> water, weak broth and such refuse meat as he thinks
> fit. He has the right to force him to do any work, no
> matter how disgusting, with whip and chains. If the
> slave is absent for a fortnight, he is condemned to
> slavery for life and is to be branded on forehead or
> back with the letter S; if he runs away three times, he
> is to be executed as a felon. The master can sell him,
> bequeath him, let him out on hire as a slave, just as
> he can any other personal chattel or cattle. If the
> slaves attempt anything against the masters, they are
> also to be executed. Justices of the peace, or
> informants, are to hunt the rascals down. If it
> happens that a vagabond has been idling about for three
> days, he is to be taken to his birthplace, branded with
> a red hot iron with the letter V on his breast, and set
> to work, in chains, on the roads or at some other

> labour. If the vagabond gives a false birthplace, he
> is then to become the slave for life of that place, of
> its inhabitants, or its corporation, and to be branded
> with an S. All persons have the right to take away the
> children of the vagabonds and keep them as apprentices,
> the young men until they are 24, the girls until they
> are 20. If they run away, the are to become, until
> they reach these ages, the slaves of their masters, who
> can put them in irons, whip them, etc. if they like.
> Every master may put an iron ring around the neck, arms
> or legs of his slave, by which to know him more easily
> and to be more certain of him.[74]

The harshness of these laws against vagabondage--which, again,
were just as strong in James I's time as in Edward's--is
especially striking when one considers that the enclosure of the
commons under Henry VII created literally thousands of such
"vagabonds" out of dispossessed agriculturalists. The implicit
advantage of these laws for the rising industrialists of Bacon's
time is clear--"vagabonds" either offer themselves as
wage-laborers, or suffer the unsavory legal consequences.

It is true that Bacon never resorts to such harsh language
in support of his vision of the sane society (notwithstanding the
fact that, as Lord Chancellor, he readily supported similar types
of legislation). But it is quite clear that he shared the
general conviction of the middle class that the ideal society is
one in which bourgeois structures--economic, normative and
theoretical--are predominant. In an epistle to James I entitled
"Of the True Greatness of the Kingdom of Britain," Bacon painted
an idealized portrait of England that would have appealed to the
most intractable of burghers. His ideal was of a nation

> ...whose wealth resteth in the hands of merchants,
> burghers, tradesmen, freeholders, farmers in the
> country, and the like; whereof we have a most evident
> and present example before our eyes, in our neighbours
> of the Low Countries, who could never have endured and
> continued so inestimable and insupportable charges,

either by their natural frugality or by their
mechanical industry, were it not also that there was a
concurrence in them of this last reason, which is, that
their wealth was dispersed in many hands, and not
engrossed into few; and those hands were not much of
the nobility, but most and generally of inferior
conditions.[75] ["Hands of inferior condition" here
refers to bourgeois, not labouring, hands.]

Bacon's only attempt to sketch this ideal society made up
of "merchants, burghers and tradesmen" (and, it is reasonable to
assume, "technicians") appears in his fragmentary New Atlantis.
This work, probably written in 1624 but only published the year
after Bacon's death, provides us with an idea of the "utopian"
character of a society based upon the tenets of instrumental
reason, a society which has eliminated irrationality by taming
external (physical) nature as well as internal (human) nature.

The New Atlantis, or "Bensalem," as its principle city is
called and which serves as a representative encapsulation of the
character of the entire society, strikes one as a research
institute writ large. Its primary rule of thumb is that "the
laws of nature are thine own laws,"[76] the implication being that
natural law applies equally to the physical and sacred realms.
This fidelity to the discovery and harnessing of natural law has
most immediately resulted in an amazing number of inventions,
both luxurious and practical, in New Atlantis--perfumes,
mechanical labor-saving devices, almost miraculous medicines and
weather-simulating machines that regulate whimsical climatic
conditions. Practical, applied scientists are revered within the
new society in a way that is analogous to the traditional
veneration of saints in Catholic cultures. It is the custom of
the land, in fact, to lavishly reward those citizens who make
advances in the mechanical arts: "...upon every invention of
value, we erect a statue to the inventor, and give him a liberal
and honourable reward."[77] This adulation of the suppliers of

mechanical innovation is a direct reflection of the high premium
which the ideal New Atlantis society places upon instrumental
reason.

The respect which those individuals who reveal and tame
nature's laws enjoy is accentuated by the fact that the entire
country is under the direct control, not of professional
politicians, democratic institutions, or even royal mandate, but
of a caste of professional scientists and technicians who live
and work at an institute known as "Salomon's House." Salomon's
House is a research foundation and central ruling body which, as
Bacon says, is "dedicated to the study of the Works and Creatures
of God," and is "the lanthorn of this kingdom."[78] The express
goal of Salomon's House, as expressed by one of its principle
luminaries (a member of an elite group of technicians known as
the "Fathers"), is Baconian to the core: "The End of our
Foundation is the knowledge of Causes, and secret motions of
things; and the enlarging of the bounds of Human Empire, to the
effecting of all things possible."[79]

The Fathers of Salomon's House, in addition to wielding
considerable political authority over New Atlantis (which I
shall discuss more fully later), also enjoy the genuine
approbation of its citizenry and are treated with the pomp and
circumstance which European countries of Bacon's time reserved
for their royalty. The following description of a visit to
Bensalem by one of the Fathers gives a pretty good indication of
their status in the New Atlantean sane society.

He was carried in a rich chariot without wheels,
litterwise; with two horses at either end, richly
trapped in blue velvet embroidered; and two footmen on
each side in like attire. The chariot was all of cedar
gilt, and adorned with crystal; save that the fore-end
had pannels of sapphires, set in borders of gold, and
the hinder-end the like of emeralds of the Peru colour.

> There was also a sun of gold, radiant, upon the top...;
> and on the top before, a small cherub of gold, with
> wings displayed. The chariot was covered with cloth of
> gold tissued upon blue. He [i.e., the Father] had
> before him fifty attendants, young men all, in white
> sattin loose coats to the mid-leg; and stockings of
> white silk; and shoes of blue velvet; and hats of blue
> velvet; with fine plumes of divers colours, set round
> like hat-bands. Next before the chariot went two men,
> bareheaded, in linen garments down the foot, girt, and
> shoes of blue velvet; who carried the one a crosier,
> the other a pastoral staff like a sheep-hook; neither
> of them of metal, but the crosier of balm-wood, the
> pastoral staff of cedar...[80]

And so on and on. The description of the pomp surrounding
the person of a Father continues, with the most exacting of
details, in a quite wearisome way. No doubt part of the reason
for the elaborate ceremonial description can be chalked up to the
ex-Lord Chancellor's intoxication with official court protocol.
But it is also reasonable to suppose that Bacon so emphasized the
richness of the Father's retinue to underscore the latter's
supreme importance in New Atlantis. Notice that there is an
almost religious flavor to the descriptions of the Father's
symbols of office: a crosier on the one hand, a pastoral staff
on the other. The implication is obvious: the Fathers of
Salomon's House--i.e., the leading technicians and champions of
instrumental reason within the confines of the sane
society--possess not only political but also spiritual authority.
Within their hands is concentrated the means of providing for the
well-being of New Atlantis precisely because they know the
secrets of recalcitrant nature. Just as a shepherd looks after
the interests of his flock, sometimes even to the point of
prodding them in directions which they don't want to go, so the
Fathers mandate and supervise the lives of their charges, the
inhabitants of New Atlantis.

The Fathers of Salomon's House, for instance, keep a tight

rein on the scientific research that goes on within the borders
of New Atlantis, as well as on the public appearance of new
inventions. It is not uncommon for them to hold back from
general consumption new mechanical contrivances which have been
constructed in the Salomon institute. The assumption is that it
takes time for the average person to absorb technical innovation.
Exposure to it, consequently, should proceed in gradual stages.
Otherwise, the technocratic elite runs the risk of introducing
new mechanical arts which, although theoretically in the material
interest of all humankind, might be abused by an immature and
unsophisticated populace which, if the truth were told, is in
constant need of strict supervision by their betters. Moreover,
inasmuch as all technological and scientific research is
performed under the auspices of Salomon's House, the Fathers have
final say as to what constitutes "good" science and what
constitutes "bad" science. Needless, perhaps, to say, given the
earlier stated aim of the institute to "enlarge the Human Empire"
by "effecting all things possible" in the mechanical arts, only
those scientific projects which promise to promote the utility in
the Atlantean sane society are granted an imprimatur.

But the authority of the Fathers extends far beyond the
technological realm. They mandate the annual types and
quantities of commodities which will be produced and consumed
within the society. They regulate, with the strictest of
controls, the numbers of natives which can leave the confines of
the New Atlantis and those of foreigners who might wish to enter.
And they punish with swift and harsh justice the isolated
instances of dissent or nonconformity which, left unchecked,
might threaten the equilibrium of the community.

The Fathers' last role as civil magistrates is one which is
only infrequently assumed in the New Atlantis. Human and

societal relationships have been fashioned and controlled by
institutional, rationalized techniques just as much as have
scientific research and mechanical invention. The entire social
structure is strongly hierarchical--indeed, patriarchical--with
each individual having clearly designated duties and social
functions as defined by his or her place within the community.
This rationalization of interpersonal relationships usually
precludes the possibility of dis-equilibrating behavior--so much
so, in fact, that the average inhabitant of New Atlantis takes on
a curiously automoton-like persona. When, for instance, the
Father of Salomon's House makes his entry into Bensalem, the
populace, rather than greeting him with the jubilant enthusiasm
which the ceremonial pomp of his entourage would seem to warrant,
display an orderliness and decorum which is, to say the least, a
bit eerie: "the street was wonderfully well kept; so that there
was never any army had their men stand in better battle-array,
than the people stood. The windows likewise were not crowded,
but every one stood in them as if they had been placed."[81] This
military-like, dispassionate control is revealing. It symbolizes
Bacon's assumption that the well-run society, like the well-run
research institute, is emotionless, rational and orderly, under
any and all circumstances. The rationalized society, just like
rationalized scientific method, has no room for inutile emotional
spontaneity.

The rational character of the New Atlantean sane society is
further encouraged by the rigid hierarchical and patriarchical
character of the community. Just as the Fathers of Salomon's
House exert absolute supervisory authority over the whole of the
society, ensuring that general economic, scientific and social
relations are strictly regulated, so the father of each nuclear
family (known as the "Father of the Family") likewise enjoys
absolute domain over his dependents. He is served by his male

children, who always approach him upon bended knee, and over
whose destinies he has final control. His female children, in
addition to all the other women of his household, are even more
closely bound by his authority. They assume an entirely passive
role within the confines of the home--and, indeed, throughout
society as a whole. In public functions, when their presence is
even tolerated, they are allowed only to "stand about [the
patriarch], leaning against the wall."[82] Under no circumstances
are they permitted to actively participate in either the process
of decision-making or the performance of ceremony. Even at
meals, the women of a household are required to eat apart from
the males, behind a screen. Age enjoys no privilege in this
regard; the mother of an entire family enjoys no more rights than
her younger, less "productive" relatives. At meals, "if there be
a mother from whose body the whole lineage is descended, there is
a traverse placed in a loft above on the right hand of the chair,
with a privy door, and a carved window of glass, leaded with gold
and blue; where she sitteth, but is not seen."[83] The
justification for the hierarchical and patriarchical structure of
both family and social life in New Atlantis is, so far as Bacon
is concerned, obvious: hierarchical assignations of duties and
functions minimize the possibility of irrationality and whimsy in
the social fabric, thereby maximizing the orderliness which is
necessary for a truly rationalized community. The patriarchical
devaluation of women stems from the fact (for Bacon) that females
in no way contribute to an enrichment of the mechanical arts,
most probably because they are "by nature" incapable of the
dispassionate attitude necessary for an objective inquiry into
the secrets of physical reality. As such, their value in a
society that prizes instrumental reason above everything else is
at a low premium. That women are viewed by Bacon as being too
"emotional" to engage in the mechanical arts has been
convincingly argued by Carolyn Merchant in her The Death of

Nature,[84] in which she demonstrates that Bacon ascribes the same
metaphorical predicates of capriciousness, whimsy and jealousy to
womankind as he does to nature itself. Both must be bent to the
will, and hence tamed, by male reason.

The mores and normative codes which permeate New Atlantis
are also conducive to the ultimate rationalization of the
society. Sexual norms are especially stringent; as one of the
New Atlanteans proudly declaims, "You shall understand that there
is not under the heavens so chaste a nation as this of Bensalem;
nor so free from all pollution or foulness. It is the virgin of
the world."[85] "Masculine love" is condemned as an
abomination,[86] as is heterosexual intercourse outside the bounds
of matrimony. This ubiquitous valuation of "purity" is not a
consequence of the New Atlanteans seeing sexual loyalty as an end
in and of itself, however. Marriage is viewed as a good because,
through it, the stabilizing patriarchical (i.e., "rational")
structure of the community is maintained and strengthened. Even
in the realm of morals, then, the final aim of Bacon's New
Atlantis is to promote instrumentality.

A high value is placed upon the possession of private
property in New Atlantis, and is used to further solidify the
patriarchical family structure which is seen as a necessary
condition for a well-run, orderly society. Children born out of
wedlock have no property rights whatsoever, and their parents are
materially penalized for their transgression of societal mores.
Moreover, couples who marry without the consent of their
parents--a consent which, obviously, is viewed as an essential
function of a hierarchical community--are indirectly penalized.
Their offspring enjoy fewer property rights than do the children
of sanctioned unions. As Bacon says, "Marriage without consent
of parents [the New Atlanteans] do not make void, but they mulct

it in the inheritors: for the children of such marriages are not
admitted   to   inherit   above   a   third   of   their parents'
inheritance."[87]

Finally, the social stability of New Atlantis is ultimately
cemented by a Christian religion which obviously possesses a
moral   code and   hierarchical organization   analogous   to   that of
the Church of England in Bacon's time.   The inhabitants of New
Atlantis, just like Bacon himself, are confident that the right
to dominate and manipulate nature has been granted them by the
deity,   and that, consequently, their emphasis upon both the
mechanical   arts and   the material affluence which they produce
enjoys divine approval.   This god-given mandate is adequately
expressed in one of the traditional prayers of the Atlanteans:
"Lord God of heaven and earth, thou hast vouchsafed of thy grace
to [us], to know thy works of creation, and the secrets of
them..."[88] The implication is obvious: knowledge of nature's
secrets has been vouchsafed so that the dominion of humankind
over creation can be solidified through the production of good
works--i.e., the creation of new inventions.

In this brief sketch of the character of Bacon's ideal sane
society, one characteristic stands out: the supreme value
placed upon instrumentality. Social functions are deemed worthy
only to the extent that they promote the same   "rationality"
within the social fabric that Bacon espouses in scientific
investigation.   Just as scientific research should be closely
supervised, with a clearly designated division of   labor,
responsibility and authority, so the sane society should likewise
be one in which overall political, economic and moral supervision
closely regulates the lifestyles and tasks of all strata within
the community. Furthermore, just as the best results in science
are the consequences of a dispassionate, objective and orderly

method of inquiry, so the best societal structure is one which
likewise instantiates these virtues by eliminating passion,
spontaneity and nonconformism. The way to conquer physical
nature is to bind its seeming whimsicalities to scientific method
and supervision. Analogously, the way to eliminate social
caprice and irrationality is to apply identical constraints to
individual behavior. That, in the final analysis, is the lesson
to be derived from Bacon's New Atlantis.

Bacon obviously presented his allegorical community as an
exemplar of what the ideal society should be--i.e., as a utopia.
In point of fact, however, the imaginary ideal is ideological.
It mirrors the interests and values of the ascendent middle class
of Bacon's time--as does, of course, his entire "new" scientific
canon. The primary virtue in New Atlantis is instrumentality,
both in the mechanical arts and in social functions. Material
prosperity and the coincidental valuation of private property is
assured through the House of Salomon's strict supervision of the
research behind and production of new labor-saving and
revenue-creating devices. Social stability is promulgated
through political and normative institutions which encourage
strong authoritative structures that promote the efficiency and
orderliness a society must enjoy in order to maximize its
material prosperity. Class dissent is checked via the
hierarchical supervision of economical and political activity;
private property and economic gain is used as an incentive for
fidelity to establish social standards; and "nonproductive"
elements of society--most notably women--are relegated to a
passive and hence essentially powerless role in the community.

In short, the New Atlantis sane society is a seventeenth-
century middle class ideal in which profit-generating technology
and socially stabilizing institutions are deemed the keys to the

good life for all inhabitants. The rub, of course, is that the
values which it espouses are applicable only to a society in
which but one class--the bourgeoisie--is materially dominant.
That the entire image of New Atlantis strikes the reader as a
middle class Shangra-la is not accidental. As I have tried to
argue throughout this section, the hidden normative assumptions
lying behind Bacon's vision of both "correct" scientific method
and the ideal social structure are directly reflective of the
interests of the materially ascendent class of his day--the
middle class.

IV

I started this chapter by posing a question: how is it
that Bacon's vision of a new logic has proven to be such a
pervasively influential ideal of the modern era, notwithstanding
the fact that it suffers from serious philosophical flaws? I
have argued that Bacon's influence was as strong as it was
because of the fact that his system gave systematic expression
and intellectual justification to the values and aspirations of
the increasingly empowered middle class of the seventeenth,
eighteenth and nineteenth centuries. As such, neither his
methodological assumptions nor his blueprint of the ideal--or
"sane"--society are objective. Tied as they are to specific
class interests, even while claiming universal applicability for
all social strata, they reveal themselves as ideological in
nature. The ultimate social function of Bacon's system,
notwithstanding its sincere reformist aspirations, was to
consolidate the hegemony of the materially ascendent class both
during his lifetime and afterwards, and to likewise strengthen
the purview of conventional capitalist values and conceptual
models. Furthermore, it is clear in retrospect that the sane
society social agenda implied by his system failed, precisely
because of its mistaken assumption that what were merely

classbound values were in fact universal ones, truly conducive to the welfare of <u>all</u> humankind.

Bacon's assumptions that instrumentality was the ultimate goal of all correct science and that the sane society was one which rigorously applied the same "objective" (and hence utility-laden) methods to social relations as the natural philosophers applied to physical phenomena, were to prove far-reaching in their historical consequences. As I shall argue in the next two chapters, the theoretical models of the <u>Great Instauration</u> and the social agenda of <u>The New Atlantis</u> served as the bedrock upon which the putatively utopian sane societies of the nineteenth century would rest.

CHAPTER 3

THE IDEOLOGICAL NATURE OF THE SANE SOCIETY OF NINETEENTH-CENTURY UTOPIAS: HISTORICAL BACKGROUND AND OVERVIEW

> Really the mechanical science of this period has not mechanized human conduct. Rather, it has given freedom. Humanity was never before so free in dealing with its own environment as it has been since the triumphs of modern science. The ability to look at the world in terms of congeries of physical particles actually has enabled men to determine their environment.
>
> George Herbert Mead,
> Movements of Thought in the Nineteenth Century

> I have heard that there is a Society for the Diffusion of Useful Knowledge. It is said that knowledge is power and the life. Methinks there is equal need of a Society for the Diffusion of Useful Ignorance, for what is most of our boasted so-called knowledge but a conceit that we know something which robs us of the advantages of our actual ignorances.
> Henry David Thoreau,
> Journals, February 8, 1851

I

The nineteenth century gave rise to an explosion of putative utopian novels. Indeed, more self-proclaimed utopian fantasies appeared during this period than in all the years prior to it. These novels, with very few exceptions, reflected the nineteenth century's exhuberant confidence in its ability to inaugurate a genuine golden age--or "sane society"--in which traditional social irrationalities would finally be eliminated. Notwithstanding the fact that this optimistic faith in inevitable progress might appear smugly inflated to the wearier twentieth-century mind, the nineteenth-century imagination felt its exhuberance more than justified by the startling advances it witnessed in scientific theory, technology, medicine, economics and geo-political relations. The wonder and pride with which the century regarded its achievements, in addition to its confident assurance that the decades to come would bring even more amazing developments, strongly influenced the optimistic credo expressed in the period's booming utopia industry.

The character of the nineteenth-century "utopia" was also heavily colored by the period's assumption that, as the inheritor of the Baconian worldview, it had radically broken with the stultifying traditions, both scientific and normative, of the pre-modern past. One of the strongest reasons for the period's faith in itself was its impression that it had jettisoned the irrational material conditions bequeathed to it by earlier, technologically unsophisticated generations. It envisioned itself as striking out afresh, uncluttered with superstitions or illusory beliefs, and thereby capable of finally instantiating Bacon's sane society exemplar which would in turn revolutionize the entire social, economic and theoretical world order. It is unlikely that any century thus far has enjoyed a stronger sense of its own manifest destiny than did the nineteenth.

Finally, the nineteenth century had no doubts about the

absolute universality of the values and theoretical models which constituted its worldview. Liberated as it believed itself to be from the technological immaturity which had retarded previous eras, it was confident in its ability to clearly and without bias analyze the nature of both physical and social reality. The unquestioned assumption was that the "revolutionary" innovations which characterized the century, in both theory and technique, would usher in the good society for all humans. Nothing was plainer than that increased technological sophistication and the rationalization of socio-economic relations were the necessary conditions of a social agenda promotive of everyone's welfare, both wealthy and penurious, male as well as female. Science, so the nineteenth century believed, was value-free and interest-blind; and this almost cultish faith in the objectivity (and hence universal validity) of the scientific canon became the major leitmotif of the period's sane society literature.

The nineteenth century, then, was one which saw itself as the revolutionary catalyst for the emergence of a not-too-distant golden age. It perceived the values and theoretical models which it accepted as universal and objective in nature, and hence most appropriate and eminently realizable. The putative utopian novels spawned during this period in turn were stamped with the nineteenth century's image of itself. Such a reflection, after all, seemed to make sense. Utopias by definition point towards the future, to a vision of the perfect society, and the nineteenth century saw itself as inevitably moving towards this future, laying the necessary material conditions for the perfect sane society. It is only logical, then, that nineteenth-century "utopian" visions accepted the perceived revolutionary character of their century as the harbinger of a future golden age.

The problem, however, is that the nineteenth century was by no means as revolutionary as it fancied itself. Instead of representing a radical conceptual break with the past, the era's collective mind was firmly rooted in the normative and theoretical model legitimized by Bacon two hundred years earlier. Moreover, the set of propositions which constituted the nineteenth century's Weltanschauung was neither objective nor universal. In point of fact, it mirrored the interests of, and was consequently only properly applicable to, one class of people--the ascendent bourgeoisie. The nineteenth century was, in short, confused about its own character. It cherished a set of beliefs which were fundamentally illusory. Thus the normative and conceptual models characteristic of the century were, in Mannheim's terminology, part and parcel of the modern era's total ideological structure. And inasmuch as the welter of putative utopian novels which appeared during this time were based upon an extension of that worldview, they too were ideological. Ironically, then, the very novels which claimed to epitomize revolutionary change in both values and thought were, in fact, the culmination of a long ideological continuum. Even more ironically, they were extremely effective in justifying and propagating the existent ideological milieu by apotheosizing its classbound values as necessary and universal propositions. Nineteenth-century sane society "utopias" were, in a word, descendents of the ideological Baconian vision of "rationalizing" both societal and physical reality.

In Chapter Four I shall examine several of these literary portraits of the sane society. In the present chapter, my purpose is to set the stage for this later discussion by performing three tasks. First, I aim to give an idea of the generally exhuberant attitude of the nineteenth century and to

provide reasons for its existence. Second, I will indicate how
this   confidence   was   translated   into   a   set   of   themes
characteristic of mainstream nineteenth-century utopian visions
of the sane society. Finally, I hope to provide historical
evidence for my assertion that nineteenth-century utopias are
actually disguised ideologies. I   shall do this by arguing   that
there was a dark side to the era's apparent revolution in
technique and material prosperity, a less than utopian underbelly
which the century's cheerleaders by and large failed to take
seriously: the condition of the laboring classes.

II

The Age of Progress

If, as is often claimed, the eighteenth   century was
characterized by a general mood of optimism, the nineteenth
century's[1] attitude about itself and its accomplishments can just
as well be summed up as one of exhuberance. Styling itself "the
century of progress," its most fervently held belief was that it
represented the concrete inauguration of an era   of human
emancipation from superstition, ignorance, poverty and warfare.
It enjoyed a general mood of enthusiasm, a confident faith in its
ability to steadily improve the condition of humanity.
Furthermore, this confidence was expressed not merely by most of
the century's intellectual savants but, more significantly, by
the members of a rising socio-economic group which entered into
mature predominance in these years: the middle class. The
general sentiment was that the nineteenth century was an
historical watershed, the first significant stage in a rather
dizzying and inevitable acceleration towards a golden era of
reason and progress which the "new" science of the early modern
period, as systematized by Bacon, had made possible. True, there
were a few dissenting voices. The early German and British

Romantics,   the   American   transcendentalists,   Kierkegaard,
Schopenhauer, Nietzsche, France and Hesse were all among those
who protested against the nineteenth century's love affair with
itself. But these pessimistic prophets were by no means
representative of the era's basic self-image, and their influence
tended to be confined to relatively small and rather incestuous
groups of intellectuals and aesthetes. It was the exhuberant
cult which celebrated the inevitability of the sane society, and
not the gloomy warnings of the occasional dark prophet, that
succeeded in capturing the popular imagination.

The tragic irony is that the prophets of doom had a more
accurate appreciation of the nature of the nineteenth century's
cult of progress than did its ardent champions. Notwithstanding
their claims of emancipation and universal applicability, the
ideals of the nineteenth century were solidly grounded in the
scientific, political and normative worldview which arose in the
two immediately preceding centuries. Far from representing a
radical break with the past and an intrepid charting of hitherto
unexplored intellectual continents, the worldview of the
nineteenth century was really the logical outcome of a total
ideological structure whose roots reached as far back as Francis
Bacon. Furthermore, in spite of its assumption of universal
validity, the nineteenth century's Weltanschauung was directly
reflective and supportive of the hegemonic ascendency of the
middle class. Both the revolutionary and universal qualities
which the nineteenth century claimed for its ideals were,
consequently, illusory in nature, as was also the period's
zealous faith in the inevitable rationalization of man and
society. It would take the holocaust of the Great European War
to finally shatter the era's magic lantern confidence in itself.

Still, right until the bottom dropped out in 1914, there

were very good immediate reasons for the nineteenth century's
deceptive image of itself as the century of absolute progress.
To begin with, it provided a background of relative relief from
the destruction of large-scale warfare. From the Vienna
Congress of 1815 to the beginning of World War I in August 1914,
the Western world enjoyed almost one hundred years of peace.
Metternich's division of Europe after the fall of Napoleon
established a balance of power between the victorious Big Four
nations of Britain, Austria, Russia and Prussia such that it was
to each state's economic advantage to settle differences at the
diplomatic table rather than the battlefield. True, a few
bellicose eruptions did occur in the nineteenth century: the
Crimean War in 1854, the American Civil War in 1861, the
Franco-Prussian War of 1870 and the Boer War at the turn of the
century. But each one of these conflicts was localized,
short-lived and, with the horrible exception of the American
Civil War, led to relatively small numbers of casualties.
Compared to the earlier Napoleonic Wars which for twenty years
ruinously transformed all of Europe and half of Imperial Russia
into a slaughterhouse, these subsequent conflicts seemed, to the
nineteenth century mind, like minor skirmishes.

In addition to providing a balance of power capable of
sustaining one hundred years of general peace, the nineteenth
century also gave birth to an astounding level of industrial
progress and economic affluence. The central factor in this
almost geometric growth rate was not so much the invention of
machinery capable of mass production (such machinery had been
introduced in the eighteenth century), but rather the application
of new and plentiful sources of power with which to drive the
machines. The two most fruitful sources were coal and steam.
Their revolutionization of the production process was, to the
nineteenth-century imagination, nothing short of proof that

Bacon's earlier apotheosis of instrumental reason had been justified. The historian Geoffrey Bruun describes the phenomenal growth rate of the century's industrial capacity:

> That modern machine industry was built on coal was testified to by the rate of its consumption. Between 1670 and 1770 the annual European coal production increased only threefold. Between 1770 and 1870 (the century of the Industrial Revolution) it rose thirtyfold. But this first century of industrialism, impressive and even revolutionary though its effects proved, was only a prologue. After 1870 (until European economy was dislocated by the First World War) the average increase in coal production each decade was greater than the total increase for the preceding century.[2]

And as the century drew to a close, even more powerful sources of energy began to be exploited: "By 1881 the production of petroleum already exceeded 3,000,000 tons annually, and the oil industry had been born. More significant still, newly perfected dynamos in electric power plants were generating current for light circuits and other commercial purposes. The age of oil and electricity was at hand..."[3]

The technological innovations that arose from this explosion in productive capacity were even more dramatic, and colorfully bolstered the nineteenth century's faith in its ability to inaugurate the sane society. Furthermore, the new inventions encouraged by the rising levels of capital and mechanical expertise appeared with mind-boggling swiftness. In fourteen short years, between 1867 and 1881, the microphone, telephone, electric lamp, gramophone, electric tramcar and internal combustion engine made their first appearance. Motion pictures, dry-plate photography and primitive color photography not only amazed and delighted middle class audiences but also opened up exciting new avenues for research. The media and publishing

industries   likewise   benefited   from   the   new   technological
expertise: the introduction of the rotary perfecting   press and
the typewriter accelerated the production of printed   material by
a   hundredfold.   (Amusingly   enough,   Nietzsche,   who despised
almost   everything   the   age represented,   was   one   of the   first
European   intellectuals   to   acquire   a   typewriter,   which   he
laboriously   taught himself   to use   in order   to   pound   out the
hundreds   of   letters   he sent   each   year   to acquaintances   and
relatives.)   Nor, as Bruun points   out,   was   the explosion   in
mechanization confined to industry alone.

> The improved   reaper and binder   enabled the farmer   to
> expand his   acres while chemical   fertilizers increased
> the yield.   Transportation   costs fell while the   speed
> and regularity of   the carriers improved; the   airbrake
> solved   the   problem   of   deceleration;   and   railroad
> tunnels   through   the   Alps (Mont Cerus,   1871;   Saint
> Gothard,   1882)   reduced   the   journey   from   Italy   to
> Germany or France from days to hours.   The   Suez Canal,
> which enabled   vessels to pass   from   the Mediterranean
> to   the   Red   Sea   and   Indian   Ocean,   and   the   first
> transcontinental   railway   to   cross   the   United States,
> were both opened   in the same year (1869).[4]

The increasing ease with which this explosion of technology
both rationalized the production process and promised to once and
for   all   decide   the   battle   between   recalcitrant   nature   and
industrious man, both delighted and amazed the nineteenth-century
mind.   Even   more   significantly   it   reinforced   the   growing
assumption that   no achievement was   beyond the purview   of human
ability.   Man as   the master   technician   ultimately capable of
subduing the forces of nature had been a common leitmotif of the
West, as we saw in the previous chapter, at least as far   back as
Bacon's   apotheosis   of   instrumental   reason   in   the   seventeenth
century.   The   arrival   of the   machine   age   in   the   nineteenth
century only   enhanced, with spectacular   concrete   results, that
self-image.   As early   as 1827   this growing   confidence   in   the

manifest destiny of <u>homo faber</u> had been forcefully expressed by
J.A. Stumpff, the royal British harpmaker, when he captured the
mood of the age with the following paean to the newly-invented
steam engine:

> The shiny metal moves up and down,
> It animates all parts behind
> A single goal. The huge construction
> Always obeys the master's mind.[5]

The advent of the new technology in the nineteenth century,
then, reinforced the assumption that instrumental reason both
could and should rationalize human existence by subduing nature
to the "huge constructions" of the "master's mind." But it also
served to popularize another idea that had been in vogue for the
previous two centuries, namely that nature itself was
exhaustively and best understood in totally quantitative,
mechanistic terms. The mechanistically lawlike character of
physical reality in turn implied that nature was capable of being
systematically exploited for profit. If the natural world was
perceived by the no-nonsense industrial imagination of the
nineteenth century as being imbued with any beauty at all, it was
the cold beauty of a well-oiled machine whose parts operated with
a geometrical precision.

The thesis that nature is imbued with law-like regularity,
and hence ultimately controllable through instrumental reason's
harnessing of it via the mechanical sciences was, as we saw in
Chapter Two, the nucleus around which Bacon's new system
revolved. The Baconian ideal of extending the empire of man
through the manipulation of nature received new impetus in the
nineteenth century when physicists announced to the world that
nature itself was nothing more nor less than a vast reservoir of
energy--a giant machine, as it were--waiting to be tapped by

ingenious entrepreneurs. Helmholtz was especially influential in
bestowing a scientific imprimatur upon this conception of nature
with his popularization of a mechanistic worldview based upon the
postulation of the law of the preservation of energy.   The
instrumental implication of this formulation was that nature is
best regarded as a repository of energy capable of being both
mechanically transformed and technologically preserved by being
harnessed in the interests of industry. In a revealing passage
from his "On the Interaction of Natural Forces and the Latest
Pertinent Findings of Physics," a popular lecture given in
Koenigsberg in 1854, Helmholtz gives succinct expression to the
era's utilitarian attitude towards nature as well   as its
confident assurance of nature man's right to bend nature to his
desires:

> We human beings cannot create work energy for human
> purposes, we can only take possession of it from
> nature's general storehouse.   The woodland brook and
> the wind that drive our mills, the forest and the
> mineral-coal deposits that fuel our steam engines and
> heat our homes, are all merely bearers of a part of
> nature's huge energy reserve, which we exploit for our
> purposes and whose effects we try to maneuver according
> to our will.[6]

For both Helmholtz and the nineteenth-century scientific
worldview, it was a simple step from this ascription of a
machine-like nature to physical reality to the analogous
assumption that organic reality, both human and nonhuman, could
best be explained in exclusively mechanistic terms. In the same
lecture cited above, Helmholtz elaborates upon the analogy:

> Having learned about the origin of work energy by
> observing the steam engine, we must ask: Is it any
> different with human beings?   In point of fact,
> survival is tied to the continual intake of
> nourishment, combustile substances that, when totally
> digested, enter the blood, then undergo a slow burning
> in the lungs, and from wellnigh the same combustions

with the oxygen in the air as would arise from burning
in an open fire. Since the amount of heat generated by
combustion is independent of the length of turning and
its intermediary stages, we can calculate on the basis
of the material   consumed how much heat   or its
equivalent in work can thereby be produced in the body
of an animal. Unfortunately, the difficulties of such
experiments are very great; yet within the limits of
precision hitherto attained, research shows that heat
generated in an animal body matches that supplied by
chemical processes.   The body of an animal thus does
not differ from a steam engine in the fashion in which
it gains heat and energy; it does differ, however, in
the purpose and the manner for which and in which it
then uses the energy gained. Moreover, in its choice
of fuel, it is more restricted than the steam engine.[7]

It is important to note that the message of the preceding
passage is not simply that man is a natural creature and hence
subject, like all things which exist, to natural laws.   If such
was Helmholtz's only point, his assumption would be one of those
too general statements which are true by default but rather
trivial (such as, for instance, Voltaire's insistence that "it
would be very odd if laws which governed the universe made an
exception of man, that minute inhabitant of a planet"[8]).
Instead, the point that Helmholtz is making is much stronger.
His claim is that a living creature, just like the overall nature
of the inorganic physical order, has the functional
characteristics of a machine, and hence is exhaustively analyzed
in quantifiable, mechanistic terms. If the analogy limps at all,
so far as Helmholtz was concerned, it is only because an organic
machine is ultimately "more restricted," and hence less
efficient, than an inorganic one.

The influential Helmholtzian ascription of a mechanical
nature to man, whose every motion, "voluntary" or "involuntary,"
can be explained in terms of energy distribution, was reinforced
in the nineteenth-century imagination by discoveries in the
biological and social sciences. In the first half of the century

Bichot argued that the human body was merely the sum total of its component cells. Shortly thereafter the Dutch biologist Van Beer demonstrated that the fertilized egg, far from being a fully developed homonculus, was in fact an energy cell which served as the necessary condition for the development of human tissue in general. "From then on," as Charles Moraze claims,

> biology was no longer limited to natural history: the study of the cell became its chief occupation. Certainly, the study of the substance of the egg and of the cell was not yet free from the vitalist principles which had permeated eighteenth-century biology, much as phlogiston had in the realm of physics. Nevertheless, biological experimentation was already moving towards the principle of the conservation of energy, which was fairly generally recognized in that field after 1850.[9]

There were other perceived verifications of the mechanistic nature of man in the biological sciences which were even more dramatic and which consequently especially captured the century's popular imagination. Lister's introduction of antiseptic surgery in 1865 established the causal relationship between bacteria and infection. Pasteur and Koch strengthened the theory by demonstrating that discrete, isolatable varieties of germs were the direct causes (rather than the mere concomitants) of disastrous diseases such as anthrax and tuberculosis. And in the last quarter of the century bacteriologists identified the sources of infection for diseases such as diptheria, cholera, leprosy and malaria. The new science of immunology to which these and other discoveries gave impetus provided overwhelming practical evidence for Helmholtz's depiction of reality as the quantifiable transformation and preservation of energy.

The chemical sciences also appeared to lend support to the uniformly mechanistic worldview of the nineteenth century. In 1830 Justus Liebig conducted research which led to the discovery of the carbon cycle, demonstrating that chlorophyll used solar

energy to return to the earth the carbon which it extracted from
organisms. This specific cycle was seen as a microcosmic
encapsulation of the entire process of energy transformation and
preservation which informed all of reality.   When Mendeliev
published his Periodic Law of Elements in 1869, arguing that
elements ranged according to their atomic weights display a
periodicy such   that each eighth   element   reveals similar
properties, the century's assurance that both   organic and
inorganic reality behaved in a rational and hence manipulatable
manner was still further strengthened.

The nascent social sciences of the time also eagerly adopted
the Helmholtzian worldview as their starting point.   If human
reality operated under the same laws and was characterized by the
same mechanistic functions as nonhuman reality, the structure
and organization of social groupings were, by implication,
capable of ultimate rationalization. Accounts of so-called moral
and psychological processes would inevitably reduce to
descriptions of relations between matter and energy, explainable
in precise, deterministic terms, ultimately eliminating the
disconcerting existence of theoretical ambiguity and concrete
noncontrollability in the social arena. The ideal sane society
thus came to be seen as yet another machine-like structure whose
well-oiled components interacted with one another in a maximally
efficient way.

Saint-Simon and   Comte were the   first major thinkers after
Bacon to systematically draw out the social implications of the
mechanistic analysis of human reality which Helmholtz would later
popularize. If, as Saint-Simon argued, individual behavior was
ultimately explicable in terms of ironbound laws directing the
motion of matter, it only stood to reason that groups of those
same individuals--or societies--were likewise explicable in terms

of lawlike regularities.[10] Economic, political, familial, religious and sociological structures, no less than nonorganic ones, could be analyzed and hence refashioned (given, of course, sufficient amounts of data) with exact, mathematical precision. As Comte, following Saint-Simon's lead, later confidently asserted,

> We shall find that there is no chance of order and agreement but in subjecting social phenomena, like all others, to invariable natural laws, which shall, as a whole, prescribe for each period, with entire certainty, the limits and character of political action: in other words, introducing into the study of social phenomena the same positivistic spirit which has generated every other branch of human explanation.[11]

Human behavior, both individual and group, came to be regarded as ultimately rationalizable--i.e., manipulatible--in the moral arena as well. Early utilitarians such as Bentham and James Mill set the stage with their assumption that individual and group behavior, motivated by the pursuit of pleasure and the avoidance of pain, could be directed by controlling environmental conditions such as social sanctions. The Felicific Calculus was, after all, much more than a convenient sliderule for the ranking of pleasures. It was also an at least implicit device to use in encouraging or discouraging specific types of social behavior--and to do so, once again, with quantifiable, mathematical precision. Since degrees of pleasure or pain were ultimately dependent upon automatic responses to "social considerations," the key to moral behavior was the control, in a rational, lawlike way, of the social environment.[12]

The latter half of the nineteenth century saw the rise of a new "scientific" sociology which claimed to wed the Helmholtzian mechanistic worldview to the Darwinian concept of natural selection. This movement, which has come to be known as "Social

Darwinism," accepted the earlier Baconian assumption that the nature of social structures could be understood in the same mechanistic terms as physical phenomena. But it also claimed to provide theoretical justification for the nineteenth century's assurance that both individual members of the species and social groupings were steadily progressing--i.e., becoming more strong, rational, efficient, moral and intelligent. The assumption was that the mechanism of natural selection was inevitably operant in the development of societal structures just as much as in that of biological species. Natural selection, so the theory had it, weeded out nondesirable biological characteristics in a species' evolutionary struggle for survival and selected only those traits most conducive to the well-being of the species as a whole. Analogously, societies also underwent an evolutionary process in which unhealthy structural characteristics and segments of the population were eventually discarded, ultimately resulting in a society free from irrationalities and retrogressive anamolies. Herbert Spencer, by far the century's most influential spokesman for Social Darwinism, claimed that the starting point of his cosmic evolutionary schema was the law of the conservation of energy--or, as he styled it, "the persistence of force." Throughout all levels of reality, Spencer claimed, there exists the incessant redistribution of matter and motion, a redistribution that serves as the motor for the evolutionary process. Evolution is the progressive integration of matter and the concomitant dissipation of motion: it is the continuous flow from incoherent, chaotic homogeneity to a coherent, rational heterogeneity. Furthermore, this movement is necessary. Owing to the persistence of force, homogeneity is inherently unstable, since the various effects of persistent force upon it inevitably lead to differentiation in its once seamless character. Heterogeneity is the inevitable result of this process. Thus the key to Spencer's Social Darwinism, as Richard Hofstadter says, is the "progress from homogeneity to heterogeneity--in the formation of the earth from a nebular mass, in the evolution of higher, complex species from lower and simpler ones, in the embryological development of the individual from a uniform mass of cells, in the growth of the human mind, and in the progress of human societies..."[13]

For Spencer, then, all of reality is necessarily moving towards a state of ultimate rationalization--or "equilibrium." Adaptation of both individuals and society, in their progression towards more and more coherent states of heterogeneity, is as logically certain as a piece of deductive reasoning. As Spenser himself says in his Social Statics, "the ultimate development of the ideal man is logically certain--as certain as any conclusion in which we place the most implicit faith; for instance that all men will die... Progress, therefore, is not an accident, but a necessity. Instead of civilization being artificial, it is a part of nature; all of a piece with the development of the embryo or the unfolding of a flower."[14] It is no mere coincidence, given the prevalent metaphor of the nineteenth century, that Spencer's characterization of the perfectly sane society as a well-integrated, fully rational and completely efficient nexus of heterogeneous parts, could just as well fit the description of a sophisticated mechanical device whose "shining metal," as Stumpff said, "moves up and down," animating "all parts behind/A single goal."[15]

Helmholtz's argument for the uniformly mechanistic character of reality, with its consequent assumption that nature was exhaustively analyzable in quantitative terms and thereby ultimately manipulatible, provided one conceptual legitimation of the sane society ideal. So did Social Darwinism's putative theoretical justification for the claim that the evolution of

society was necessarily progressive. But the popular imagination
of the nineteenth century could not have been so captured by the
normative and theoretical implications of these models had it not
been for the common perception that concrete material conditions
provided evidence for their truth.   I have already indicated a
few of those conditions: a long period of peace, the harnessing
of new energy sources, the resulting technological explosion,
the dramatic conquest of nature, and the stunning advances which
medicine began to make against the scourge of various infectious
diseases.   In addition to these material indicators that the
"scientific" worldview of Helmholtz and Spencer (and Bacon before
them) was basically correct, there existed another cause for the
nineteenth century's exhuberant confidence that it was ushering
in a new age: an apparent enrichment of everyday social
existence.

     In the first place, statistics seemed to indicate that
individuals were living longer and healthier lives.   At the
beginning of the nineteenth century, for example, the number of
deaths in France was approximately 28 per 1,000 persons; only
thirty years later the ratio dropped to 25 per 1,000.   In the
British Isles, and especially in Ireland, the decline was even
greater.[16]   The drop in the death rate was also apparently
reflected in a complementary increase in population in the first
half of the nineteenth century. Again, the most dramatic change
occurred in England and Ireland: between 1800 and 1830, their
combined population rose from sixteen to twenty-five million.[17]
And although the decline in death rate and rise in population
differed from country to country and lacked a consistent growth
curve, the generation at the end of the century had more members
and enjoyed better health than had its great grandparents at the
beginning.

The change in vital statistics was undoubtedly due in part to the advances in the medical sciences which characterized the period. But it was also seen as the indirect consequence of an increased general affluence, of a change for the better in the average gross national incomes of both the United States and the major European powers (most notably Great Britain, France and Germany). The assumption was that the acceleration of a country's gross national income necessarily meant a general rise in the individual standard of living of each inhabitant of that country.

It can hardly be denied that the heavily industrialized nations of the West were acquiring quantities of wealth hitherto unimagined. This dramatic leap in national incomes is best illustrated if measured in terms of national growth rates in machine production and finance investment. In the nineteenth century, primarily because of the explosion of industrial capacity in the wake of steam and coal power, these two indices became the most significant gauges of a nation's economic power. Those countries which could produce and export machinery or machine parts were guaranteed a virtually unlimited world market. Likewise, those nations which could afford to invest monies in foreign projects could be assured not only of generally high premiums (owing to cheaper production costs), but also a strengthening of the range of their geo-political influence.

Using the production and exportation of machines or machine parts as an index, we see that by 1880 three nations produced four-fifths of the machinery sold on the world market: Great Britain, the United States and Germany. Furthermore, the monopoly which these three powers enjoyed continued right up to the Great War, although there occurred fluctuations in the order of rank. In 1880, for instance, the order of precedence for the

exportation of machinery was Great Britain, Germany and the
United States; by 1913, the order was Germany, the United States
and Great Britain--an ominous reversal of the European balance of
power, by the way, which Metternich had established at the
Congress of Vienna in 1815.[18] Germany's general economic growth
in the second half of the nineteenth century, in fact, proved to
be the most dramatic of all the major powers. Between 1851 and
1870, its overall productive rate doubled; after the
consolidation of the Reich in 1870, the rate doubled again in
the space of twenty years; and between 1890 and 1914, it again
enjoyed a skyrocket increase of just over 70%.[19]

One can also get a feel for the huge capital gains made by
the period's leading national powers by considering the
astronomically high production increases which arose as the
result of the bitter Anglo-German trade rivalry in the last two
decades of the century. The huge percentage jumps in productive
capacity that seesawed between competing nations throughout this
rivalry is dramatic enough. Just as significant, however, is the
indication that a handful of nations had become so affluent by
the end of the era as to control over half of the world trade.
Geoffrey Bruun stresses both these factors:

> In 1880-4 German steel mills produced only half as much
> steel as the British; by 1900 they were producing 20
> per cent. more. British exports of cotton manufactures
> dropped between 1880 and 1900, while German exports
> doubled. British pig-iron production and consumption
> remained almost stationary during these twenty years,
> but German output and consumption increased over 100
> per cent.
>
> ...The opening of the twentieth century found Britain
> still in the lead with 21 per cent. of international
> trade. Germany came second with 12 per cent., the
> United States third with 11 per cent., and France
> fourth with 8 per cent. In the next thirteen years
> world trade doubled and the percentage shifted... When

the First World War commenced the figures stood: Britain 17 per cent., the United States 15 per cent., Germany 12 per cent., and France 7 per cent.[20]

Foreign investment was also largely concentrated among the same powers, although the United States sadly lagged behind its European neighbors--particularly Great Britain, which easily retained its lead up to the beginning of the Great War. Between 1880 and 1913, British foreign investments multiplied threefold. A full quarter of its total national wealth was exported to various parts of the empire. French and German foreign investments, relative to British, were only one-half and one-third as much, respectively. But even those lower percentages represented immense investment sums which brought in proportionately huge rates of interest.

In addition to the assumption that increases in national income meant increases in per capita income, there was also the general impression that the nineteenth century's explosion of affluence resulted in other benefits for the population-at-large. An increase in literacy in Europe and the United States was seen as the direct result of national governments possessing the economic resources to finance free public schools at the primary level. There was an obvious proportionality between the decline in a country's illiteracy and the increase in its industrial power, a factor which further bolstered the belief in a trickle-down of benefits from gross national incomes. At the beginning of the century it is estimated that fully one-third of the men and one-half of the women in Britain, one half the adult population in France, and an even higher percentage of adults in Germany, were unable to read or write. By 1900, the estimated illiteracy rate had fallen to below 5% in each of these countries. Analogous figures also held for the United States: between 1880 and 1900, the illiteracy rate for those over ten

years of age fell from 17% to under 10%.[21] It is quite possible
that these figures were somewhat exaggerated by individual
nations eager to highlight the progressive consequences of their
meteoric rise to positions of world power, but it is doubtful
that a great deal of inflation occurred. One indication that the
percentages are more or less correct is the dramatic demand for
newspapers in Europe during the last two decades of the century.
Between 1880 and 1900, the number of European newspapers actually
doubled, suggesting the existence of a proportionately growing
market for written material.[22]

I have indicated several causes of the nineteenth century's
confidence that the average standard of living was inevitably
improving: an increase in life-expectancy and general health,
the assumption that national affluence entailed individual
affluence, and the dramatic decrease in illiteracy. I have also
suggested that these concrete phenomena were probably more
effective in convincing the popular imagination that the century
was one of progress than the theoretical constructs of a
Helmholtz or a Spencer, although it can't be denied that as
literacy levels rose, popularizations of the mechanistic
worldview also served to strengthen the era's overall feeling of
exhuberance and self-confidence. There is one more concrete
cause for the common man's faith in the progressiveness of his
century that must be mentioned, a factor that in the long run may
have been the most influential in consolidating the general
attitude of optimism. It is the assumption that the least
privileged of the industrial nations' population--the laboring
class or proletariat--was acquiring, in addition to a general
rise in real wages, a concomitant increase in political and
social privileges.

National social insurance, for example, appeared on the

scene towards the end of the century. Increasingly industrial Germany was the first country to inaugurate a systematic program of guaranteed benefits for laborers (largely due to Bismarck's desire to placate the powerful German socialist movement).[23] A Health Insurance law was approved by the Reichstag in 1883 which provided an annual maximum of thirteen weeks' medical care to injured workers, with labor unions covering two-thirds and management one-third of the total cost. A year later the Accident Insurance law replaced the earlier mandate, requiring employers to cover the full cost of disability insurance. Finally, in 1889, the Old Age and Invalidity law provided pensions for retired and fully disabled laborers, the cost to be shared by unions, management and the German government. In the last decade and a half of the century, over 50,000,000 claims were paid to retired, ill and injured workers.[24]

The other European economic powers soon followed Germany's example, although Great Britain, the last one to enact a national insurance law (the 1897 Workmen's Compensation Act) sought to limit the number of compensatory accidents by including the rather vague provision that only injuries not caused by the "gross carelessness of the worker" were actionable. Of all the major powers, only the United States lagged in introducing some type of state insurance for the working class. Institutionalized benefits on the American continent really never materialized until the inauguration of Franklin Roosevelt's "New Deal" program in the 1930s.

Another factor which the popular imagination took as an indicator of the improvement in living conditions for the working class was the relaxation of laws against union organizations in the last quarter of the century. By 1900 trade union membership exceeded two million in Great Britain and one million each in

Germany and the United States. The political clout which the unions claimed was further strengthened by the gradual extension of the vote to a larger electorate. In Germany and France universal male suffrage was granted in 1871; in Great Britain the Reform Acts of 1884-85 raised the enfranchised portion of the male population from 3,000,000 to 5,000,000. Confidence in the imminence of a golden era of equality reached a feverish pitch when even traditionally repressive states such as Spain (1890), Imperial Russia (1906) and Turkey (1908) granted partial political concessions to their restless populations.[25]

Finally, the emergence of industrial corporations in the nineteenth century encouraged the belief that the members of the European laboring class were acquiring an increasingly loud voice in the economic direction of their respective countries. So-called "Company Acts" passed by Britain in 1844, France in 1867 and Germany in 1870, legalized the formation of companies financed by and supposedly answerable to hundreds and sometimes thousands of small stockholders.[26] Although actual management of these corporations was usually highly centralized, their appearance and phenomenal growth in the last five decades of the century assured the era that the supply of available wealth was becoming less concentrated.

All in all, then, the nineteenth century's exhuberant confidence in itself seemed to be more than justified by the period's remarkable achievements in both theoretical and concrete arenas. The conceptual model of reality as a tightly organized and highly rational machine guaranteed that social irrationalities were ultimately eradicable, and this theoretical optimism was dramatically bolstered by the general increase in technological innovation and perceived levels of affluence that characterized the period. The century's assurance that it had

discovered the key to the final perfectability of society was
obviously the fundamental premise with which the era's more
ardent cheerleaders justified their optimism. But this faith in
inevitable progress was also shared by some who were less
sanguine about the era's claims of universal improvement in
political and social conditions. Nineteenth-century critics of
liberal economy such as Proudhon, the "idealistic" socialists
and, of course, Marx, seemed to have no doubt about the
ultimately mechanistic and hence controllable nature of reality.
They objected only to the ways in which the social machine was
being manipulated by what they perceived as classbound interests.
Indeed, the underlying assumption of their criticisms of the
existing order was that economic maldistribution and material
scarcity were no longer necessary, given man's new awareness of
the rationality of natural and sociological laws. The continuing
presence of these phenomena, so far as they were concerned, was
indicative of society's failure to fully rationalize itself, not
of a radical flaw in the theoretical model itself. True, there
was a very small group of nineteenth-century reformers who turned
their backs on the ideal of increasing technologization,
championing instead a retrogressive return to a life of
simplicity and bucolic "purity." But these latter-day
machine-breakers exerted no lasting influence upon the temper of
the times. The vast majority of the period's social critics
agreed that it was as impossible as it was undesirable to turn
the clock back. The sane society, for them, could only arise on
the basis of increased productive capacity and the
rationalization of distribution. Consequently, one of the most
common leitmotifs of nineteenth-century reformism was an analysis
of how the future perfect society would use its technological
expertise to insure distributive justice.

III

Characteristics of the Nineteenth-Century Sane Society Ideal

Along with its title of the "age of progress," the nineteenth century can also lay claim to the rubric of the "age of the utopias." Between 1800 and 1914, an astonishing number of utopian novels appeared in Europe and the United States--more, in fact, than were written in the four preceding centuries. In the fifteenth century, three utopias appeared; the sixteenth century gave rise to a total of sixty-six; the seventeenth and eighteenth centuries respectively contributed 131 and 175 utopian fantasies. In the nineteenth century, however, the number of self-proclaimed utopian novels skyrocketed to 515. Furthermore, the appearance of nineteenth-century utopias accelerated as the century progressed; fully half of them were written _after_ the publication of Bellamy's Looking Backward in 1888.[27]

It can hardly be denied that one of the reasons for the upsurge of utopian fantasies in the nineteenth century is that the novel as a literary form came into its own during this period, a phenomenon which, in turn, is doubtlessly linked to increasing levels of literacy in the West. But, as I have indicated in the previous section, the most significant impetus to blueprinting the ideal sane society was the exhuberant confidence with which the nineteenth century viewed its present achievements and anticipated its future ones. The widespread optimism which the period's apparent technological, economic and medical accomplishments stimulated, coupled with the reassurance on the part of natural and social scientists that reality was ultimately rational and hence controllable, created a mood of enthusiasm which was reflected in the growing number of utopian novels written for a popular audience. The very ubiquity of the demand for these imaginary images of a perfect society is indicative that confidence in the century's ability to usher in the new age was not the exclusive possession of a handful of technocrats and savants. Rather, it permeated the nineteenth-century imagination, cutting across all class strata.

In the next section of this chapter, I will defend my earlier suggestion that these sane society images are ideological in character (or, in Mannheimian terminology, that they are symptomatic of the total ideological structure that characterized the period). In the present section, however, I should like to discuss the general themes, values and assumptions of the nineteenth century's rash of "utopian" images. This overview will serve, I trust, as a helpful prolegomenon to the detailed analysis of specific utopian novels which appears in Chapter Four. Although the general characteristics discussed here are not predicable of <u>all</u> nineteenth-century utopias--the most obvious exceptions being what Lewis Mumford calls "pastoral utopias"[28]--they are shared by the era's <u>mainstream</u> sane society images, and consequently enjoyed the greatest popularity.

The Scientization of Society

The overriding characteristic of mainstream nineteenth-century utopian images was their vision of the "scientization" of society--the assumption that social groupings are susceptible to the same theoretical models, methodology and control which is appropriate to the understanding and manipulation of the physical order. As we saw in Chapter Two, Francis Bacon was the first influential thinker to provide a "scientific" legitimation to this assumption. He argued, recall, that human, social reality is conformable to the same laws or "Forms" as is physical reality and suggested in the <u>New Atlantis</u> that the nature of the properly ordered society is analogous to the strict supervision, dispassionate discipline and division of labor characteristic of a research institute. This proposition was given new impetus in the nineteenth century by, on the one hand, Helmholtz's suggestion that human nature and social groupings shared the mechanistic quality of the physical realm and, on the other, by Social Darwinism's thesis that the evolution of any given society could be predicted (and hence, to a certain extent, directed) with almost mathematical precision. The virtues of this scientization of society were apparent to both Bacon and the nineteenth-century utopian novelists. Social irrationalities such as commodity scarcity, distributive inequality, illiteracy, disruptive social dissent and individual or group passions that periodically overrode the dictates of reason, are the result of unscientific, haphazard social structures. As such, they are eliminable. All one had to do was to "rationalize" the economic, normative and psychological tendencies within the social fabric that encouraged these debilitating phenomena. That rationalizing process in turn depended upon an awareness of those natural laws (as, for instance, the Helmholtzian law of the transformation of energy) which were equally applicable to both physical and human reality. Once these laws had been isolated and defined, the causal connections pertaining between physical properties as well as social properties would be rendered transparent and hence manipulable.

This ideal of the complete scientization of society on the part of nineteenth-century utopias had embedded within it an implicit assumption about human reality--namely, that it is malleable, flexible and ultimately dependent upon the environment. The nineteenth-century imagination was particularly captured by Locke's metaphorical description of the human mind as a _tabula rasa_, a mere _potentia_ that, beginning at birth, was influenced and eventually fashioned by the experiences it acquired during its lifetime. Psychological associationists in the eighteenth century such as Hartley, and ethical behaviorists in the nineteenth such as Bentham and James Mill, only reinforced the assumption that the way in which humans form ideas and the particular manner in which humans behave in social and interpersonal settings are the direct result of their interaction with environmental stimuli. The implication of these epistemological and ethical "givens" seemed clear to the nineteenth-century prophets of the sane society. If individual behavior was directly shaped by the character of external conditions, the way in which to stimulate "correct" and discourage "incorrect" behavior was to refashion the social environment in such a way as to eliminate the material conditions which gave rise to psychological and normative irrationalities in the first place. Indeed, one of the fundamental premises of Social Darwinism, a movement whose influence upon the sane society architects was enormous, was the pervasive importance of adaptation to the environment on the part of both biological species and social institutions. One of the practical consequences drawn from this assumption was that the evolution of societies could be "helped along" by a careful manipulation of environmental factors.

The upshot of the sane society's emphasis upon the scientization of society, and its underlying assumption that human nature is ultimately plastic and hence dependent for its character upon environmental conditions was, in a curious way, the desubjectification of man. Human beings in nineteenth-century "utopian" novels display an almost automaton-like stiffness. They rarely if ever display emotions or act spontaneously or passionately, much less freely. They are well-controlled, orderly and pre-eminently rational robots.

Specific instances of this will be discussed in detail in the
next chapter. For now, one only need harken back to the passage
from Bacon's New Atlantis cited in Chapter Two, in which the
inhabitants of Bensalem "welcome" the Father of Salomon's House
with a rigid, military absence of normal enthusiasm, to get a
feel for the automaton nature of utopian man.

Disconcerting as this depiction of human reality may be, it
really should come as no surprise. Given the sane society's
ideal of societal scientization, in which human beings are
reduced to objects (even if sophisticated and cunningly-made
objects) which possess no fundamental distinctions from physical,
non-organic things, it only stands to reason that they should
drop the trappings of subjectivity. The point, in fact, can be
put even more strongly. From the perspective of
nineteenth-century utopias, it is not only logical that the
inhabitants of the sane society should be desubjectivized; it is
also desirable. Subjective foibles such as passion, emotional
reactions, individual idiosyncracies and spontaneity of action
all lead to the irrationalities, on both an individual and a
social level, which discourage the equilibrium so vital to the
instantiation of the ultimately sane society.

In short, the putative utopian images of the nineteenth
century eliminated subjectivity in order to guarantee social
order. In so doing, however, they tended to strip away the very
human qualities which one presumes the truly ideal society would
cultivate. The following passage from E.A. Burtt is an attempt
to capture the effects of Newton's mechanistic worldview upon
eighteenth-century man's self-image; but it could just as well
apply to the consequences of the nineteenth-century sane
society's attempt to scientize social groupings. Burtt argues
that the mechanization of human behavior

...was squarely behind the view of the cosmos which saw
in man a puny irrelevant spectator (so far as a being
whole imprisoned in a dark room can be called such) or
the vast mathematical system whose regular motions
according to mechanical principles constituted the
world of nature... The world that people had thought
themselves living in—a world rich with colour and
sound, redolent with fragrance, filled with gladness,
love and beauty, speaking everywhere of purposive
harmony and creative ideals—were crowded now into
minute corners of the brains of scattered organic
beings. The really important world outside was a world
hard, cold, colourless, silent and dead...[29]

The Apotheosis of Instrumental Reason

The sane society images of the nineteenth century, just
like Bacon's novum organum two hundred years earlier, had very
little patience with what they took to be "merely" speculative
thought, whether it was in the scientific, the psychological or
the ethical realm. Speculative thought was identified with
inutile thought, and inutility was considered to be a sufficient
condition for the disdainful rejection of any proposed model of
explanation. Instrumental reason—i.e., a methodology for
pragmatic, utility-laden problem-solving—and not the vain,
abstract meanderings of metaphysics, was the key to the ultimate
scientization of society.

This valuation of instrumental reason has, as we have seen,
a long tradition. Bacon's main criticisms of the earlier
Aristotelian and School logic centered around what he took to be
its intoxication with syllogistic validity rather than a
"correct" emphasis upon the invention of new "arts." The mind of
the nineteenth century was also captured by the ideal of
instrumental reason, with Helmholtz's mechanistic model of

reality serving as as impressive theoretical justification.

The emphasis upon instrumental reason in the "utopias" of the nineteenth century led to their painting the ideal sane society as one in which technology reigned supreme. The utopian society, for these visionaries, was rationalized only insofar as it was capable of resolving technical problems concerning production quotas, distribution, the harnessing of natural resources and the eradication of the causes of social discontent. Just as with Bacon's fragmentary New Atlantis, the working assumption of the nineteenth-century sane society was that more technology is better. The ultimate goal was the complete automization of the world.

An obvious consequence of this technological exemplar is the proliferation of mechanical gadgets in sane society models. Production has been streamlined, with different machines performing the division of labor necessary to create unlimited supplies of commodities. Mechanical means of transportation have reduced the hitherto risky and time-consuming business of world travel. Medicines and surgical techniques have all but eliminated disease and the infirmities of old age. And marvelously engineered skyscrapers with sanitary and commodious residential quarters have transformed the character of urban life.[30]

A less obvious but just as important consequence of the sane society's emphasis upon technology is its elimination of wild, untamed nature from the surface of the planet. Unharnessed nature represents, to the sane society imagination, an inutile waste of resources. Even more pertinently, it presents a threat to the overall plan of ultimate rationalization which defines the new order. Its very existence serves as an uncomfortable reminder that the "empire of man," as Bacon would have put it,

has not yet succeeded in consolidating its hegemony over the
natural world. Common motifs in the sane society "utopias,"
then, include the transformations of desert regions into garden
spots; the stringing of electric lights and railway tracks into
regions such as tropical forests; the colonization of the
planet's oceans, via the construction of underwater communities
and agricultural centers; and the artificial control of climatic
conditions. Moreover, rural existence is almost always
de-emphasized in these novels. Urban areas are extended in size
and connected by new, swift means of transportation that
transform the entire society into one huge megalopolis, while a
minimum of rural life is reluctantly retained as the necessary
means towards agricultural efficiency. The overall tenor of the
nineteenth-century sane society is remarkably cosmopolitan in
flavor.

There is another general characteristic of the nineteenth-
century "utopian" novel which arises from its emphasis upon
instrumental reason--one, moreover, which is closely connected
with the earlier discussed goal of scientizing all of society.
Instrumental reason, whether it is instantiated through
technology or through administration, seeks to produce systems
which are maximally utility-laden and hence best able to
alleviate the "irrationalities" which plague unplanned
communities. We have already seen how instrumental reason
promotes mechanical utility by its pervasive emphasis upon
technology. In the administrative arena, the dictates of
instrumental reason necessarily point to the need for strict
supervision, on the part of a technocratic elite, of the
economic, political and normative activities of the ideal
community. The members of the sane society who make up this
elite ruling class are usually industrialists, the possessors of
investment capital, and technicians, the inventors and operators

of the machines which guarantee the conquest of the natural world. Just as a mechanized factory must have foremen and engineers to guarantee the efficiency of the production process, so the machine-like society must have its supervisors to guard against debilitating social irrationalities that could upset the equilibrium of the delicately tuned works. It must not be supposed, however, that this ruling elite is a group of self-serving individuals whose exercise of power is devoted to an exclusive augmentation of their own interests. Rather, the industrial and technical supervisors of the sane society, like the Fathers of Salomon's House in New Atlantis, are devoted to the general welfare of the society in which they live. The assumption is that the members of the ruling elite are by definition wise, dispassionate and objective enough to subordinate their individual ambitions to their supervisory responsibilities. As such, they often appear as an ascetic group of individuals who willingly forego personal advancement for the sake of the sane society's interests. In point of fact, however, their sacrifice is not as great as it might at first appear to be. In the sane society, individual and social interests converge. In laboring for the good of the community, the individual maximizes his own happiness.[31]

The Identity of Individual and Social Interests

Nineteenth century "utopias" see no conflict between the interests of the ideal society and the interests of individuals within that society. The working assumption is that what is conducive to the well-being of the society at large must likewise be conducive to the well-being of individuals. Individuals, after all, are merely parts of the social machine, and to overhaul a machine is to improve both the quality of its overall function and the health of its components.

An identity between social and individual interests in the
sane society is posited because of the assurance that the
character of the new order has become completely rationalized.
Personal ambition, greed, selfishness and similar
counter-productive traits have been expunged from the psyches of
the inhabitants of the sane society. They have been so
desubjectivized that their values and interests necessarily
mirror those of their societal environment. Just as the ideal
social structure is one in which administrative irrationality and
technological inefficiency have been eliminated, so the ideal
inhabitant is one who has rid himself of the chaotic traits of
passion, emotion and individuality. Because of the convergence
of group and individual identities, the person who labors for the
good of his society simultaneously increases his own chances for
happiness. As we saw in the preceding section, this assumption
of isomorphism between the societal good and individual
well-being was readily accepted by the enthusiastic nineteenth
century, which interpreted general rises in national revenues as
indicators that per capita incomes for all individuals within
society were also on the upswing.

One of the obvious implications of this assumed identity of
social and personal interests in the sane society is that
behavior which doesn't enhance the clockwork efficiency of the
social structure is, in the long run, self-destructive.
Individualism, which the utopian novelists seem to define as an
attitude in which the subject misguidedly places his presumed
interests before those of society, is strongly condemned. It is
seen as an illness, as an atavistic remnant of pre-utopian
egoism, which deludes and harms both society and its members. A
high premium is placed upon conformity to the "scientific"
standards of the social structure, since it is only in obedience

to those putatively rational standards that instrumentality can
be maximized. The failure to act in accordance with
conventional norms is not looked upon as merely idiosyncratic but
harmless behavior. Instead, it is seen as an irrational refusal
to maximize both individual and social well-being, and is
consequently discouraged in the same way as other kinds of
self-destructive activity would be.

This emphasis upon "objective" reason as the necessary
condition for the good individual life as well as for the orderly
functioning of society as a whole underscores the sane society's
insistence that an elite class of social supervisors is an
essential safeguard for maintaining the health and equilibrium of
the new order. The supervisors, be they industrialists,
technicians, or a combination of both, represent the epitome of
instrumental rationality. They are those individuals best
qualified to objectively determine the steps which ensure the
maximum efficiency and overall well-being of the entire
community. Their actions are self-interested only to the extent
that they realize that what is good for the society as a whole
will also be good for themselves and other citizens. As such, no
right thinking individual within the sane society could possibly
disagree with either the necessity for their authority or the
virtue of their decisions. Given the assumptions that
instrumental reason is the basis for the well-run society, that
the elite supervisory class is the group of individuals most
qualified to instantiate instrumentality, and that the well-being
of the individual is directly proportionate to the well-being of
the social structure, it follows that a disregard for the
standards established by technocratic authority is both perverse
and dangerous.

"Revolutionary" Social Agendas

One of the most striking themes in all the mainstream sane society "utopias" of the nineteenth century is their claim to have radically broken with the traditional irrationalities which have hindered human progress. Each of the novels insists that its theoretical worldview and consequent social agenda are revolutionary in character--i.e., that they are programmes for the absolute transformation of both social and individual reality.

It is true that nineteenth-century "utopias" by and large accept the mechanistic worldview characteristic of the modern era. But they claim to "revolutionize" the model by applying it to <u>all</u> aspects of existence. The social structure, according to the sane society, will never realize maximum efficiency or overall well-being until it is transformed into an elaborate and sophisticated machine, in which each element is in co-ordinated synchronicity with all others. Likewise, individual humans must be trained in such a way as to eliminate eratic, subjective tendencies in their behavior. The achievement of these two goals will lay the necessary conditions for the complete scientization of society, which is the ultimate goal of the new order. Technological advances in the nineteenth century had rationalized the production process. The mathematical precision of the engineer's blueprint, when applied to social relationships in the future sane society, would at last allow this technology to come into its own by eliminating the possibility of irrational human administration.

There is another reason why nineteenth-century sane societies consider their social agendas to be revolutionary. They all argue that the new order is one which directs the evolution of the species, both biologically and socially.

Earlier generations, the assumption runs, had been at the mercy of natural evolutionary processes, primarily because of their inability to understand and control the laws of nature. Consequently, true progress in the ultimate rationalization of society--i.e., the construction of social relations in conformity to natural, mechanistic laws--was, at best, an uneven affair, a hit-and-miss strategy which unfortunately hindered development more often than not. But scientific expertise provided by the judicious application of instrumental reason in the new order allows for the possibility of consciously improving upon nature's evolutionary schema. In the biological realm, the evolutionary process can be accelerated by advances in medicine, hygiene and eugenics--a science, by the way, which all of the nineteenth-century sane societies ardently defended. Weaknesses in the species can be eliminated through selective breeding or, as a final resort, the sterilization of evolutionarily unsuitable individuals. Likewise, biological strengths can be maximized by a rational program of what we would today call "genetic engineering." Nor is the social arena outside of the purview of evolutionary prodding. "Antisocial" tendencies can gradually be eliminated by discouraging (or, in extreme cases, preventing) reproduction by persons who perversely cling to individualism. Similar social irrationalities, which it might take natural selection eons to weed out of the population, likewise can be artificially eradicated in the space of a few generations. The revolutionary claims of nineteenth-century "utopias," then, are continuations of Bacon's. In the new order, the entire spectrum of nature is finally subordinated to the dictates of instrumental reason. This change, for the sane society, represents a radical and irreversible break with the past.

The Perfectability of Man and the Universality of Values

The notion of controlled evolution, which was defended by nineteenth-century Social Darwinists such as Herbert Spencer, only served to solidify the assumption on the part of the advocates of the sane society exemplar that humankind was on the road to inevitable perfection. The ultimate elimination of irrationalities in the realms of science, social relations, ethics and economics was vouchsafed by the increasing grasp and consequent manipulation of natural laws guaranteed by the growing purview of instrumental reason. The final goal of the sane society--the complete scientization of the social machine--would produce a race of humans strong in body and spirit, unhindered by passions, jealousies, physical illnesses or ignorance.   It would also insure the existence of a social structure free of economic scarcity, crime and dissent, a social milieu which for the first time in the history of the species could provide the necessary conditions for the well-being of all men.

The ultimate perfectability of man, according to nineteenth-century sane society visions, was ultimately based upon two presumptions. In the first place, human and social reality was inevitably headed towards perfection through the gradual rationalization of social relations and the concomitant eradication of structural weaknesses.   Instrumental reason, applied to both technological and administrative problems, was more than able to engineer a maximally efficient, utility-laden social edifice. This rationalization entailed, furthermore, that individual and social happiness was capable of perfect, ultimate fulfillment. The most immediate reason for this utopian faith in the maximization of felicity is the sane society's assumption that what is good for the society as a whole is equally good for the individuals who dwell within that society.   The instrumental overhauling of the social structure, then, so far as nineteenth-century "utopias" were concerned, could only result in a proportionate increase in happiness for its inhabitants since, in point of fact, their "subjective" states would be reflective of the character of their environment.

But there is another reason why sane society visionaries presumed that the instantiation of their social agendas would guarantee a perfect felicity. It is their ascription of universal applicability to the values and social norms they defended. Bacon had argued in the seventeenth century that the continual technologization of society was to the advantage of all segments of citizenry. Similarly, the nineteenth-century sane societies reasoned that the scientization of society, the strict supervision of production and distribution, and the accelerated mechanization of everyday life were conducive to the ultimate well-being and happiness of all social classes. There was never any suspicion on the part of the sane society visionaries that the values they predicated of the new order were classbound. After all, they appeared to be based directly upon the objective, interest-blind nature of physical laws. Even as the laws of gravity held for all bodies in motion, so also were the "scientific" strategies for rationalizing society applicable to all collections of people.

IV

The Darker Side of the "Century of Progress"

I have attempted to show that the general characteristics of nineteenth-century "utopias" were immediately based upon the optimism that arose from the period's mechanistic worldview, technological expertise and socio-economic structure--in short, that the ideals of the sane society intimately reflected the material conditions that the era perceived as being genuinely "progressive" and inevitably conducive to the well-being of all individuals in all classes. In what follows, I shall provide evidence for my earlier assertion that the worldview of the nineteenth century was ideological. I shall argue that its ideals were illusory because they failed to recognize their classbound, contextual nature, claiming instead a universal validity. Instead of promoting the well-being of all members of society, these ideals were in fact directly reflective and supportive of the interests of the ascendent, bourgeois class. Consequently, the putatively revolutionary social agendas which they defended, far from encouraging significant social innovation, in reality served to solidify the century's economic and social status quo. Because the sane society images of the nineteenth century were so reliant upon the total worldview of their period, they too were ideological, rather than genuinely utopian, in character. Chapter Four is devoted to an elucidation of the specifics of these sane society visions. In what follows, my purpose is to indicate the illusory nature of the nineteenth-century exhuberance which they reflected by showing that there was a dark side to the socio-technological revolution of which the period was so proud.

The nineteenth century's ascription of a mechanistic nature to reality served as the basic foundation for its confidence that both physical nature and social groupings were ultimately susceptible to "rational" manipulation and control. The perfect society was seen as one whose technological conquest of nature gave birth to unlimited material rewards as well as the final extirpation of social irrationalities that might impede the steady administration of production and distribution. This "scientific" ascription of a machine-like nature to society--as defended, recall, by thinkers such as Helmholtz and Spencer--provided an intellectual legitimation for economic, normative and social measures which were deemed necessary for the ultimate instantiation of the "good" society. Furthermore, it was assumed that this scientization was in the interests of all individuals. In point of fact, however, the ideals and social agendas which it encouraged, far from proving conducive to the felicity of all classes, actually served to consolidate the hegemony of the bourgeoisie at the expense of other social segments. It supplied a theoretical justification for unbridled capitalist expansion. It is no accident that most of the "utopian" novels of the nineteenth century came from Britain, Germany and the United States--the three superpowers which most profited from the period's technological explosion and capitalist centralization.

One of the common assumptions of the nineteenth century, as indicated earlier, was that an increase in a country's industrial capacity led to a rise in overall national revenue, which in turn trickled down to improve the per capita standard of living. It is quite true that the nineteenth century's technological expertise generated a general improvement in living conditions. But it is also obvious that the material benefits of such industrialism accrued primarily to that class which owned and controlled the means of production--which, in the nineteenth century, happened to be the industrial bourgeoisie. The lot of the laboring class was improved only relatively, while the capitalist class enjoyed an absolute improvement in its material affluence and political power. As W.J. Reader points out, in speaking of the material conditions of nineteenth-century Britain,

> By the middle of Queen Victoria's reign there seemed to be fairly good grounds for believing that the economic system would in the long run get rid of poverty automatically, without very much more than a shove here and a prod there from a Parliament elected on a

democratic franchise. For anyone could see, and if he
could not see there were plenty of statistics to tell
him, that more working class people than ever before
were able to live in something like comfort, and that
their number was increasing. This was true... At the
same time it was also true that the comfortable working
class had only recently emerged in any considerable
numbers, that only a thin line divided them from
poverty, and that old age, sickness, trade depression
or some other quirk of fortune might at any time push
the individual and his family back into it again.
Poverty lay at the root of working class life and had a
powerful influence on the ways of life and habits of
thought of the whole new race of town-bred working men.
Even when they found themselves more or less securely
above the line of want, they did not easily shake off a
dread of falling back into the slough they had climbed
out of.[32]

In short, real wages for laborers _did_ rise in the nineteenth
century. But this increase was far from proportionate to the
increasing levels of wealth generated as a result of their
manipulation of the machinery of production. According to
Geoffrey Bruun,

The rise in real wages between 1800 and 1900 was only
20 to 25 per cent, in Great Britain, Germany, and
France, whereas the average worker's productive
capacity, thanks to the machines, increased more
rapidly, and the proportionate wealth of the capitalist
employer rose more rapidly still.[33]

These figures, striking as they are, do not really provide
an adequate idea of the disproportionality of the rewards
created by an economic system whose ideals claimed to be in the
absolute interest of all classes. A bare statement of the
distance between the rise of real wages for labor and the
increase in profits for the middle class fails to capture the
generally squalid material conditions created for the nineteenth
century's working class as a result of the era's concentration of
capital, industry, population and power.

The core around which the nineteenth century's centralization of economic power revolved was the factory, with its streamlined and closely supervised production of huge quantities of commodities. The explosion of the factory system in the nineteenth century was perhaps the most important factor in the phenomenal growth rate of urban areas (not to mention the concomitant dismissal of rural life by such thinkers as Marx as one of "idiocy"--i.e., low productive capacity). The upsurge of the factory system dispossessed thousands of craftsmen and small manufacturers, thereby encouraging an enormous influx of job-seeking immigrants from country to town which assured the industrialists of the period with a seemingly limitless supply of cheap labor. This huge migration of labor into urban industrial centers had two consequences. It kept factory wages low and working conditions harsh, in addition to so overcrowding already saturated urban areas as to generally give rise to living conditions much worse than those from which the rural dispossessed had fled.

To begin with, unemployment within the urban factory centers was chronic. It has been estimated that the percentage of unemployed laborers in nineteenth-century industrial Britain ranged from 4% in a "good" year like 1850 to 9.5% in a "bad" year like 1886. Furthermore, unemployment levels for certain skilled and semi-skilled professions often ran much higher than the overall unemployment statistics. In the "bad" year of 1886, for example, 13.9% to 22.2% of ironfounders, blacksmiths, boilermakers and iron shipbuilders were out of work--in addition to what was probably a much higher percentage of unskilled workers.[34] These fluctuating but generally high levels of chronic unemployment would continue right up to the advent of the Great War.

In addition to the chronically unemployed segment of nineteenth-century Britain's working class, there also existed a high level of underemployment. For factory workers, underemployment usually took the form of short-time labor, "so that what was just about a living wage on full time would fall short."[35] A great deal of work available to the class of unskilled laborers was seasonal, and irregular even then. The often deliberate (because wage-saving) managerial policy of underemployment in this period was so widespread that one commentator surmises that "many men...can never have known what steady employment was."[36]

Despite the problems of chronic un- and under-employment, however, there were plenty of laborers in the industrial centers who did procure more or less steady work. But both the real wages and the working conditions afforded by this employment were atrocious--so much so, in fact, that W.J. Reader argues that there were more people in poverty in Britain at the end of the nineteenth century than at its beginning:

> Charles Booth, in the nineties, thought that about one-third of the population might then have been in poverty, with an income of 21s. or 22s. a week for a small family or 25s. or 26s. for a large one. People at this level, as he put it, might not be in actual want, but "would be better for more of everything." Not far below this level "actual want" would presumably set in, and it has to be borne in mind that in the nineties the population of England and Wales was some thirty million people, so that we are dealing with figures of the order of ten millions or so. Sir William Giffen, who was not a pessimist in these matters, calculated that on the basis of figures for 1885 some fifty-nine per cent of grown men earned 25s. or less a week, and he thought the average earnings of all grown men might run to about £60 a year, which would imply a great many getting a good deal less.[37]

The factory work environment was generally as dismal as the

average wage paid to laborers.   Lack of ventilation and proper lighting, huge levels of noise and temperature from steam-driven machines, the almost total absence of safety features on the machinery production, long shifts--not uncommonly involving a full twelve hours--and relentless supervision and discipline: these were regular features of the nineteenth century's factory system. Generally squalid and unhealthy working conditions were the norm in most urban industrial centers. Many factory owners possessed capital only for the immediate necessities of production, with little or none to spare for the improvement of the factory environment itself. Moreover, most factory owners felt no need, either economic or ethical, to provide safer and less dehumanizing working conditions for their employees. The contract between laborer and employer was considered to be one which revolved exclusively around wages and output.   The quality of life on the production point, not to mention the happiness and fulfillment which the laborer might or might not derive from his work, were entirely beside the point.[38]

The low wages paid to the huge army of urban industrial workers, in addition to the generally abysmal living conditions created by the crowding together of families into ghetto-like areas, resulted in unsanitary, malnourished and disease-ridden existences for approximately one-third of the citizens of nineteenth-century Britain. Notwithstanding the fact that mortality statistics and the frequency of infectious diseases improved for the middle and upper classes of the period, the working class continued to live short and unhealthy lives right through the end of the century.

Environmental conditions in working class neighborhoods were almost completely lacking in sanitation. Entire families were often crowded into single rooms in large tenement buildings.

Sometimes the occupants of these rooms included swine or goats which dispossessed rural workers had brought with them in their exodus from the countryside. Privies were usually insufficient, shared by several households, and plagued by inadequate drainage. In a report on one London parish published by the Royal Commission on Housing in the 1880s, the conclusion was that "it seems to be no uncommon thing for the [water] closets to be stopped and overflowing for months." Furthermore, it was discovered that "in some parts of London they are used as sleeping places by the houseless poor."[39] Sanitary conditions in other industrialized urban centers were no better. "In Bristol privies actually exist in living rooms: and elsewhere in the provinces there are instances where no closet accommodation at all is attached to the dwellings of the labouring classes."[40]

Adequate water supply was also hard to come by in working class tenement areas. In London, for example, the water mains ran only under the city's principle streets, and inhabitants of the poorer districts were forced to fetch their water from standing pipes located long distances from where they lived. Failing this, they could collect rain, sleet or snow, depending upon the season, or rely upon the horribly polluted Thames for their drinking and cooking water. The absence of readily available and clean water resulted, predictably enough, in an exacerbation of already unhygienic conditions. Given the physical difficulties involved in fetching water from distant pumps, few laborers were willing to waste the precious commodity by using it for bathing. "A Lancashire collier [in 1842] said he never washed his body; he let his shirt rub the dirt off, though he added, 'I wash my neck and ears and face, of course'. The sense of smell was stunned, and observers remarked how little the working class seemed to be discommoded by the mixture of stenches in which they had to live."[41]

Needless to say, the unsanitary living conditions created by inadequate sewage disposal and the lack of pure drinking water, in addition to the general level of malnutrition encouraged by low wages, led to chronic disease and periodic outbreaks of infectious epidemics in the working districts. Cholera was finally brought under control in Britain'a urban areas in the late 1880s, but other infectious diseases such as typhoid, typhus, tuberculosis and diphtheria continued virtually unabated. Rickets and other maladies brought about by chronic malnutrition were also at epidemic proportions--not surprisingly, given the average diet of weak tea, oatmeal and potatoes (with bacon once or twice a week)[42] upon which most laborers and their families lived. Although diet, sanitary conditions and the overall health of the propertied classes continued to improve throughout the century, the material conditions of the British working class remained virtually unchanged from when one Southwood Smith described it in 1844 in these words:

> The poorer classes. . .are exposed to causes of disease and death which are peculiar to them; the operation of these peculiar causes is steady, unceasing, sure; and the result is the same as if twenty or thirty people were annually taken out of their wretched dwellings and put to death, the actual fact being that they are allowed to remain in them and die.[43,44]

The children of working class parents were generally ground in the same mill as their parents, thus reproducing in subsequent generations the low level of health characteristic of the class as a whole. Children from the poorer districts rarely attended school. Instead, economic necessity compelled them to enter the work force at the earliest possible age. As late as 1880, according to the Royal Census of 1881, over 20% of the British population was illiterate (although, granted, the illiteracy level had been 40% thirty years earlier). Children

too young to hire themselves out--mainly infants, since it was
not uncommon for four and five year olds to be employed--were
habitually drugged during the daytime with opiate derivatives to
save their parents the expense of sitters. The favorite of these
concoctions was one "Godfrey's Cordial," whose indiscriminate
use, as stated by an 1844 commission report, caused "great
numbers of infants [to] perish, either suddenly, from an
overdose, or, as more commonly happens, slowly, painfully, and
insidiously."[45] Children who managed to withstand the effects of
Godfrey's Cordial long enough to enter the workforce were little
better (if any) off. A British Children's Employment Commission
of the 1860s concluded, among other things, that over 11,000
children in the ceramic industry worked "under conditions which
undermine their health and constitution." What that meant,
according to W.J. Reader, was that "small boys between six and
ten years old were carrying moulds from the potters to the
'stoves' (small rooms at a temperature of 120 degrees or so) for
about 11 1/2 hours a day nominally, but in fact for as much as
14, 15 or 16 hours, and they were getting perhaps as much as
half a crown a week for doing it."[46] Nor was standard factory
work the only brutalizing task which children regularly
performed. From the 1830s through the 1860s, one of the more
common jobs for young, underfed (and hence small) boys was
chimney-sweeping. The work involved climbing up soot-covered
flues, balancing oneself all the while with knees and elbows, and
chipping away at the encrusted residue with chisels and stiff
brushes. The brutality of the job can be measured by the
following account of the "training" programme for perspective
chimney sweeps, as described by a Nottingham master sweep named
Ruff:

> No one knows the cruelty which a boy has to undergo in
> learning. The flesh must be hardened. This is done by
> rubbing it, chiefly on the elbows and knees, with the

strongest brine, close by a hot fire. You must stand
over them with a cane, and coax them with the promise
of a halfpenny, etc., if they will stand a few more
rubs. At first they will come back from their work
with their arms and knees streaming with blood, and the
knees looking as if the caps had been pulled off; then
they must be rubbed with brine again.[47]

Just as telling as the above testimony is Charles Dickens'
description of the lot of chimney sweeps in his time. In <u>Oliver
Twist</u> Dickens describes how the orphan boy Oliver is almost
apprenticed from the public workhouse to a professional chimney
sweep by the name of Mr. Gamfield. Gamfield, in defending his
line of work before the workhouse board of trustees, is asked by
one of the presiding officers if it isn't the case that young
boys are often smothered in chimneys while cleaning them. The
unsavory Gamfield responds

'That's acause they damped the straw afore they lit it
in the chimbley to make 'em come down agin'... that's
all smoke, and no blaze; vereas smoke ain't o' no use
at all in makin' a boy come down, for it only sinds him
to sleep, and that's wot he likes. Boys is wery
obstinit, and wery lazy, gen'lmen, and there's nothink
like a good hot blaze to make 'em come down with a
run. It's humane, too, gen'lmen, acause, even if
they've stuck in the chimbley, roasting their feet
makes 'em struggle to hextricate theirselves.'[48]

Finally, it was not uncommon for children to be abusively
overworked by their own parents, who often relied upon piecework
done at home as a necessary supplement to family incomes. One
young woman, after describing how her younger sister was
inaugurated into the mysteries of piecework stitching at the age
of 5 1/2, went on to describe this sort of labor in more general
terms:

Little children are kept up shamefully late, if there
is work, especially on Thursday and Friday nights, when
it is often till 11 or 12. They have to make two days
out of Friday. Mothers will pin them to their knee to

keep them to their work, and, if they are sleepy, give
them a slap on the head to keep them awake. If the
children are pinned up so, they cannot fall when they
are slapped or when they go to sleep. ...The child has
so many fingers set for it to stitch before it goes to
bed, and must do them. [49]

It should be clear by now that the exhuberant confidence
which the nineteenth century felt in its ability to totally
rationalize society, thereby alleviating economic scarcity and
political injustice, was dubious. Although the harsh conditions
which I have described here are taken from the pages of British
history, parallel abuses could easily be cited from German,
French or American accounts of the nineteenth century. True, the
industrial revolution in   power sources, the increase of
commodity production, the rapid rise of national revenues, the
startling advances in the medical sciences and the decline in
illiteracy which the century prided itself upon, did occur. Of
that there can be no doubt. What is also clear, however, is that
the benefits derived from these accomplishments were enjoyed by a
discrete segment of the population--the owners of the means of
production--and not by all classes of individuals. In fact, the
case can be put even stronger. Not only did the material changes
which the nineteenth century inaugurated fail to usher in
universal betterment, since a significant portion of the
population failed to benefit by them; they in fact actually
improved the lot of the empowered industrial middle class at the
expense of the working class. There is little doubt that the
lifestyle of the laboring class in the nineteenth century,
abysmal as it had been in earlier generations, actually declined
during this period of capitalist expansion and concentration. As
such, the upswing in affluence pointed to by the period's
champions was not representative of the actual condition of all
classes in the "Century of Progress," but only that of the
industrial and mercantile middle class.

I argued earlier that the mechanistic worldview of the nineteenth century served as an intellectual justification for the period's centralization of economic and political power. The instrumentalist assumption that humankind is best benefited by increasingly sophisticated industrial technology is the practical consequence of supposing physical reality to be an utterly rational machine capable of manipulation and limitless profit. As such, this nineteenth-century revitalization of the Baconian vision of industrial technique as the key to the instantiation of a new, perfect order was particularly appealing to the capitalist imagination. But there is another reason why the nineteenth century hegemony so enthusiastically accepted the mechanistic worldview. In addition to legitimizing the exploitation of natural resources for profit, it also provided a "scientific" justification for maintaining the exploitative nature of the capitalist social system.

Keep in mind that luminaries of the century such as Helmholtz and Spencer believed there was no fundamental distinction between human reality and physical reality. Since both conformed to identical mechanistic laws, both were capable of ultimate rationalization. The rationalization of physical reality, according to this view, necessarily led to the conquest of nature and the eradication of scarcity through an increase in technological sophistication (or what Bacon referred to, in the seventeenth century, as the invention of new "arts"). But technological expertise alone was incapable of ushering in the perfect new order. Unless social relations themselves were coaxed into conformity with objective, mechanistic laws of nature, the administration of the new technology would be at the mercy of the structural irrationalities that had plagued earlier social groupings. The social agenda of the mechanistic worldview, then, took as its primary desideratum the inauguration of a social setting which was free of subjective passions, individualism, and unpredictable--hence irrational--behavior. Those values and theoretical models which encouraged individual conformity to the status quo and, in the long run, absolute social equilibrium, were consequently defended by the epigones of the period as standards which best promoted individual and societal felicity. The ultimate goal of these models, and of the social agendas based upon them, was the total objectification of man. This in turn depended upon the elimination of any and all behavioral tendencies which were nonconducive to the clockwork efficiency of the social machine.

Helmholtz at mid-century had done much to popularize the notion that the human individual was nothing more than an energy-conversion machine--and, furthermore, one that was capable of accelerated levels of conversion under proper direction and supervision. The basis of the period's factory system seemed to agree. As W.J. Reader points out, the middle and upper classes habitually praised the factory system not simply because it generated huge quantities of profit, but also because it exercised a salutory "steadying" effect upon the undisciplined and emotional masses.[50] The rigors of factory work demanded conformity to strict schedules and unbending regulation. They forcibly instilled standards of orderliness and efficiency within a social class that was perceived as being habitually unruly and hence threatening to the health of the body politic. Factory discipline maximized the class's hitherto untapped instrumental potential. It also served to stamp out those subjective irrationalities which stood in the way of the working class's genuine happiness. The discipline of factory life consequently came to be seen as a concrete catalyst to the mechanistic goal of ultimately bringing social existence into conformity with natural law--a conformity which, once again, was seen as both "scientifically" correct and morally justifiable because of its maximization of social instrumentality as well as individual happiness.

The "steadying" effect of strictly supervised factory work was raised to new heights towards the end of the century with the advent of the "science" of scientific management known as "Taylorism," named after its founder, Frederick W. Taylor. The goal of Taylorism was to create conditions at the production point which would maximize commodity production, or instrumentality. The key to this maximization was the total objectification of workers by training them to perform as automatic, machine-like cogs in the vast industrial apparatus. Harry Braverman describes the "revolutionary" character of Taylorism in the following way:

> Control has been the essential feature of management throughout its history... But Taylor raised the concept of control to an entirely new plane when he asserted as an <u>absolute necessity for adequate</u> management the dictation to the worker of the precise <u>manner in which work is to be performed</u>. [Braverman's emphasis] That management had had the right to "control" labor was generally assumed before Taylor, but in practice this right usually meant only the general setting of tasks, with little direct interference in the worker's mode of performing them. Taylor's contribution was to overturn this practice and replace it by its opposite. Management, he insisted, could only be a limited and frustrated undertaking so long as it left to the worker any decision about the work. His "system" was simply a means for management to achieve control of the actual mode of performance of every labor activity, from the simplest to the most complicated.[51]

The fidelity which this new management strategy showed to the mechanistic goal of desubjectification is highlighted by three cardinal principles which Taylor held to be central to his system. First, Taylor argued that industrial efficiency is maximized by completely eliminating the dependence of the actual production process upon the individual skills of production point workers. As he said, "The managers assume...the burden of gathering together all of the traditional knowledge which in the past has been possessed by the workmen and then of classifying, tabulating, and reducing this knowledge to rules, laws, and formulae."[52] The actual mechanics of work, regardless of the situation, should be so streamlined and completely engineered that any worker able to follow instructions can perform them. This rationalization of the labor process has the double advantage of not only maximizing production quotas by eliminating subjective input, but also of rendering any single worker expendable by insuring that his specific task is performable by anyone else. The ideal human industrial machine, just like the ideal mechanical one, has easily replacable parts.

Second, Taylor insisted that maximum efficiency in the factory necessarily depended upon the complete separation of conception from execution. Ideally, the laborer should have no input into the theoretical aspects of his activity. "All possible brain work," as Taylor says, "should be removed from the shop and centered in the planning or laying-out department."[53] The job of the worker is not to think about what he is doing; reflection merely slows down his productive capacity. His duty is to perform the specific task assigned to him, preferably in as mindless and automatic a way as possible. The Helmholtzian goal of transforming the inefficient organic machine into one which is as totally objective and "bug-free" as a mechanical one is translated here into a law of mangement.

Finally, Taylor argued that the control necessary for the maximization of the production process could be acquired only if the workers were absolutely prohibited from understanding the techniques and long term planning that served as the formal conditions for commodity production. There is a total separation of mental from manual labor in the ideal factory system. Cogs in the machine have no need to understand what it is they're doing. Their only function is to perform the tasks assigned to them by the master blueprint. This third principle, like the preceding two, aims at objectifying human labor to such an extent that the individual worker has no opportunity either to use his own initiative or any way deviate from established procedure. His only role--and his sole possibility for utility-laden behavior--is to mechanically follow to the letter the instructions given him. As Taylor says,

> Perhaps the most prominent single element in modern scientific management is the task idea. The work of every workman is fully planned out by the management at least one day in advance, and each man receives in most cases complete written instructions, describing in detail the task which he is to accomplish, as well as the means to be used in doing the work.[54]

Taylor's campaign to scientize the workplace through the desubjectivization of production point workers captured the imagination of the late nineteenth and early twentieth century to a greater extent than any other proposed theory of management. Especially appealing was Taylorism's claim to mathematize, with absolute precision, the quantities of human energy involved in the labor process. Advocates of the system argued that such qualifications would result in a total utilization of individual energy. By consigning a specific arithmetical value to every production point action, "wasted" time and effort in the workplace could be ultimately eliminated. This ideal of scientizing the workplace, based as it was upon the "essential effort to strip the workers of craft knowledge and autonomous control and confront them with a fully thought-out labor process

in which they function as cogs and levers,"[55] may well have
increased profit for the industrialist. But it did so by
reducing workers to the status of mindless machine parts.

Both Taylorism and earlier less "efficient" strategies of
workplace management were intended to do much more than simply
maximize conformity on the factory line. Just as importantly,
the hope was that the "steadying" influence of industrial
discipline would trickle down to the social and private lives of
members of the unruly working class. The ideal was to Taylorize
all aspects of existence among the lower classes, to insure--for
both their own and society's good--that they became as
predictably clocklike in the social arena as they were in the
factory. Only then, so the social scientists of the nineteenth
century presumed, would society reach the end towards which it
was necessarily moving.

This desire to scientize the personal lives of the lower
classes is strongly reflected in the constant efforts on the part
of the period's middle class to "clean up" the lifestyles and
personal morals of the working class--or, in a word, to bring it
into conformity with the bourgeois ideal of "steadiness." The
tendency on the part of the worker to resort to drink in his
spare moments was seen as a manifestation of his essentially
irresponsible nature. Most teetotalling reformers of the day
assumed that the abysmal living conditions of the average factory
worker was a direct result of his intemperance. The harsh
economic system in which he found himself was rarely seen as a
contributing factor to either the workman's habitual patronage of
bars and gin houses or his squalid lifestyle. The period's
middle class moralistic mentality, which valued thrift and
steadiness above all other virtues, was continually shocked over
what it perceived as the working man's addiction to unsavory

pleasures which squandered wages and energies, and encouraged anti-social behavior.

Similarly, the loose sexual standards of the nineteenth-century working class likewise scandalized the period's bourgeoisie, providing more evidence that the rabble was in constant need of moral supervision. Even Engels was disturbed by the working man's refusal to conform to Victorian sexual mores; "next to intemperance in the enjoyment of intoxicating liquors," he laments, "one of the principle faults of English working-men is sexual license."[56] Most middle class commentators of the day agreed that conventional marriage bonds between working class individuals were either shaky or nonexistent. For a class which highly valued the sobering effects of marriage and family life, this sexual nonconformity was much more than merely offensive; it was downright frightening. It represented yet another example of the natural perversity and need for constant supervision of the working class.

The point that most middle class reformists of the period missed was that the unrelentingly harsh material conditions of the laboring class rendered it by and large indifferent to the values which the more comfortable bourgeoisie took as self-evidently universal. The "nether world"[57] of the worker shared nothing in common with the respectable and secure world of his bourgeois counterpart. It is hardly surprising, then, that the latter's ideal of "steadiness" was so conspicuously absent in society's lower strata. W.J. Reader sums up the situation quite nicely when he says that working class society was

> a world which the accepted [middle class] scale of
> values and ideas of right behaviour hardly penetrated.
> Thrift meant nothing to people so poor that they could
> live only for the day. "Self-help" and individual
> ambition were alike a mockery to people so weighed down

by circumstances over which they had no control. How
could conventional morality make any sense to people
sleeping seven or eight to a room? In fact, there was a
good deal of prostitution, the marriage bond was fairly
loose, and illegitimate children were easily accepted
into their mothers' families. Of religious belief,
except of the vaguest kind, there was practically none
except among the Catholic Irish, the Jews and
occasional pockets of far-out nonconformity. The law
was a doubtful protection, the property of the rich a
more or less legitimate target, and the police
potential oppressors. In any case, life in gaol might
be more comfortable and would certainly be healthier
than life outside.[58]

In addition to "scientific" techniques for the supervision
of behavior in the factory and the home, the nineteenth century
also gave rise to a mechanistic sociology which claimed to not
only explain but--even more importantly--to justify the
increasing disproportionality of material conditions existing in
different economic strata. This sociology, which I discussed at
the beginning of this chapter, was Social Darwinism. Using a
distorted version of Darwinian natural selection as its
fundamental premise, it argued that elements within society, just
like biological species in nature, compete for existence. Those
societal elements which are strong enough to survive do so, and
rise to the top of the social hierarchy. Those elements which
are unsuitable fall to the bottom of the social ladder and
eventually die out. In short, society, just like nature, is "red
in tooth and claw." From an emotional and short-sighted
perspective, it may appear unfortunate that certain groups of
individuals are doomed to a life of material failure and quick
extinction, but from an evolutionary perspective the process is
both inevitable and, "objectively speaking," desirable. The
selecting-out of social elements unable to viably compete is
evolution's way of weeding undesirable segments from the body
politic, a culling process that only encourages the ultimate

health of society as a whole. Herbert Spencer, the century's
leading cheerleader for the doctrine of inevitable social
perfection, summed up the basic tenets of Social Darwinism in his
Principles of Sociology:

> Not simply do we see that in the competition among the
> individuals of the same kind, survival of the fittest
> has from the beginning furthered production of a higher
> type; but we see that to the unceasing warfare between
> species is due both growth and organisation. Without
> universal conflict there would have been no
> development of the active powers.[59]

Social Darwinism's defense of social selection meshed quite
nicely with the century's attempts to rationalize society
through management strategies of disciplined conformity to the
status quo.   Thrift, steadiness, and an unwavering fidelity to
the work ethic were the desiderata of the ultimately scientized
society, precisely because they were seen as the vehicles most
conducive to the maximization of both profit and social
equilibrium. The ascendent middle class, of course, perceived
itself as instantiating these virtues.   The "proof" was its
obvious dominant position within the social and economic
hierarchy. It campaigned to instill and encourage the same sense
of social responsibility in the lower classes through the factory
system--which, recall, possessed the two desirable
characteristics of generating the profit upon which the bourgeois
hegemony rested while at the same time disciplining the unruly
(and hence unhappy and poverty-stricken) masses.   Those elements
of the working class which were fit to rise to the occasion and
better themselves would.   Those which were unfit would die out.
Any artificial efforts to improve the material conditions of the
lower classes, so Social Darwinism argued, represented a
deliberate retardation of the inevitable evolution of society.
Spencer was especially vocal in his condemnation of social
welfare programs designed to succor the poor, arguing that such

strategies only prolonged the misery of those social elements doomed to extinction while at the same time lowering the quality of existence for society as a whole. Even Darwin, who was by no means a Social Darwinist of the same ilk as Spencer, at times expressed sentiments that smacked of this general orientation. In The Descent of Man, for example, Darwin implied that the artificial maintenance of "undesirable" social elements would prove detrimental to the entire human race:

> We civilised men. . .do our utmost to check the process of elimination; we build asylums for the imbecile, the maimed, and the sick; we institute poor-laws; and our medical men exert their utmost skill to save the life of every one to the last moment. ...Thus the weak members of civilised society propagate their kind. No one who has attended to the breeding of domestic animals will doubt that this must be highly injurious to the race of man.[60]

The influence of the "science" of Social Darwinism upon the latter half of the nineteenth century served to consolidate, along with Taylorism, the assumption that society not only could but should be understood in wholly mechanistic terms. Likewise, it provided a comfortable intellectual justification for the disproportionality of economic and political privilege that was becoming more and more apparent as the century neared its end. It was through no fault of the social system that poverty existed. Rather, the cause of both wealth and penury was chalked up to the impersonal mechanisms of evolutionary process. The tenets of Social Darwinism also legitimated the capitalist class's valuation of competition, the social analogue to the biological "struggle for survival," as the cutting edge that separated viable from nonviable social elements. It was the mechanism, as Spencer said, that encouraged the "development of the active powers" of the race, thereby promoting the instrumentality which was the necessary condition for the ultimate scientization of society.

In this last section I have tried to provide historical
evidence for my assertion that the worldview of the nineteenth
century was ideological in character. Recall that Mannheim's
functional description of a total ideology includes three
primary characteristics. First, its normative and conceptual
models, although claiming universality, are in fact contextual,
dependent for their very genesis upon the material conditions of
the environment in which they arise. Second, its values and ways
of interpreting the world are directly reflective of the
interests of the economically and politically ascendent class and
are consequently supportive of the social status quo. Finally,
its social agenda, based as it is upon the illusory assumption of
universality, is incapable of concrete actualization. In spite
of both the nineteenth century's actual achievements in the
mechanical sciences <u>and</u> its rhetorical claims to a revolutionary
social agenda, I hope I have indicated that there was a darker
side to the picture. The era's mechanistic worldview, with its
valuation of the complete scientization of society through the
extension of instrumental reason, resulted in both technological
and social consequences which were far from conducive to the
general well-being of all segments of the population. True, the
upsurge in technique did bolster national revenues and commodity
production. But the direct beneficiary of this change was
clearly the ascendent industrial middle class. The material
conditions of the lower classes generally not only did not
improve, but actually worsened. Furthermore, the period's ideal
of a machine-like society, as we have seen, was concretely
expressed in ways that were detrimental to both the social status
and the actual physical well-being of the lower classes.

Discounted as unruly, emotional and ignorant threats to the
equilibrium of the new society (with "equilibrium" here being
regarded as fidelity to the established social order), the lower
classes were systematically subjected to social strategies
which, it was hoped, would maximize their instrumentality and
minimize their potentially disruptive tendencies. These
strategies were all based upon a campaign of
desubjectification--i.e., the extirpation of subjective qualities
in members of the working class which prevented them from
assuming the functional roles of orderly, predictable and
controllable cogs in the social machine. Moreover, the ultimate
rationalization of society in general and the lower classes in
particular was guaranteed, in the nineteenth-century mind, by
the "science" of Social Darwinism, which itself provided
intellectual justifications for the capitalist structure of
society.

The aspirations of the nineteenth-century capitalist
worldview, in short, were ideological through and through. They
gave expression to the interests of the period's hegemonic
structure, they were not imbued with the universality claimed for
them, and the social agenda which they gave rise to simply did
not succeed. The condition of humankind was not improved by the
century's technological "revolution"; one class--the bour-
geoisie--was. Just as Bacon's "utopian" New Atlantis was an
image of the perfect seventeenth-century middle class society, so
likewise the nineteenth century's ideal of the ultimately
rational society was one that only properly fit its own middle
class.

The mainstream "utopian" novels that sprang up in the
nineteenth century wholeheartedly accepted the ideological claims
of their period. Their vision of the future sane society was one

in which all of the nineteenth century's values and mechanistic assumptions about the nature of reality were adopted and carried through to their logical conclusions. The "utopian" sane society was one in which social relations had been "scientized" to the same extent as mankind's relation to physical reality. Instrumental reason, the catalyst for this process of scientization, had eradicated subjective human foibles to the extent that individual and social interests had finally converged. Industrial capacity had been "revolutionized" through the unlimited growth of technology--a growth which, in turn, was conducive to the universal betterment of all people. And the perfect society, that pinnacle of social stability and material plenty which was the goal towards which millions of years of evolution had directed itself, had finally been reached.

Resting as firmly upon the values and theoretical assumptions of an ideological worldview as the putative utopias of the nineteenth century did, they themselves, from the very start, were likewise ideological in character. Far from breaking with the ideological continuum of their era, they actually reinforced it by bestowing upon its models the standard of utopian perfection, much as Francis Bacon had reinforced the ideological worldview of his own day. In the next chapter, we shall examine in some detail the specific characteristics of three of these nineteenth-century visions of the sane society.

CHAPTER 4

THREE NINETEENTH-CENTURY UTOPIAS

> How many goodly creatures are there
> here! How Beauteous Mankind is! O
> Brave new world, that has such people
> in 't!

> William Shakespeare, "The
> Tempest" (v,i)

> We are the priests of material
> development, of the work which
> enables other men to enjoy the fruits
> of the great sources of power in
> nature, and of the power of mind over
> matter. We are the priests of the
> new epoch, without superstitions.

> George Morison, in the
> keynote address to the
> 1895 convention of the
> American Society of Civil
> Engineers

I

The sane society metaphor came into its own in the nineteenth century, capturing the imagination of the layperson as well as the intellectual. Although blueprints of the fully rationalized social structure were sometimes straightforward treatises, the more common form of presentation was the "utopian" novel. The popularity of the sane society image, accordingly, can be measured by the number of putative utopian stories that were published and devoured by the reading public during this

period. As we saw in the last chapter, more "utopian" visions of
the perfect society were penned in the nineteenth century than in
all the centuries previous to it.

As I have argued throughout this study, mainstream
nineteenth-century "utopias" display a circumspect list of
characteristics and values. They agree that social sciences
should be modeled after the natural sciences; that instrumental
reason, with its emphasis upon concrete problem-solving, is more
valuable than "inutile" speculation; that the interests of
society are identical to the interests of the individual; and
that the human race is capable of ultimate perfection through the
correct application of the theoretical principles of
technological science and Social Darwinism. Moreover, we have
also seen that they perceived themselves as defending a
revolutionary social agenda whose instantiation would usher in
the good life for all human beings. This latter claim, as I have
tried to show, is an ideological one. Instead of offering
blueprints of the future community which are truly innovative and
serve as genuine alternatives to the values of nineteenth-century
industrial society, the sane society motif in fact mirrors and
reinforces the capitalist status quo. This subtle defense of the
ideological hegemony is apparent in those novels which are
outspokenly capitalist in tenor, as well as in those, ironically
enough, which claim to be socialist.

In the previous chapter, I argued that nineteenth-century
"utopian" novels are disguised ideologies and hence extensions
of the Baconian sane society vision. I defended this thesis in a
general way, showing that the characteristic features of
nineteenth-century "utopias" parallel the concrete ideals and
ideological constructs of the period. In this chapter, I wish to
elaborate upon that argument by examining three of these putative

utopias in some detail. They are Edward Bellamy's Looking
Backward: 2000-1887 (1888), M. Auburre Hovorre's The
Milltillionaire (1895), and Alexander Bogdanov's Red Star
(1908).

It might be objected that my sampling is too small, given
the fact that at least 515 self-proclaimed utopian novels were
written in the nineteenth century. But in fact these three
novels are quite representative of the different types one finds
in the mainstream sane society genre. Bellamy's vision espouses
a version of state capitalism; Hovorre's rather bizarre little
vignette defends monopoly capitalism as the economic structure of
the future perfect society; and Bogdanov champions a sane society
which is strongly centralized and disciplined along Leninist
lines. All of the other "utopian" novels written during the
century by and large fall into one of these three categories.

Furthermore, at least two of these novels (Looking Backward
and Red Star) were immensely popular in their time and served as
prototypes for a rash of imitative novels which repeat, almost ad
nauseaum, the same themes and value assumptions. Indeed, the
"utopian" novels that appeared before Bellamy and Bogdanov were
likewise cut from the same cloth; as Frank and Fritzie Manuel
put it, "for the most part these novels...are derivative,
syncretistic, and infinitely boring."[1] It is hard to see how
they could have been otherwise. Caught up as each of them was in
the nineteenth century's enthusiasm for technology, the
scientization of social relations, and instrumental reason, it is
not surprising that the same social model is defended time after
time--almost as if one and the same blueprint was used in each
construction.

Bellamy, Hovorre and Bogdanov, then, serve as adequate
representatives of the entire tradition of nineteenth-century

sane societies. We could just as well have focused upon Theodor
Hertzka's _Freeland_, H.G. Wells' <u>A Modern Utopia</u>, N.G.
Chernyshevskii's <u>What Is To Be Done</u>?, or any number of other
nineteenth century "utopias." But to have done so would have
only added to the cast of characters and fictional scenarios; the
overall themes and values would have remained unchanged.[2]

II

Edward Bellamy's <u>Looking Backward: 2000-1887</u>

There is no doubt that Bellamy's <u>Looking Backward</u>, first
published in the United States in 1888, exerted more influence
upon the popular imagination than any other sane society vision
of the nineteenth century. Indeed, the only novel in this genre
which even comes close to the popularity enjoyed by <u>Looking
Backward</u> is H.G. Wells' <u>A Modern Utopia</u>, which appeared in the
first decade of the twentieth century. But Wells was the
literary giant of his generation, and any book published under
his name was assured of wide distribution and avid consumption.
Bellamy, on the other hand, was a relatively unknown American
journalist when his sane society blueprint appeared.
Notwithstanding its author's obscurity, however, the book sold
some 200,000 copies in its first year. Furthermore, by the end
of the century, it was the most purchased novel in America except
for <u>Uncle Tom's Cabin</u>, published some forty years earlier.[3]

Bellamy's novel obviously served as the prototype for the
"utopian" images that followed it. As mentioned in the previous
chapter, the bulk of the nineteenth century's sane society
images appeared after the publication of <u>Looking Backward</u>. Many
of them were transparently modeled upon the blueprint of
Bellamy's new order--so much so that, granting the obvious

dissimilarities in plots and characters, to have read one of them
is to have read them all. It is true that others--although not
many--were written in reaction to the picture of the ideal
society which Bellamy presented. But with very few exceptions,
these "anti-Bellamy" novels shared a set of values and
theoretical assumptions quite similar to those which Bellamy
defended in Looking Backward. As a result, they by and large fit
into the mainstream of nineteenth-century "utopias."

The influence of Looking Backward can also be gauged by the
fact that it served as one of the primary inspirations for the
growth of American nationalist political sentiment in the last
decade of the nineteenth century. One of the most
characteristic themes of Bellamy's "utopia" was its defense of
the centralization of a country's economic structure--what we
today, following Lenin,[4] would call "state capitalism." The
latter, of course, is an economic system in which the material
means of production are owned and managed by the state, rather
than by private entrepreneurs on the one hand, or the laboring
class on the other. Bellamy's defense of the nationalization of
industry rang an especially sympathetic chord for the American
petit bourgeoisie and agriculturalists who served as the basis
for the short-lived "Populist Party" of the 1880s and 1890s.
Moreover, Bellamy's sane society vision also appealed to the
growing number of individuals in the United States who believed
that the maximization of economic efficiency could be attained
only through the creation of a rigidly hierarchical, strongly
centralized and militarily disciplined work force. This
movement, known to its advocates as "Nationalism," mushroomed in
the closing years of the century, largely due to the enormous
popularity of Bellamy's novel, and campaigned for a social agenda
which closely paralleled the new order in Looking Backward. The
concrete and widespread influence of this Bellamy-inspired

movement is described by Arthur Lipow:

> The popular response of Bellamy's contemporaries to
> Looking Backward was phenomenal... Looking Backward
> sold by the hundreds of thousands and its ideas were
> widely discussed and debated in the 1890s. It quickly
> became the ideological foundation of an organized
> political movement. 'Nationalism' consciously ap-
> pealed, with considerable success, to educated
> middle-class people, especially to the "new" property-
> less middle class, and to displaced professionals and
> intellectuals...
>
> In 1888, a group of retired army officers attracted by
> Bellamy's military solution to the labor problem formed
> the first Bellamy Club. A short time later the
> membership expanded and the First Nationalist Club of
> Boston was founded. The Nationalist, published by the
> First Club, became the official periodical of the new
> movement. Clubs began to spring up throughout the
> country and the constitution and declaration of
> principles of the First Boston Club became the model.
> Be the end of 1890 there were 158 Nationalist clubs in
> twenty-seven states. Sixty-five were in California and
> sixteen in New York City. The peak of the movement was
> reached in 1891 when there were 165 clubs chartered.[5]

True, both the Nationalist and Populist movements lost their
political viability towards the close of the century. But the
enormous (albeit short-lived) influence which their Bellamite
social agendas enjoyed testifies to the accuracy with which
Bellamy's sane society image captured the popular middle-class
sentiments of the day. The fame of Bellamy's work did not rest
upon the introduction of novel, thought-provoking ideas which
redirected the century's basic worldview. Rather, its popularity
was due to its expertise in giving succinct and systematic
expression to ideas and values already present in the social
milieu of middle class America.[6]

The plot of Bellamy's Looking Backward, as with so many
other putative utopias of the period, is simplistic and, indeed,
somewhat crude. Both the story progression and the personalities

of the main characters are little more than weak, contrived props upon which to hang the blueprint of the sane society.   In brief, the plot's action revolves around one Julian West, a member of Boston's propertied leisure class in the last quarter of the nineteenth century.   West suffers from chronic insomnia.   In the hope of curing his malady, he constructs a sound-proof bedroom in the basement of his Bostonian mansion and hires a Svengali-like physician by the name of Pillsbury to hypnotically put him into a comatose sleep which only Pillsbury can break.   One night in 1887, Pillsbury puts his patient under, disappears, and West, miraculously preserved by his trance-like state, sleeps through the twentieth century until he is discovered in his basement room and awakened in the year 2000. The rest of the novel consists of didactic (and rather tedious) accounts of the new order which West has awakened to: the sane society of the twenty-first century, as seen through the eyes of a displaced nineteenth-century man.

The social order which West discovers is one which has been totally rationalized.   Technology has provided the material wherewithal for the elimination of both economic scarcity and physical disease; crime is almost nonexistent; manual labor has virtually disappeared, and the work that remains is easy to do and doesn't require much time or effort.   Individuals usually retire at the age of forty-five and their final years are devoted to "fulfilling," "creative" activity.   There is no social dissent, no warfare, and no significant interpersonal conflicts to disrupt the equilibrium of the new order. It runs with the clockwork efficiency of a vast machine that maximizes both collective instrumentality and individual happiness--not surprisingly, since the two are considered to be synonymous.

The necessary condition for the inauguration of this

marvelous new society has been the elimination of rampant
individualism, on both the social and economic levels. The
individualism of West's chaotic century, so he is told by one of
the inhabitants of the new Boston, "was inconsistent with much
public spirit. What little wealth you had seems almost wholly to
have been lavished in private luxury."[7] This "primitive" desire
to promote one's own interests at the expense of society's
resulted in a harshly competitive world in which community
stability and collective betterment could hardly flourish. The
new Boston of A.D. 2000, however, has managed to eliminate
individual egoism to such an extent that the well-being of the
individual is identified with the well-being of the state. The
felicity of the collective ensures the happiness of the
individual. Consequently, wealth within the confines of the
society is channeled into public rather than private enterprises:
"Nowadays. . .there is no destination of the surplus wealth so
popular as the adornment of the city, which all enjoy in equal
degree."[8]

In point of fact, however, the distinction between "private"
and "public" enterprise within the confines of Bellamy's sane
society is a specious one, precisely because the former no
longer exists. In the new order, the state owns all property
except personal possessions; as such, it controls the development
and distribution of commodities, services and by-products from
natural resources. The state, in short, comprises one huge trust
which centralizes--and hence rationalizes--the economic relations
of the new society. Bellamy compares it to a gigantic monopoly
syndicate which co-ordinates the entire nation's productive
capacity into a maximally efficient machine. During the
formative stages of the new society,

> the movement toward the conduct of business by larger
> and larger aggregations of capital, the tendency toward

monopolies, which had been so desperately and so vainly
resisted, was recognized at last, in its true
significance, as a process which only needed to
complete its logical evolution to open a golden future
of humanity.

Early in the [twentieth century] the evolution was
completed by the final consolidation of the entire
capital of the nation. The industry and commerce of
the country, ceasing to be conducted by a set of
irresponsible corporations and syndicates of private
persons at their caprice and for their profit, were
intrusted to a single syndicate representing the
people, to be conducted in the common interest for the
common profit. The nation, that is to say, organized
as the one great business corporation in which all
other corporations were absorbed; it became the one
capitalist in the place of all other capitalists, the
sole employer, the final monopoly in which all previous
and lesser monopolies were swallowed up, a monopoly in
the profits and economies of which all citizens shared.
The epoch of trusts ended in The Great Trust.[9]

Bellamy emphasized the centralization of commodity
production and distribution in his futuristic novel as an
antidote to what he took to be the irrationalities of unplanned
economic relations in his own time. According to Bellamy, the
nineteenth century's "system of unorganized and antagonistic
industries was as absurd economically as it was morally
abominable. Selfishness was [its] only science, and in
industrial production selfishness is suicide. Competition, which
is the instinct of selfishness, is another word for dissipation
of energy, while combination is the secret of efficient
production..."[10] Passages such as this one have led many
commentators, both in Bellamy's time and afterwards, to assume
that the economic model defended in the novel is a socialistic
one. This interpretation, however, rests upon the mistaken
assumption that because Bellamy condemns "competition" and
"selfishness" in the marketplace, he necessarily advocates a
system in which the means of production and determination of

quotas are owned and directed by the laboring class. But such is
not the case. Bellamy objects to competition primarily because
he thinks it encourages inefficiency and waste in the economic
arena, and hence stands in the way of the ultimate
rationalization of society. He _is_ concerned about management's
exploitation of workers; of that there is no doubt. But the
reason for his concern is that such exploitation is
characteristic of an anarchic economy which lessens the
possibility of equilibrium in social relations. This point is
indicated in the following passage, where Bellamy argues for the
advantages of a centralized state economy not on the grounds of
suffering labor, but rather on the basis of maximized
instrumentality:

> The wastes which resulted from leaving the conduct of
> industry to irresponsible individuals, wholly without
> mutual understanding or concert, were mainly four:
> first, the waste by mistaken undertakings; second, the
> waste from the competition and mutual hostility of
> those engaged in industry; third, the waste by
> periodical gluts and crises, with the consequent
> interruptions of industry; fourth, the waste from idle
> capital and labor, at all times. Any one of these four
> great leaks, were all the others stopped, would suffice
> to make the difference between wealth and poverty on
> the part of a nation.[11]

In contrast with the irrational and de-stabilizing
individualistic economy of the nineteenth century, the new
economic order of the twenty-first century is one that has
arranged itself according to organizational plans and production
techniques that work with mathematical precision. Nothing is
left to chance or individual whim in this monolithic structure.
In fact, the very condition of its success is that it has rid
itself of the subjective foibles which hampered the progress of
earlier models. It enjoys, in short, the qualities of an
impersonal and autonomous machine, and as such is maximally

efficient: "the [economic] machine...is indeed a vast one, but
so logical in its principles and direct and simple in its
workings that it all but runs itself; and nobody but a fool could
derange it..."[12]

   The advantages of the new order's economic machine are
revealed in both the production and distribution of commodities.
The centralized economy has at its exclusive disposal the
nation's supply of natural   resources and its material means of
production--factories,   research   facilities,   and   so   on.
Production quotas for each year are determined by statistical
comparisons of the previous year's distribution range and the
growth or decrease in demand and population size. This
centralized supervision of natural resources and   modes of
production insures that strict controls are   placed upon
technique, while the statistical analysis of distribution
patterns guarantees a minimum of wastage in both material and
labor-power. Bellamy describes the latter process in the
following manner:

> Now that every pin which is given out from a national
> warehouse is recorded, of course the figures of
> consumption for any week, month, or year, in the
> possession of the department of distribution at the end
> of that period, are precise. On these figures,
> allowing for tendencies to increase or decrease and for
> any special causes likely to affect demand, the
> estimates, say for a year ahead, are based.[13]

The strictly supervised process of production, with its
eradication of individualistic (i.e., irrational) tendencies, is
paralleled by the new order's distribution strategy. Currency is
no longer the medium of exchange; nor are goods sold at private
establishments. Instead, "a credit corresponding to his share of
the annual product of the nation is given to every citizen on the
public books at the beginning of the year, and a credit card

issued him with which he procures at the public storehouses, found in every community, whatever he desires whenever he desires it."[14] Private exchange of commodities between individuals is not only unnecessary in Bellamy's sane society; it is also impossible: "everything was procurable from one source"--the state-owned public warehouses--"and nothing could be procured anywhere else."[15] To either accommodate the possibility of or encourage private exchange, in the eyes of the inhabitants of twenty-first century Boston, represents an atavistic retreat into individualism which could re-open the doors to irrational social relations. Strictly controlled and centralized distribution, just like production, is a necessary ingredient of the Bellamite sane society.

An interesting consequence of the method of distribution in the new Boston is that it aids in the erosion of individuality by reducing the number of stimuli with which humans come in contact. Each one of the public warehouses has precisely the same stock; to visit one of them is to visit all. Although there is a variety of commodities in each, of course, there is no possibility of exposure to significantly alternative styles, brands, or fashions, because there are no private productive agencies in competition with the state. The resulting uniformity of available goods both reflects and strengthens the emphasis upon conformity in the society. Pick-ups can be made quickly, with little reflection, and there is no need for elaborate decision-making. Neither, however, is there much opportunity for personal style or creativity.[16]

The "benefits" of institutionalized conformity are perhaps nowhere better illustrated in Bellamy's "utopia" than in the so-called "industrial army" that comprises the society's workforce. Distribution ratios and production techniques can be

mapped out with absolute mathematical precision, but unless there
is a body of disciplined drones closely supervised by an ever
watchful cadre to instantiate that precision, the blueprint is of
little instrumental value. Bellamy meets that need by creating a
rigidly hierarchical industrial army. It is explicitly based on
a military model. At the top of the echelon is the President of
the United States, whose "most important function...is the
headship of the industrial army."[17] Underneath him are the
generals and colonels who supervise various departments (or
perhaps "battalions" would be more appropriate) of the
centralized economic structure. They also co-ordinate the
activities of the lieutenants and NCOs of industry, who for their
part are the immediate supervisors of the greater part of the
industrial army--the "privates," if you will. Each caste or rank
grouping within this army has a specific function in the
industrial process, and each likewise enjoys different
privileges. The division in caste and social function is
rigorously maintained, even to the point of assigning each its
own particular "uniform":

> [each has] its emblematic device...and this, in the
> shape of a metallic badge so small that you might not
> see it unless you knew where to look, is all the
> insignia which the men of the [industrial] army wear,
> except where public convenience demands a distinctive
> uniform. This badge is the same in form for all grades
> of industry, but while the badge of the third grade is
> iron, that of the second is silver, and that of the
> first is gilt.[18]

The assignation of emblems (unobtrusive as they may be)
representing different industrial caste underscores the
disciplined and strict hierarchical nature of Bellamy's
industrial army. The army is meant to be the axis upon which the
health of the sane society revolves. As such, it must be as
precise in its activities, as statistically objective and hence

manipulatible in its functions, as is a vast mindless machine. There is no uneasy suspicion in Bellamy's mind that the individuals who comprise the bulk of the industrial army might be unhappy or unfulfilled in their particular situation. Maximum instrumentality and efficiency, so far as he is concerned, is the means of insuring a society's interests, and the interests of society are identical to the interests of the individual. Consequently, the most certain route to both individual and societal felicity is through the rigorous, centralized supervision of human behavior, because such supervision is a necessary condition of instrumentality. As Bellamy says,

> the organization of the industry of the nation under a single control, so that all its processes interlock, has multiplied the total product over the utmost that could be done under the former system. The effectiveness of the working force of a nation, under the myriad-headed leadership of private capital, even if the leaders were not mutual enemies, as compared with that which it attains under a single head, may be likened to the military efficiency of a mob, or a horde of barbarians with a thousand petty chiefs, as compared with that of a disciplined army under one general--such a fighting machine, for example, as the German army in the time of Von Moltke.[19]

The new order's centralized co-ordination of commodity production and planning has resulted not only in the elimination of material scarcity and wastage, but also in a technologized society in which inventions unknown to the nineteenth century abound. Conventional energy sources have been replaced by electricity; one of the first things Julian West notices about new Boston is "the complete absence of chimneys and their smoke..."[20] The architectural planning of urban areas within the new order has been sanitized. Both pollution and irrational distribution of living space are things of the past. Piped-in music entertains the inhabitants of new Boston, an accomplishment which delights as much as it amazes West. The medical sciences have eliminated diseases and the infirmities of old age. And automation and streamlined techniques have drastically reduced the need for human labor in many arenas of daily existence. As one of the inhabitants of new Boston tells West,

> Our washing is all done at public laundries at excessively cheap rates, and our cooking at public kitchens. The making and repairing of all we wear are done outside in public shops. Electricity, of course, takes the place of all fires and lighting. We choose houses no larger than we need, and furnish them so as to involve the minimum of trouble to keep them in order. We have no use for domestic servants.[21]

The material achievements of the new order reflect the sane society's emphasis upon instrumental reason. Every aspect of social and individual existence has been "cleaned up" through the application of the ideals and methods of the natural sciences to human behavior. The character of the new society is but "the logical outcome of the operation of human nature under rational conditions."[22] The apparent success which this approach has enjoyed has only further convinced the inhabitants of the twenty-first century of the importance of instrumental thinking and the gratuitousness of mere idle speculation. As one of them says, in a remark which nicely captures the entire sentiment of the society, "having lost its utility, [an activity] has ceased to be regarded as a virtue."[23] This credo, as we have seen, is one that both Bacon and the scientists of the nineteenth century would have heartily agreed with.

The technological accomplishments that personify Bellamy's utopia, in addition to the institutionalized emphasis upon instrumental as opposed to speculative reason, point to the presence of both a "new" society and a "new" human being. For Bellamy, as for all of the utopian novelists of the nineteenth century, human nature is plastic, the result of environmental

manipulation. The assumption is that a new race of human beings
can be created through the gradual metamorphosis of societal and
interpersonal structures. The best way to encourage "sane,"
instrumental behavior on the part of individuals, then, is to
create objective conditions of reinforcement for such behavior.
To change the human environment is to change human motivation.
As one of Bellamy's characters tells Julian West, "...the
conditions of human life have changed, and with them the motives
of human action."[24]

One of the most dramatic changes in human behavior which the
new Boston's program of social engineering has brought about is
the eradication of selfish egoism and its replacement by a
selfless fraternity. Bellamy is quite proud of the fact that his
new order has eliminated the greed and competition nurtured by
the egoism of earlier generations. He has one of his characters
express the point to Julian in the following way:

> If I were to give you, in one sentence, a key to what
> may seem the mysteries of our civilization as compared
> with that of your age, I should say that it is the fact
> that the solidarity of the race and the brotherhood of
> man, which to you were but fine phrases, are, to our
> thinking and feeling, ties as real and as vital as
> physical fraternity.[25]

This and analogous expressions of fraternity and
cooperative solidarity from the inhabitants of Bellamy's new
Boston are, on a first reading, both impressive and appealing.
It is only on closer examination that the utopia's apotheosis of
"fraternity" begins to take on a somewhat disconcerting tone. To
begin with, it gradually becomes clear that the "solidarity of
the race" depends upon the utter elimination of elements of
individuality in the social body. This eradication of individual
idiosyncracy is a social as well as a "mental and moral
improvement." As one of new Boston's citizens tells West,

"Individualism, which in your day was the animating idea of
society, not only was fatal to any vital sentiment of brotherhood
and common interest among living men, but equally to any
realization of the responsibility of the living for the
generation to follow."[26] While there is little doubt that
unbridled individualism is responsible for interpersonal
aggression and oppression, if by "individualism" one means the
nonprincipled and totally egoistic pursuit of one's own
pleasures, it also seems to be the case that "individualism" can
have less pernicious connotations. It can, for instance,
indicate nonaggressive variability or creative flair. Bellamy
seems not to have interpreted "individualism" in this more benign
way, however. For him and his new Boston, individualism was
always a negative attitude, dangerous to the well-being of
society and its institutions.

In keeping with this condemnation of individualism, Bellamy
likewise insists that the notion of self-support is both
pernicious and confused. All human beings depend upon
centralized supervision for their happiness and material
well-being. To suppose that a single person could separate
himself from the commmunity and nevertheless survive not only
flies in the face of common sense; it also serves as a dangerous
precedent for a destabilizing nonconformity, inasmuch as "true"
civilization is founded upon the eradication of self-support. As
one of the intelligentsia of new Boston puts it,

> There is no such thing in a civilized society as
> self-support. In a state of society so barbarous as
> not even to know family co-operation, each individual
> may possibly support himself, though even then for a
> part of his life only; but from the moment that men
> begin to live together, and constitute even the crudest
> sort of society, self-support becomes impossible. As
> men grow more civilized, and the subdivision of
> occupations and services is carried out, a complex

> mutual dependence becomes the universal rule. Every
> man, however solitary may seem his occupation, is a
> member of a vast industrial partnership, as large as
> the nation, as large as humanity. The necessity of
> mutual dependence should imply the duty and guarantee
> of mutual support...[27]

Given Bellamy's narrow interpretation of individualism and
self-support, what the "mutual support" referred to in the above
quotation appears to reduce to is the reinforcement of behavioral
patterns which display conformity to societal institutions and
the discouragement of behavioral patterns which tend to promote
the individual's desires above those of society's. The barometer
for evaluating an individual's actions is, in the final
analysis, his ability to work well according to the standards
established by new Boston's vast industrial machine. In fact,
the value of an individual member of society is determined solely
by the amount of time and energy which he spends in its service.
As Julian West discovers, in the utopia of A.D. 2000 "the value
of a man's services to society fixes his rank in it."[28] As such,
individual humans acquire the status of machine components in the
overall societal mechanisms, each with his own functional niche
and assigned duty: "nowadays everybody is a part of a system
with a distinct place and function."[29] The transformation of
what otherwise might be nonconforming agents into acquiescent,
well-coordinated machine parts best serves the new Boston's
instrumentalist ideals. Productive efficiency is maximized, as
is the equilibrium surrounding social relations, when
environmental conditions are so manipulated as to desubjectify
humans.

It might appear that the mechanization of both personal and
productive relations would have inaugurated a society in which
there is absolute equality between different individuals. This,
at any rate, is Bellamy's claim: "...there is recognized no sort

of difference between the dignity of the different sorts of work
required by the nation."[30] As we have seen, however, such is not
the case. The very militarization of the productive process has
ensured differences both in rank and privilege, with the obvious
implication that a colonel or captain in the industrial army is
more powerful than a private or NCO. The patterns of inequality
in power and rights which accompany division of labor under the
capitalist mode of production seem to be reproduced, then, in
Bellamy's new society.   Moreover, differences in the status and
privileges of the sexes are likewise retained. Bellamy claims
that the proper role of women in his new Boston is to
participate, on an equal basis with men, in working towards the
common weal: "our women, as well as our men, are members of the
industrial army, and leave it only when maternal duties claim
them."[31] In fact, however, the subordinate status which women
were usually bequeathed in nineteenth-century capitalism has been
retained in Bellamy's vision of the future "perfect" society.
Women are still looked at as dainty, fragile creatures who are
unable to compete with men in either strength or endurance.
Their duties in the new Boston--and, consequently, their social
positions--are fewer and less vital than those assumed by male
workers. As a new Bostonian (a male) explains the matter to
Julian,

> Women being inferior in strength to men, and further
> disqualified industrially in special ways, the kinds of
> occupation reserved for them, have references to these
> facts.   The heavier sorts of work are everywhere
> reserved for men, the lighter occupations for women.
> Under no circumstances is a woman permitted to follow
> any employment not perfectly adapted, both as to kind
> and degree of labor, to her sex. Moreover, the hours
> of women's work are considerably shorter than those of
> men's, more frequent vacations are granted, and the
> most careful provision is made for rest when needed.[32]

All this is not to say that the living conditions for women in Bellamy's new Boston exactly duplicate those of the nineteenth century. Women in the new order have been freed, for instance, from the chores of housework and cooking; automation takes care of the first task, while communal kitchens cover the second. But it is clear that Bellamy's new society has removed these chores not out of concern for equal gender opportunities, but rather because automated housework and communal cooking are simply more efficient than more traditional approaches. That the maximization of labor efficiency within the society is the real goal here is evidenced, for instance, by the fact that women in the new society still bear the burden of child-rearing. It is always the mother, never the father, who leaves the industrial army on the birth of an enfant. Moreover, new Boston appears to be concerned with raising the happiness level of women primarily because such an action increases the happiness of the male inhabitants. In a most revealing passage, Julian West is told that "women are a very happy race nowadays, as compared with what they were before in the world's history, and their power of giving happiness to men has been of course increased in proportion."[33]

Notwithstanding these and similar disturbing features, new Boston sees itself as the harbinger of a golden age, in which society and individuals are finally brought into harmony through a complete identification of their interests. As one of the new order's leading clergymen says,

> It is a pledge of the destiny for us that the Creator has set in our hearts an infinite standard of achievement, judged by which our past attainments seem always insignificant, and the goal never nearer.
>
> The betterment of mankind from generation to generation, physically, mentally, morally, is recognized as the one great object supremely worthy of effort and of sacrifice. We believe the race for the

first time to have entered on the realization of God's ideal of it and each generation must now be a step upward.[34]

The primary mechanism by which Bellamy's utopia is approaching ever nearer to the "realization of God's ideal of it" is evolutionary selection. The new Bostonians are firm in their commitment to the tenets of Social Darwinism. For them, the evolution--i.e., "progress"--of human traits, industrial capacity and social stability is an inevitable consequence of Darwin's theory of natural selection. Undesirable characteristics, both individual and social, will be weeded out because of their inability to compete in the struggle for survival. The natural evolutionary process can be accelerated, moreover, by social engineering's judicious manipulation of the social environment. Those traits most conducive to social stability--conformity, for example--are encouraged by a system of behavioral rewards and admonitions. By such strategies, social selection and natural selection become one, and for the first time human beings work hand-in-hand with the evolutionary process. As one of the new Bostonians tells West during a discussion about the genesis of the utopia to which he has awakened,

> The solution came as the result of a process of industrial evolution which could not have terminated otherwise. All that society had to do was to recognize and cooperate with that evolution, when its tendency had become unmistakable.[35]

One of the more obvious ways in which the new order has aided natural evolution in its drive towards the ultimate perfection of society is by increasing the intelligence level of individuals to a degree unimaginable in the nineteenth century, West's own time. His utopian host informs him, for example, that "one generation of the world today represents a greater volume of intellectual life than any five centuries ever did before."[36]

This improvement of the species has resulted from several strategies for aiding the evolutionary process. Environmental conditioning has created external inducements towards stability by discouraging nonconformity (Bellamy, it should be noted, at times seems to endorse Lamarckian selection). Mild forms of eugenic engineering have created healthier bodies and more comely physical appearances, and education--the continuous sharpening of the mind from generation to generation--has produced a race which, for all practical purposes, is free of mental and emotional disease. As a new Bostonian tells Julian, "...an improvement of the species ought to follow such [changes]. In certain specific respects we know, indeed, that the improvement has taken place. Insanity, for instance, which in the nineteenth century was so terribly common a product of your insane mode of life, has almost disappeared, with its alternative, suicide."[37]

Criminal behavior, just like physical ugliness and mental slowness, has been selected out of the new Boston. One of the first things that West discovers about his new surroundings is that entrances to private residences are not locked, "indicating that burglary was not among the perils of the modern Boston..."[38] The absence of crime is due to the success of the new order's social engineering. It has eliminated the material and psychological conditions which serve as the catalysts for crime. Those rare instances of criminal behavior which occasionally do pop up are viewed as atavistic remnants of irrationality in man, and are treated as ailments: "we have no jails nowadays. All cases of atavism are treated in the hospitals. ...Crime is nowadays looked upon as the occurrence of an ancestral trait."[39]

Economic plenitude, social stability, individual tranquillity--these are the fundamental characteristics of

Bellamy's sane society. As he himself boasts, his new order is "a paradise of order, equity, and felicity."[40] But the cost of this paradise, it might be argued, has been too great. Equilibrium has been paid for with individual creativity; an increase in economic wealth has brought with it a class system just as rigid as the one which existed in Bellamy's nineteenth century; and the rationalization of the social order has been purchased with social freedom. Far from being a vision of the good society, in which all humans flourish, Bellamy's Looking Backward is a fantasy which by and large reflects the character of the conventional power relations during Bellamy's time. It is revolutionary only in appearance; in reality, it is a subtle ideology. As Frank and Fritzie Manuel succinctly put it, "Bellamy's characters even in their emancipation are still buttoned-up Bostonians..."[41]

I have devoted a considerable amount of space to an analysis of the ideological character of Bellamy's Looking Backward because it is generally agreed that the novel is the nineteenth-century utopia par excellence. It gives adequate expression to the scientific and industrial ideals of the nineteenth century, it encapsulates the values and imaginary social structures of the "utopian" novels that preceded it, and it served as a phenomenally effective inspiration for the sane society images that immediately followed its original publication. It is little wonder, then, that the following analyses of The Milltillionaire and Red Star will sound so familiar. To have read Bellamy's Looking Backward is, in a very significant way, to have read all of the nineteenth century's sane societies.

M. Auburre Hovorre's The Milltillionaire

This short utopian vignette first appeared as a privately printed (and carelessly proofread) pamphlet in Boston. The exact date of publication is uncertain but is generally believed to have been 1895.[42] Nothing is known about the author except that the name which appears on the title page is pseudonymous; his real name was Albert Waldo Howard.

The Milltillionaire is one of the nineteenth century's most unusual utopian sketches, in both form and content. Structurally, it is only thirty pages in length--a refreshing break from the usually overlong and monotonous pieces typical of the genre--and divided into three different chapters or parts which seem to have no significant connection with one another. The first chapter is but a few lines; the second is just over two pages; and the third chapter, which begins and ends with startling abruptness, comprises the rest of the pamphlet. Moreover, there is no plot to the vignette--not even the minimal plot most favored by other utopian authors--and the style of writing is extremely uneven and punctuated with an army of upper case letters, exclamation points and ellipses. In short, the piece has the appearance of a hastily written manifesto.

The content of The Milltillionaire is also somewhat idiosyncratic. Although it falls within the mainstream tradition of nineteenth-century utopian novels, it also claims certain features for its vision of the future--free love and public nudity being the two most dramatic--which are not found in most other novels of the same genre. As such its author shows much more imagination than, for example, Bellamy. These idiosyncracies are not strong enough, however, to warrant excluding the piece from the period's set of ideological

"utopian" novels. The majority of values defended in it clearly
reflect those of nineteenth-century capitalism.

The setting of the vignette is earth, some time in the
distant future ("late in the Age of the Planet Earth,"[43] as
Hovorre puts it).   An individual whom Hovorre calls the
"Milltillionaire," "a being of such colossal and illimitable
wealth and power, one might say he was a very god--or God," has
purchased the entire planet. His unlimited wealth enables him to
create a "paradise" of prosperity, technological sophistication
and culture. He controls the planet--which Hovorre, for reasons
that are never entirely clear, calls "the Bardic State,"[44]--with
magnanimity; "the only revenue the Bardic State requires from any
individual after attaining the age of twenty-five years is that
he allot a minim [sic] portion of his time daily to the
continuance of the Universal Welfare of the Planet."[45] This
tribute in turn binds all of earth's inhabitants to "render equal
service to the Bardic State." The equality of duty, according to
Hovorre, demonstrates that "slavery" doesn't exist in the new
order.[46] It might be argued that equally distributed servitude
is servitude nonetheless; but this is a point that seems to have
escaped Hovorre. For him, the equality of status enjoyed by the
inhabitants of the Bardic State somehow guarantees individual
freedom, notwithstanding the fact that the Milltillionaire,
"virtually owning the Earth, controls or sways the nations at his
pleasure, or could annihilate or transform them at his
option."[47]

The Milltillionaire's unimaginable quantities of wealth
have revolutionized the scientific and technological realms. To
begin with, conventional energy sources such as steam and animal
power are things of the past; they have been completely
supplanted by the "Bardic" energy sources of electricity and

magnetism: "...no Horse or Steam-power is allowed, electric and
magnetic forces now supplying all powers of locomotion other than
human. In point of fact, horses, cattle, dogs, cats and so forth
are only to be seen in the Zoological Parks as curiosities or
pets."[48] Furthermore, it seems as if Bardic science has also
almost completely replaced electricity with the new power of
"magnetism." This latter energy source, discovered by a science
underwritten by the Milltillionaire's trillions, has two
manifestations. On the one hand, it is a physical energy of much
stronger intensity than mere electricity. As Hovorre describes
it for his readers, "all of [the Bardic State's] artificial
illumination is effected by a magnetic current so powerful that
one lamp will illumine an area ten miles square almost as
brilliantly as sunlight."[49] On the other hand, magnetic power
also manifests itself as psychic energy--or "psycho-omni-
magnetism"--which acts upon persons rather than inanimate
objects:

> By Psycho-omni-magnetism a man who has omni-
> magnetically qualified himself is not only able to
> magnetise a few individuals but is able to omni-
> magnetise his entire environment of whatever persons
> it may be composed so that they will be impelled to
> harmoniously co-operate with him in the prosecution of
> any enterprise.[50]

In short, "Magnetism supersedes Electricity and psycho-omni-
magnetism transcends Hypnotism"[51] in the Bardic State.

It is tempting to dismiss Hovorre's description of
psycho-omni-magnetism as the farfetched fantasy of a wild
dreamer. After all, the very notion of a psychical energy
capable of hypnotizing large numbers of people into harmonious
cooperation is as unlikely today as it must have seemed to the
nineteenth century. But the introduction of such a phenomenon
is, I believe, significant. Psycho-omni-magnetism represents

ultimate control over human behavior just as physical magnetism represents ultimate control over natural forces. Science and technology have thereby achieved their final goal: the rationalization of all reality through the systematic extirpation of untamed nature as well as radically individualistic human behavior. Just as the forces of the physical world have been harnessed in the interests of man, so likewise has the human mind been "impelled" by psycho-omni-magnetism to cooperate "in the prosecution of any enterprise." This double guard against irrationality can only serve to strengthen the prosperity and stability of the perfect Bardic State.

The concrete, material results of magnetic energy are spectacular. Most of the inhabitants of the planet, with the sole exceptions of "savages and barbarians who still adhere to their native swamps, but who are fast becoming extinct like other wild animals,"[52] live in beautiful cities, each of which is circular in form, with a radius of one hundred miles.[53] Although there are about twenty such cities on the face of the earth, with the consequence that the population of each runs into the "quadrillions," pollution, overcrowding and mechanical inefficiency have been completely eliminated. Bardic architecture is based upon a colossal scale, with apartment buildings that "tower several thousand feet in the air, the smallest of which is capable of housing comfortably and luxuriously one million citizens."[54] Connecting the shops, businesses and apartment buildings is the main artery of inner-city transportation, the "Triple Canopied Highway." The highway is 1000 feet in width, with 200 feet of pavement and 400 feet of recreational lawn on either side. It has three different levels; the first two are for electrically powered vehicles and the top tier is for cyclists and pedestrians. This uppermost level not only provides splendid vistas for the enjoyment of travelers; it also protects them from the elements, covered as it is with a glass canopy "as secure from all storms and dust and heat as the marbled hall of any palace."[55] Moreover, huge subways underneath the city accommodate heavy vehicles loaded with freight, thereby preventing noise and air pollution.

In addition to the inner-city Triple Canopied Highway, each Bardic city also enjoys the services of the Viaduct Railway, a transportation system that connects one city with another. Towering an amazing 15,000 feet in the air and "built upon the principle of a gigantic suspension bridge," the Railway can propel its electrically-driven vehicles at a velocity of one thousand miles per hour.[56] This huge velocity is attainable in part because of the unbroken surface of the Viaduct; being as high as it is, "and thus having no barriers in the way of hills or mountains to surmount or wind around, [it] enjoys a level stretch of steel from city to city..."[57] If a Bardic citizen is in a real hurry, however, he can bypass the Viaduct Railway and journey by Aerial Ship, an airplane propelled by magnetic energy which can "actually circumnavigate the planet in about two hours, flying through space at the tremendous rate of ten thousand miles per hour."[58]

Outside the confines of the various Bardic cities, Milltillionaire-financed technology has gone a long way in taming nature. As indicated earlier, all "civilized" inhabitants of the Bardic State have foresaken the countryside for the geometrical perfection of the cities. But the now uninhabited countryside is nevertheless brought into the service of the state. It is "devoted exclusively to State Agriculture and Horticulture, Gardens and Parks."[59] There is very little need for direct human contact with the land at these Horticultural

centers; the tasks of sowing, cultivating and harvesting are
performed by sophisticated automation:

> by all potent power of electricity, man is now able to
> convert an entire continent into a tropical garden at
> his pleasure. The gardens are manipulated by vast
> automatic machines, but requiring the pressure of a
> knob to translate their immobility into instantaneous
> and incessant action... Thuswise is the soil tilled
> and drilled automatically in a moment of time; thus
> all vegetable produce is harvested...[60]

In addition to fully automated agricultural techniques,
Bardic science has also elaborated a method whereby the weather
can be controlled. The "Science of Calorification and
Refrigeration" has provided means to both cool tropical
environments and warm frigid ones: "By Calorification of a
Calorifico-Electric Ether...frigid climes [are] rendered
temperate and tropical ad libitum. ...Even the tropic seas may
be frozen at our pleasure by permeating the waters
with...irresistible [Refrigeration] Element."[61] Moreover, the
amount of rainfall is as much within the power of the Bardic
State's science as is the temperature. It is "not only able to
produce rain, as the incipient rainmakers of yore anticipated,
but what is more, to prevent showers deluging us when their
advent is undesired."[62]

Along with Hovorre's description of psycho-omni-magnetism,
the "science of calorification and refrigeration" might be
dismissed, as one commentator puts it, as the fantastical
"daydream of one who found his own world wanting, but had no real
ability to change it."[63] Once again, however, I would suggest
that such an interpretation misses the more significant meaning
behind the description. The final conquest of nature, obviously
enough, promises to once and for all eliminate scarcity while
enthroning man as master of the planet. But there is another

consequence, one that is of primary importance to the sane
society: the removal of any arena of experience which might
possibly   encourage   or   awaken   individuality,   passion   or
imagination.   Wilderness   areas,   natural   beauty   and   natural
awesomeness defy the utopian social engineer's desire to subject
all of existence to sanitized, geometrical blueprints.   To
"rationalize" wilderness is to completely destroy it, to so
subject it to human standards of orderliness and efficiency as to
fundamentally change its character.   But such an extensive
project has never been imagined by even the most sanguine of
utopian authors.   The second best but more manageable strategy
is to so mechanize society's relationship to nature as to expose
fewer and fewer individuals to its pernicious influence.   The
Bardic State has succeeded in this enterprise to a remarkable
degree.   Earth's inhabitants live in antiseptic but geometrically
beautiful and maximally efficient cities, protected not only from
wilderness areas but even from the weather. Moreover, even the
need for human contact with the soil for agricultural purposes
has   been   eliminated;   machines   have   assumed   traditional
agricultural tasks.   The physical distancing of humanity from the
disequilibrating effects of nature is but another way in which
the Bardic State in particular and the sane society in general
consolidates their hegemony.

     That social   stability and individual conformity are among
the chief values of the Bardic State is also clear from the fact
that   the   Milltillionaire's   system   encourages   "personal"
lifestyles that are most conducive to the   elimination of
individualism.   There exist, for example, laws which require
persons "to keep themselves scrupulously clean, well-dressed and
well-deported."[64]   In addition, "both men and women array
themselves in uniform styles, with the option of choosing the
color of cloth they prefer to wear."[65]   Violators of these

mandates are reckoned to be mentally unsound, incapable of "properly caring for themselves," and confined to hospital. This strict enforcement of dress codes is disconcerting enough; even more ominous, however, is the Bardic State's right to regulate "deportment"--i.e., social activity. But the progression makes sense. It is, after all, only a short step from the censor of "publicly unacceptable" dress to the censor of nonconformist and hence "dangerous" behavior.

It is true, as indicated earlier, that the Bardic State allows certain types of behavior which are unusual in nineteenth-century "utopian" novels. The inhabitants of the Bardic State, for example, are vegetarians: "our science and experience have discovered to us not only the superfluity of such meat dishes, but the utter beastliness and barbarism of indulgence in a meat or fish dish."[66] They practice "free love" and public nudity, and no one in the society is "shocked or abashed, or shy"[67] about such activities. And they have dropped Christianity as the predominant faith, replacing it with a sort of "Bardic" deism which claims that god is "Pure Love"--or, one suspects, magnetism.[68] But these idiosyncracies have become institutions within the context of the Bardic State. Instead of challenging the status quo, they represent it; as a result, conformity to them is conformity to the system.

In point of fact, there is very little dissatisfaction or manifestations of frustrated individualism within the Bardic State as a whole. The Milltillionaire's "benevolent" despotism has eradicated scarcity, perfected science and eliminated international conflict. In addition, the application of psycho-omni-magnetic techniques to either single persons or groups of people allows the State to "persuade" dissidents of the error of their ways. Consider Hovorre's description of the

Bardic State's treatment of "criminals":

> we have also disposed of all Prisons, and Insane
> Asylums... We perceive that the so-termed "criminal"
> is rather mentally diseased, and labors under a
> temporary illusion which leads him to commit an
> abnormality, and accordingly we place him in the Mental
> Hospital where he receives philanthropic treatment,
> being omni-magnetized by his physician, until brought
> back into his normal condition of being, when the
> patient naturally feels very grateful for the service
> rendered him,..and leaves the Hospital a truly
> reformed man.[69]

Here the ultimate technique for encouraging social
conformity--i.e., for "deporting" oneself correctly--has been
perfected. Anti-social behavior is an illness for which there is
a prescribed course of treatment: omni-magnetism. The
implication, of course, is that "patients" can be omni-magnetized
against their wills, since contrariness under such circumstances
is itself undoubtedly symptomatic of the presence of disease.
Angry, frustrated and frightened attitudes, then, are
trivialized, dismissed as mere symptoms of illness. Instability,
on either a social or an individual level, is an indication of
disease, not of oppressive social conditions.

In a word, the entire institutional and value structure of
the Bardic State is directed towards the maintenance of maximum
stability and efficiency. As Hovorre's Bardic narrator puts it,
"Today we have no waste and no opportunity for it allowed. In
verity all our departmental affairs of State, thus essentially
embody, and are regulated by the beautiful Economy and Harmony of
a Bardic State."[70] It might be objected that the achievement of
"Bardic Harmony" has been paid for with the loss of individual
identity and integrity. But that is a criticism for which
Hovorre would have very little sympathy. For him, as for all
other mainstream nineteenth-century "utopian" authors, the

interests of the state and the interests of the individual
coincide. To stabilize the social structure necessarily improves
the individual. And the stabilization of the former,
paradoxically, demands the elimination of the latter.

Nevertheless, it can scarcely be denied that Hovorre
considers his blueprint of the future perfect society to be
genuinely reformist in nature, representing a radical departure
from the social structure and value assumptions of the nineteenth
century. In point of fact, however, the portrait of the Bardic
State seems to display more continuity than dissonance with
Hovorre's own time. The valuation of capitalism is still very
much present. The only difference is that a shift has been made
from competitive to monopoly capitalism, with the cartel of the
Milltillionaire representing what is, quite literally, the
monopoly of the future. Nor are class divisions really erased in
Hovorre's fantasy; instead, they simply change their character.
In the Bardic State, there is the ruling and owning class--which
is comprised of the Milltillionaire and no one else--and the
nonowning, laboring class, made up of everyone else. The
fundamental acceptance of capital as the necessary condition for
social improvement, along with the inevitability of social
classes, places Hovorre's fantasy squarely in the nineteenth
century--notwithstanding his defense of free love and public
nudity.

Hovorre's intoxication with technological wherewithal and
instrumental reason as the saviors of society likewise reveals
his "utopia" to be a sane society ideology. Perhaps in no other
putative utopia of the period does the notion that "bigger is
better" come through more clearly. All of the engineering and
technological accomplishments of the Bardic State are larger
than life: 15,000 foot high railroads, cities with

accommodations for a quadrillion souls, skyscrapers that hold one million residents, and so on. The immensity of these achievements only underscores the importance that Hovorre attributes to technology's role in perfecting society. He never seems to have reflected upon whether or not one million people would want to live with one another in the same building, or if the human imagination could flourish separated from wilderness and nature. For him, the technological ability to change necessarily entails the psychological readiness to change. Individual desires follow technique, not the other way around.

This leads us to the final point, namely Hovorre's desire to establish a failsafe society, a social structure which is stable at any cost. Hovorre, like so many of the other nineteenth-century advocates of the sane society, had a very limited notion of social stability. In the final analysis, stability means stasis, nonmovement, tradition. Individuals who compose a society's populace should be encouraged in placidity, equilibrium and nonindividualism, precisely because such characteristics are seen as contributing to the maintenance of the established social order. Stability is never perceived as dynamism, either by Hovorre or his "utopian" colleagues. Although dynamism might encourage growth and confidence in a society, thereby "stabilizing" it against the dangers of dryrot, it might also lead to changes in the power structure. And that is a _truly_ revolutionary agenda that Hovorre, no less than the other nineteenth-century disguised ideologues, fails to defend.

Alexander Bogdanov's Red Star

Bogdanov's Red Star was first published in St. Petersburg in 1908, reissued in Petrograd and Moscow ten years later, and once again in 1922. It was easily one of the most influential novels in Russia during the 1920s. Popular demand for it was so great that it was reprinted at least five times in the Soviet Union immediately after the Revolution, with a circulation estimated in the hundreds of thousands. Soviet critics praised it as the "first utopia embellished with proletarian pathos," and although Lenin disliked the work for what he perceived as its "Machian" tendencies, the Russian reading public obviously concurred with the critics.[71] Moreover, non-Russian readers likewise appeared to agree. Red Star was well received outside of the Soviet Union, being translated into several languages--including Esperanto--in the early 1920s.

It is true that Red Star's popularity as a vision of the future social order peaked only after the Great War of 1914-1918. Nevertheless, the novel reflects the ideals and values characteristic of nineteenth century sane society utopias. It does so, moreover, in a manner that is especially interesting, inasmuch as it explicitly claims to be a socialist utopia. As I shall show, however, the novel's emphasis upon technologization, social stability and individual conformity, in addition to its espousal of the doctrine of Social Darwinism, clearly reveals it to be a disguised apology for the same ideological status quo defended by Bellamy and Hovorre.

Red Star's author, a physician whose real name was Alexander Alexandrovich Malinovski (1873-1928), intended his novel as a concrete illustration of a theoretical worldview which he called "tektology." The idea, which Bogdanov adopted from

Ernst Haeckel, held that all of reality could be subsumed under a general natural science that would clarify the regulatory processes which hold for both animate and inanimate matter. Bogdanov, like Haeckel, Helmholtz and the nineteenth-century intelligentsia in general, was struck by what he took to be the systematic analogies between mechanistic explanations of natural phenomena and sociological explanations of interpersonal relations. As an individual concerned with social reform, Bogdanov's primary goal was to contribute to the formulation of this united science by discovering how natural law determined and regulated social relations. Such a discovery, Bogdanov felt, would represent the first step towards the ultimate rationalization of society. Accordingly, one of the purposes of Red Star, with its elaborate blueprint of social stability, was to provide Bogdanov with a nontechnical outlet for his ideas.[72]

The plot of the novel, like most utopian plots, is simple. The main character, a Russian Marxist revolutionary named Leonid, is chosen by an advance patrol of Martians to accompany them back to their planet. He is "to serve as a living link between the human races of Earth and Mars"[73] by familiarizing himself with the Martian way of life and then relaying it to his fellow earthlings. Leonid in particular has been selected because of his accomplishments as both a scientist and a socialist--the dual outlook most in keeping with the values and worldview of the Martians.[74] The main body of the novel deals with Leonid's stay on the "red star," thereby affording the reader a detailed picture of Martian society.

Notwithstanding the fact that Bogdanov's novel appears for the most part to follow conventional utopian standards, it does have two unusual features. First, the vision of the perfect society is not located in earth's future. Instead, the perfect

society   is   situated   on   a   planet   different   from   but
contemporaneous with earth. Bogdanov's purpose in locating his
sane society on Mars is identical, however, to the goal of those
utopian authors who place theirs in a distant future on earth.
By locating the good society "nowhere," the suggestion is that it
could actually occur "anywhere."

More interestingly, Bogdanov's picture of the future sane
society is self-avowedly socialist. We saw earlier that Bellamy,
without explicitly saying as much, envisioned his new Boston to
be socialist in structure. But we also saw, notwithstanding
Bellamy's intention, that his new order was patterned more along
the lines of state capitalism than socialism.   A similar
criticism can be made of the Martian social order in Red Star.
Although claiming   to be the   concrete   exemplification of
"scientific socialism," the Martian society in fact resembles one
in which state control rather than collective ownership is
predominant. We have in this particular work, then, a most clear
illustration of how nineteenth-century "utopian" novels tended to
disguise their ideological character by self-deceptively posing
as blueprints for reform.

All nineteenth-century   "utopian" visions of   the sane
society play up the importance of applied science for the
achievement and maintenance of the stable social structure. But
Bogdanov's Red Star carries the tendency further than most. Like
Bacon's New Atlantis, the Martian society described in Bogdanov's
novel revolves around technological science.   Values, both
ethical and aesthetic, are based upon the science of engineering,
and the most admired members of the Martian society are likewise
engineers, technicians and applied scientists.

Needless to say, the Martian science to which Leonid is
introduced far surpasses that of nineteenth-century earth. Space

travel, of course, is a _fait accompli_ for the red planet. It has been made possible through the discovery of an anti-gravitational substance which the Martians call "minus-matter." As one of Leonid's hosts explains to him,

> Our society is far ahead of the academic world [of earth] in many questions. We knew about radioactive elements and their decay long before Curie and Ramsay, and our analysis of the structure of matter has come much further than theirs. We foresaw the possible existence of elements that are repelled by the planetary bodies and subsequently succeeded in synthesizing this minus-matter, as we briefly designate it. After that it was easy to develop and implement technical applications for the discovery--first, flying machines for movement within the atmosphere, and the vehicles for travel to other planets.[75]

The discovery of this minus-matter element, and of its synthesis into "a liquid which is repelled by the bodies of the solar system,"[76] has enabled the Martians to construct vast fleets of airships which explore the solar system and increase their stores of both knowledge and raw materials (in the form of ores and minerals). These spaceships, known as "etheronephs," are representative of the overwhelming control of nature which Martian science has bestowed upon its practitioners. Their capacity to circumnavigate the heavens at amazing velocities is testimony to the merits, so Bogdanov thinks, of a society based upon the advancement of instrumental reason.

A description of the etheroneph will illustrate more specifically the command over the forces of nature which Martian science has made possible. An etheroneph is "almost spherical, being flattened at the lower end rather like Columbus's egg. Such a shape, of course, provided for the greatest volume with the least amount of materials and the smallest cooling surface. The etheroneph was...made mostly of aluminum and glass."[77] This description of the structure of the etheroneph is overshadowed,

however, by Bogdanov's meticulous explanation of how the airship
works:

> The motive power of the etheroneph is provided by a
> certain radioactive substance which we can obtain in
> great quantities. We have discovered a method of
> accelerating its decay by hundreds of thousands of
> times. This is done in the engine by means of certain
> fairly simple electrochemical processes which release
> an enormous amount of energy. As you know, the
> particles of decaying atoms fly apart at a speed tens
> of thousands of times greater than that of an artillery
> shell. When these particles are allowed to issue from
> the etheroneph in only one direction, that is, through
> a passage whose walls they cannot penetrate, the entire
> craft is propelled in the opposite direction.   Thus it
> is the same principle that operates in a recoiling
> rifle or artillery piece. You can easily calculate
> that in accordance with the well-known law of kinetic
> energy, a tiny fraction of a milligram   of such
> particles per second is quite sufficient to give our
> etheroneph its evenly accelerated movement.[78]

Although the etheroneph is without doubt one of the most
dramatic technological achievements of the Martian society, it
is by no means unique. Technological knowhow has also resulted
in the construction of beautiful cities, in which pollution and
overcrowding have been eliminated; in the advancement of medical
arts, which have pushed back death and the infirmities of old
age; in the perfection of mining techniques, whether on the solid
crust of Mars or the volatile, molten surface of Venus; and in
the general conquest of the recalcitrant forces of nature.

This last technological achievement is significant. Recall
that one of the key characteristics of the nineteenth-century
sane society (and, indeed, of Bacon's seventeenth-century one) is
its hostile attitude towards nature.   There is the conviction
that there is a struggle to the death between humans and the wild
which must be fought continually by man with all the
technological contrivances at his command. Natural riches must

be violently grasped from intransigent nature. Wilderness area, with its lack of planned precision and geometrical rationality, must be eradicated lest it serve as an incentive to instability and individualistic behavior. And human beings (or, in Bogdanov's case, Martians) must be urbanized in protective, antiseptically unnatural cities.

This mixture of fear and hostility towards nature is representative of the Martian temperament. The Martian populace is convinced that if it ever lowers its guard, wilderness will claim back the territory which has been wrested from it; consequently, constant vigilance is necessary. As one of the Martian engineers tells Leonid, "True, peace reigns among [us], but there can be no peace with the natural elements."[79] Indeed, the very depletion of natural resources, as the result of overmining, is considered to be yet another assault on the part of the wild upon the sovereignity of man. As the Martian engineer goes on to say, "Even a victory over such a foe can pose a new danger.   During the most recent period of our history we have intensified the exploitation of the planet tenfold, our population is growing, and our needs are increasing even faster. The danger of exhausting our natural resources and energy has repeatedly confronted various branches of our industry."[80] When Leonid rather naively suggests birth control as an answer to the decreasing deposits of natural resources, the Martian is incredulous. "Check the birth rate?" he asks.

> Why, that would be tantamount to capitulating to the elements. It would mean denying the unlimited growth of life and would inevitably imply bringing it to a halt in the very near future. We can triumph as long as we are on the offensive, but if we do not permit our army to grow, we will be beseiged on all sides by the elements, and that will in turn weaken faith in our collective strength, in our great common life.   The meaning of each individual life will vanish together

> with that faith, because the whole lives in each and
> every one of us, in each tiny cell of the great
> organism, and each of us lives through the whole. No!
> Curbing the birth rate is the last thing we would
> resort to, and if it should happen in spite of us, it
> will herald the beginning of the end.[81]

The perceived need to conquer nature because it poses a threat
to the unity of the social organism, the insistence that to make
any concessions to ecological considerations would represent a
capitulation to the enemy, the faith that the individual's
identity is bound up with that of society's--these are typical
elements which make up the sane society's characteristically
antagonistic relationship to nature.

The technological advances which have been achieved in the
fields of mining, space science and health care are paralleled by
those in the industrial realm. Martian science has fully
rationalized both the manufacture and distribution of goods. The
former function is taken care of by a largely automated,
maximally efficient production process which supplies enough
commodities to eliminate scarcity on the planet's surface. The
latter process is carried out through a central authority which
determines both consumer and production quotas.

The Martian sane society produces its goods in vast factory
complexes whose very physical structures suggest the somewhat
incongruous traits of crisp efficiency and holiness. The
description of one of these factories, for example, could just as
well be assigned to a temple. Given the veneration in which the
sane society holds technological expertise, Bogdanov's almost
religious description is, perhaps, not accidental: "It consisted
of five huge buildings arranged in the form of a cross. They
were all identically designed, each of them having a transparent
glass vault supported by several dozen dark columns in a slightly

elongated ellipse.   The walls between the columns were   made of
alternating sheets of transparent and frosted glass."[82]

    The actual working of the machines within the factory is as
beautifully precise as the architecture of the buildings.   These
machines practically run themselves.   Martian labor power   is
required only to read gauges, check pressure points, and so on.
The mechanical production process is so efficient that the
average factory laborer's workday is from one and a half to two
and a half hours.[83] There is, quite literally, no need for
nonmechanical--i.e., inefficient--labor in the Martian workplace.
Indeed, Bogdanov's description of the workings of the factory
machines is almost that of a living, independent creature:

> The   factory was   completely free   from   smoke,   soot,
> odors, and fine dust. The machines, flooded in a light
> that illuminated everything yet was by no means harsh,
> operated steadily and methodically in the clean fresh
> air, cutting, sawing, planing, and drilling huge pieces
> of iron, aluminum, nickel, and copper. Levers rose and
> fell smoothly and evenly like giant steel hands. Huge
> platforms moved back and forth with automatic
> precision.   The wheels and transmission belts seemed
> immobile. The soul of this formidable mechanism was
> not the crude force of fire and steam, but the fine yet
> even mightier power of electricity. When the ear had
> become somewhat accustomed to it, the noise of the
> machines began to seem almost melodious, except, that
> is, when the several-thousand-ton hammer would fall and
> everything would shudder from the thunderous blow.[84]

    The maximized efficiency of the production process is
worthless, however, unless it has been coordinated with an
equally efficient method for determining production quotas.   The
Martian economy has established a centralized agency to deal with
the determination of societal needs, projection of kinds and
quantities of produced goods, and the ultimate distribution of
labor tasks.   This agency is the "Institute of Statistics."   As
one of Leonid's Martian hosts explains to him,

> The Institute of Statistics has agencies everywhere
> which keep track of the flow of goods into and out of
> the stock-piles and monitor the productivity of all
> enterprises and the changes in their work forces. In
> that way it can be calculated what and how much must be
> produced for any given period and the number of
> man-hours required for the task. The Institute then
> computes the difference between the existing and the
> desired situation for each vocational area and
> communicates the result to all places of employment.[85]

It is significant that the Institute of Statistics is
concerned with the supervision of both production quotas and
labor assignments. In Bogdanov's sane society, as in all others,
the ultimate goal is to assign arithmetical values to human
activity, values that can then be factored into the clocklike
social machine. There is never any suspicion on Bogdanov's part
that the reduction of living individuals to the status of
anonymous machine parts is either offensive or in any significant
way antithetical to the happiness or well-being of the populace.
For Bogdanov, no less than for other nineteenth-century
"utopian" authors, the happiness of the individual is guaranteed
by the stability of the social structure. The latter serves as
both the necessary and sufficient condition for the former. And
social stability, in turn, is measured by the degree of
efficiency and conformity, on all levels, that exists within the
community.

The sane society portrayed in Red Star is further stabilized
by its de-emphasis of individualism--a characteristic, as we have
seen, shared by Bellamy's Looking Backward and Hovorre's
Milltillionaire, as well as all other mainstream utopias of the
nineteenth century. Just as social engineering eliminates
irrationalities in the macro-structure, so operant conditioning
eliminates irrationalities on the micro, personal level. Martian
children, for example, are raised collectively in "Children's

Colonies." They are dressed identically, regardless of sex, rewarded for behavior which conforms to public standards, and taught to identify their own good with the general good. One of the most important functions of the Children's Colonies is the eradication of individualistic tendencies, which are by and large considered to be instances of atavistic behavior. As the director of one of these state-supervised nurseries assures Leonid, "The process whereby most children in the intermediate and upper age-groups establish their self-identity often assumes vaguely individualistic forms. The approach of sexual maturity at first intensifies that element even more. Not until adolescence is the social environment [i.e., the conditioning of the Children's Colonies] finally able to conquer the vestiges of the past."[86]

The schooling in conformity which young Martians receive at the Colonies is reflected in the values which inform social relations in general. The general Martian sentiment is that the society is of more importance than the individual and that the only memory which should live on after an individual dies is the impersonal one of his achievements, rather than his personality or name. Even Martian commemorative monuments are dedicated only to important events, not to great individuals.[87] This point is brought home when Leonid is rebuked by one of his Martian friends for referring to Menni, one of Mars' greatest engineers, as a "genius" whose fame will live forever.

> I find your expressions rather vague and even
> incorrect. Every worker is a creator, but what does
> the creating is mankind and nature. After all, Menni
> had at his disposal the experience amassed by preceding
> generations and contemporary researchers, and he based
> each step of his work on that experience. Nature
> provided him with the raw materials and germs of his
> ideas, and the struggle between man and nature
> furnished the necessary stimuli. A man is an

individual person, but his work is impersonal. Sooner
or later he will die and take his joys and suffering
with him. His accomplishments are his lasting
contributions to life, and life will go on developing
forever. In this respect there is no difference
between workers. The only inequality is a quantitative
one determined by how much they have experienced and
how much they leave behind them.[88]

When Leonid remonstrates, arguing that society can benefit from a
remembrance of its great dead, his Martian interlocutor replies,

A persons's name is preserved as long as those who knew
and lived with him are still alive. But mankind needs
no dead symbols of an individual once he is no more.
Our science and our art preserve impersonally the
collective accomplishments of all. The ballast of
names from the past is useless to the memory of man.[89]

The Martian position, it must be admitted, is nothing if
not consistent. If individuals are defined primarily by virtue
of the functions they perform within the societal machine, it is
quite natural that their personal biographies would be of little
use or interest to posterity. In the sane society, anonymity is
a virtue. Concentration upon the achievements of particular
individuals is likely to lead to disequilibrating,
individualistic tendencies, to a psychological distancing on the
part of the subject from society. And such a distancing is
perceived as an unhealthy move towards inefficiency.

The Martian society's institutionalized emphasis upon
individual conformity and social stability (which, of course, are
identical in the context of a sane society) has its roots in the
red planet's centuries-old struggle to eliminate "capitalist"
greed, fruitless competition and aggression. Mars, thousands of
years earlier, had possessed a competitive social structure and
value system which stressed individualism paralleling that of
Leonid's earth. The advent of evolutionary science convinced the
Martian populace, however, that the ultimate perfection of both

society and the species entailed the deliberate instigation of a concerted program of social engineering that would eliminate the irrationalities inherent in the old system. This "revolutionary" blueprint for the future included the centralization of economic authority, the institutional discouragement of individualism and, ultimately, the inforced identification of private with public interests. It is precisely this portrait of society which Bogdanov misleadingly describes as "communism." It is, of course, more accurately labeled "statism."

The transition from an individualistic, competitive society, in which scarcity and economic equality abound, to one which is supposedly more just and rational, is one which the Martians consider to have been inevitable, dictated by the laws of social as well as biological evolution. Accompanying the change in the social structure has been the evolutionary "progression" of the species. Individuals are physically healthier, mentally superior and morally more sophisticated than either their Martian ancestors or their earthling contemporaries. Leonid, for example, discovers that the average Martian's power of concentration and brute physical strength are far superior to his own, and realized that the difference is because of the evolutionary gap between the Martian and human species. The Martian race, moreover, has eliminated a great deal of physiological diversity so far as facial and bodily appearance is concerned. Institutionalized programs of eugenics and euthanasia have tended to erase physionomic variability to such an extent that Leonid has difficulty in distinguishing between Martian genders. This similarity in physical appearance, coupled with an identity in wearing apparel, serves as a graphic symbolic representation of the Martian valuation of conformity to the status quo.

In a word, then, the Martian sane society is one that values the qualities of conformity, stability and geometrical precision above all others. These qualities are not prized simply because they are perceived as being necessary predicates of the good society. They are also valued because of their "aesthetic" nature. To the Martian sensibility, nothing is more offensive that inefficiency, waste, or imprecision. As a result, those institutions and activities which best exemplify maximum utility, which most adequately concretize instrumental reason's ideals, are also reckoned to be the most beautiful. As one of the Martians explains to Leonid, "Powerful machines and their precise movements are aesthetically pleasing to us in and of themselves, and there are very few works of art which would fully harmonize with them without somehow weakening or dissipating their impact."[90] Architecture, for example, "means not only buildings and great works of engineering but also the artistic designing of furniture, tools, machines, and all other useful objects and materials."[91] Moreover, all poetry on the planet conforms to strict meter and rhyme; as one Martian explains,

> Regular rhythmicality seems beautiful to us not at all because of any liking for conventions, but because it is in profound harmony with the rhythmical regularity of our processes of life and thought. As for rhyme, which resolves a series of dissimilarities in uniform final chords, it is intimately related to that vital bond between people which crowns their inherent diversity with the unity of the delights of love, the unity that comes from a rational goal in work, and the unity of feeling in a work of art. Without rhythm there is no artistic form at all. If there is no rhythm of sounds it is all the more essential that there be a rhythm of images or ideas.[92]

What is true of the art of poetry is true for all Martian art forms. Beauty lies in precision and mathematical exactitude, a function which in turn reinforces social unity, cohesion and

utility. As one of the Martians say when asked by Leonid whether
Martian art permits deviation from functional perfection for the
sake of beauty, "Never... That would be false beauty,
artificiality rather than art."[93]

In spite of its claims to "socialism," then, Bogdanov's
sane society is very much within the mainstream of nineteenth-
century "utopian" thought.   Its self-proclaimed reformism is in
fact superficial.   It seems to make little difference, after all,
if one replaces a "capitalist" society which stresses individual
conformity, social engineering, instrumental reason, technocratic
authority and centralization of decision-making with a nominally
"socialist" one that defends the very same values.   Bogdanov's
Red Star does break in some ways with the value structure of the
nineteenth century; like Hovorre, for example, Bogdanov defends
more liberal sexual mores.   But given the preponderance of
conventional assumptions about the world and values that appear
only slightly disguised in the novel, the occasional apology for
free love comes across as both uninteresting and unimportant.
What is important for Bogdanov is showing how social and
interpersonal relations can be reduced to modes of explanation
borrowed from the natural sciences--or, in Bogdanov's
terminology, the "tektological" correlations between social and
natural phenomena. The implications of such a reductionism, and
the ideals of stability, maximum efficiency and utility which it
reflects, are clearly a part of the nineteenth century's sane
society ideology.

III

The sane society of the nineteenth century is, as I have
argued throughout this study, an ideological construct. While
claiming to be reformist if not outright revolutionary in scope,

it in effect mirrored and dramatized, in appealing, fictional
dress, the values and social theories of its day. It defended a
subtle class system. It worshipped instrumental reason and
technological knowledge because, in the final analysis, it valued
the wealth and power which these two tools produced. It claimed
as its final goal the ultimate scientization of society, the
extirpation of unpredictable, subjective qualities that might
lead to nonconformist behavior. Moreover, it argued that the
desubjectification of humanity was most conducive to the
"happiness" and "welfare" of the individual. It firmly defended
the notion that increasing rigidity of social controls would
result in the evolutionary perfection of both society and the
human race. Finally, it advocated an entire network of values
which, while claiming universal applicability, in fact was
classbound and properly applicable to only that class of
individuals with a vested interest in the "stabilization" of
conventional power structures.

All ideological devices are effective, to one degree or
another, in consolidating the hegemony of a period's established
knowledge. The extent of this effectiveness, in the final
analysis, is the degree to which they can retain their illusory
character--i.e., masquerade as objective, universal truths. The
sane societies of the nineteenth century are, perhaps, the most
successful perpetrators of this particular charade. They claimed
to be utopian in character, pointing to a vision of the ideal
society in which all human beings are supposedly fulfilled. They
also claimed to be harsh critics of their own time, condemning
what they took to be social injustices and offering as antidotes
their various social agendas. In point of fact, of course, the
sane society "utopias" fulfilled neither function. Their vision
of the future society was classbound, and their condemnations of
the nineteenth century was directed to only a few of its specific

features, not to its overall institutions. These institutions
were by and large reproduced in the very same novels which
claimed revolutionary status for themselves. The success of
these novels in bolstering the ideological structure of their
time, then, was quite successful. They ameliorated discontent
which arose as a result of the social institutions peculiar to
the century while subtly reinforcing the sanctity, the necessity
and the social agenda of those very institutions. In short, what
Bacon did in his New Atlantis for the seventeenth century was
done by the sane society utopias for the nineteenth.

I have tried to give an impression of the specific themes of
the sane society genre by examining three of them in this
chapter. As I suspect became increasingly clear, none of the
mainstream utopias are "good" works of literature. They display
very little originality in either plot or vision, and the
characters in them are often wooden and mannikin-like, leaving
the reader with an uneasy sense of lifelessness. The unnatural
hollowness of "utopian" characters can doubtlessly be chalked up
partly to the ineptitude of utopian authors. But most of their
lifelessness, I would suggest, is the logical consequence of the
sane society structure. How else could the inhabitants of a
fully scientized, completely objectified society, act? Deprived
of their individualities and reduced to the status of complacent,
happy drones, it is little wonder that they appear stiff, unreal.
In the final analysis, the sane society is concerned with the
consolidation of power structures, not with the fulfillment of
individuals. New Boston, the Bardic State, the Red Planet--all
ultimately point to the ideal of a mechanized society in which
human beings have neither roles nor purposes, notwithstanding the
fact that they claim to be visions of the perfect city of man.
The tragic irony, of course, is that in these cities of man,
there are no human inhabitants.

CHAPTER 5

THE LEGACY OF THE SANE SOCIETY

Pragmatism, in trying to turn experimental physics into a prototype of all science and to model all spheres of intellectual life after the techniques of the laboratory, is the counterpart of modern industrialism, for which the factory is the prototype of human existence, and which models all branches of culture after production on the conveyor belt, or after the rationalized front office.

Max Horkheimer, Eclipse of Reason

Progress in this new era will consist in the laborious writing, one by one, of hundreds of equations; in the experimental determination, one by one, of hundreds of the empirical constants contained in the equations; in the devising of practically usuable units in which to measure the quantities expressed by the equations; in the objective definition of hundreds of symbols appearing in the equation; in the rigorous deduction, one by one, of thousands of theorems and corollaries from the primary definitions and equations; in the meticulous performance of thousands of critical quantitative experiments and field investigations designed with imagination, sagacity, and daring.

Clark L. Hull, Principles of Behavior: An Introduction to Behavior Theory

I

I have tried to argue in this study that one of the most influential metaphors with which the modern era consolidated its identity was that of the "sane society." First given systematic expression by Francis Bacon in the seventeenth century, the sane society image, as we have seen, reached its zenith in the nineteenth-century utopian novel. The primary characteristic which the various sane societies of the period share is the assurance that social relations are susceptible to the same methodological approaches and mechanistic explanations used by the natural sciences in their examination of physical reality. Hand-in-hand with this reduction of social relations to mechanical models is the sane society's supreme valuation of instrumental reason--i.e., problem-solving technique--and its concomitant devaluation of "merely" speculative reason. The hope of the nineteenth-century "utopian" was that the mechanization of social relations, encouraged by the judicious use of instrumental reason and concretely represented by increasing technological expertise, would usher in a completely rationalized society. Economic scarcity, wastage of human and natural resources, social dissent, crime and illness would be irretrievably banished. The good life for all men would finally arrive.

This exemplar of the perfectly sane, mechanistic society proved as popular as it did in the seventeenth, eighteenth and nineteenth centuries because it directly reflected the interests and values of that period's ascendent economic class--the bourgeoisie. Consequently, as we have seen, it was an essential ingredient in the period's total ideological structure. The capitalist middle class made amazing strides in these three centuries towards cementing its socio-economic authority and intellectual purview, and the sane society images of both Bacon and nineteenth-century "utopian" novels mirrored them. As the scope of middle class influence increased in the modern era, the sane society metaphor likewise became more entrenched, until it hit its highest point in the nineteenth century, that period par excellence of bourgeois hegemony.

Both the era of middle class optimism and the pervasive

influence of the sane society motif upon the popular imagination crumbled in the wake of World War I. The cultural and political dominance of the European middle class suffered such blows from the Great War and the economic crisis which followed it that it never, according to some historians, fully recovered.[1] Moreover, the devastation was as much spiritual as it was material. The brutality of the war and the misery of the depression shattered the era's confidence that society was becoming more rationalized and hence drawing closer to a state of inevitable evolutionary perfection. The wave of cynicism and even nihilism that is clearly reflected in much of the artistic, literary and philosophical work of those years (as, for instance, in the Weimar Republic[2]) graphically illustrates the low premium to which the nineteenth century's exhuberant self-confidence--and, by implication, the ideological vision of the sane society--sank. Although a few sane society "utopian" novels appeared during this period, they were neither as popular nor as optimistic as their nineteenth-century predecessors. In fact, most had a hollow ring of desperate artificiality about them, as if their authors were frantically trying to recapture a vision which even they no longer fully believed in.[3]

Notwithstanding the fact that the Great European War shattered the nineteenth-century middle class's self-confident hegemony, the sane society vision has, to a certain extent, remained embedded within twentieth-century Western thought. It is certainly not as apparent as it was in the last century, nor is its popular influence as pervasive. But the goal of rationalizing social relations by subjecting them to the methodology of the natural sciences has remained an ideal in certain schools of contemporary social theory. I should like to conclude this study by examining this trend. I shall approach the subject indirectly, through a discussion of the work of two of the most influential critics of this contemporary emphasis upon the sane society exemplar: Max Horkheimer and C. Wright Mills. Horkheimer criticized what he took to be contemporary social philosophy's over-reliance on what I have here called instrumental reason; Mills focused upon what he characterized as the "abstracted empiricism" or "molecular analysis" of Anglo-American sociology. As will be seen, the criticisms of both men point to the fact that the modern era's ideal of scientizing human relations is still very much a theme in contemporary socioanalysis, even if its more dramatic popular appeal has been drastically reduced.

II

Horkheimer's Critique of Instrumental Reason

Max Horkheimer is one of the leading representatives of a movement which has come to be rather misleadingly known as the "Frankfurt School" of philosophy and social criticism. Horkheimer was the first director of the University of Frankfurt's Institute for Social Research, a think tank founded in 1931 which, at various times, included such thinkers as Theodor Adorno, Walter Benjamin, and Herbert Marcuse.[4] The so-called Frankfurt School examined the connections between socio-economic structures and forms of social knowledge. As such, it represented the first contemporary effort to take the issue of ideology seriously. It focused not merely upon an examination of the content of social knowledge in contemporary Western society, but also, more importantly, upon the genesis and practical consequences of these forms. Its purpose, then, was primarily to analyze the relationship between the material conditions and the normative and conceptual models of its day.

In his examination of different contemporary approaches to
the understanding of social relations, Horkheimer concentrated
upon those schools of thought which accept as their
methodological basis what he calls "formalized" reason.[5]
Although his choice of terminology is a bit confusing, it is
pretty clear that what Horkheimer means by "formalized" reason is
what I throughout this study have called "instrumental" reason.
According to Horkheimer, instrumental or formalized reason (I
shall use the terms interchangeably) "is essentially concerned
with means and ends, with the adequacy of procedures for purposes
more or less taken for granted and supposedly self-explanatory.
It attaches little importance to the question whether the
purposes as such are reasonable."[6] This intoxication with
"correct" methodology, which Horkheimer sees as characteristic of
contemporary physical and social science, follows from formalized
reason's assumption that reality is best understood as a realm in
which both physical and human relations can be reduced to
mechanistic models, expressed in quantifiable terms and
manipulated with mathematical precision. The ultimate goal of
this methodology is to supply an "objective" understanding of
reality which can be translated into utility-laden techniques.
Given the putative objectivity of this method, questions of value
or purpose are entirely beside the point. The only aim of
formalized reason is to provide the necessary conditions for the
dissection, classification and manipulation of both men and
nature. Speculation upon the long term value of such
methodological reductionism, from either a conceptual or a
socio-political perspective, is nonexistent. As far as
instrumental reason is concerned, the correct application of
methodology and its consequent improvement in both technique and
manipulation becomes an end in and of itself.

Horkheimer singles out neo-positivism and pragmatism as the two primary loci of the contemporary emphasis upon instrumental or formalized reason. For these two schools, "reason has come to...be regarded as an intellectual faculty of co-ordination, the efficiency of which can be increased by methodical use and by the removal of any nonintellectual factors, sucha as conscious or unconscious emotions."[7] Pragmatism, for instance, measures the truth of an hypothesis solely upon the basis of its "success," and in turn employs as its chief criteria for success the notions of probability and calculability. For pragmatism, "an idea, a concept or a theory is nothing but a scheme or plan of action, and therefore truth is nothing but the successfulness of the idea."[8] Neo-positivism, as a methodology in both the natural and social sciences, likewise rests upon a programme of organization, classification and computation of data, and accepts as its sole criterion of truth the possibility of verification. Assuming as it does that all of reality conforms to one unified and largely mechanistic worldview, its aim in the sociological arena is to eliminate any discussion of "meaningless" factors such as consciousness and emotion, and to substitute in its place an analysis of human behavior which is completely formal--i.e., mathematically objective. It is, as Horkheimer remarks, the philosophy of "a society that has no time to remember or meditate."[9]

There are several features of Horkheimer's formalized reason that remind one of the instrumental conceptual and methodological models of the sane society motif. First, and probably most obviously, the proponents of formalized reason see it as the only proper vehicle for the enrichment of either the natural or social sciences. Insisting as it does on a criterion of truth based upon pragmatic success and objective verification, formalized reason discounts as nonessential those phenomena which

do not readily lend themselves to quantification and immediate
utility. As such, it, like the modern era's instrumental
reason, has little patience for what it would describe as
nonsensical or inutile speculative thought. That which is real
can be reduced to mechanistic explanation. Everything else is
dismissed as ungrounded speculation about unimportant
epiphenomena.

Furthermore, Horkheimer's formalized reason is operational
from first to last--hence one of the reasons for its emphasis
upon "correct" methodology. Ultimately, its only purpose is "to
calculate probabilities and thereby to co-ordinate the right
means with a given end."[10] This emphasis upon operational
efficacy is especially obvious in the arena of applied science
and technology, in which the correctness of a given theory is
measured in terms of the inventions and new techniques to which
it gives rise. But, according to Horkheimer, instrumental
reason extends the criterion of utility to the activity of human
beings. No action which an individual performs is seen as either
an end or as valuable in itself. Rather, it is evaluated only in
terms of the consequences which it brings about. As such, "an
activity is reasonable only if it serves another purpose, e.g.
health or relaxation, which helps to replenish [an individual's]
working power. In other words, the activity is merely a tool,
for it derives its meaning only through its connection with other
ends."[11] This operational analysis of human behavior obviously
dismisses any particular idea of action which does not
immediately result in instrumentality. No given action is
better than another except insofar as it promotes utility. Those
ideas or actions which do not promote utility are viewed as both
irrational and a waste of time. Similarly, philosophical
speculation about normative issues is totally outside the
boundaries of scientific purview, and hence consignable to the

realm of nonsense. As Horkheimer says,

> According to the philosophy of the average modern
> intellectual, there is only one authority, namely,
> science, conceived as the classification of facts and
> the calculation of probabilities. The statement that
> justice and freedom are better in themselves than
> injustice and oppression is scientifically unverifiable
> and useless.[12]

Formalized reason as a methodology in the social and
behavioral sciences, then, reduces humans to objects whose
actions, both individual and group, are absolutely quantifiable,
and hence manipulatable. Just as the physical realm is best seen
as a complicated web of causal relationships capable of precise
determination, so human reality is likewise interpreted as
mechanistic and objective. Psychology is reduced to analysis,
prediction and control of individual behavior; sociology is
translated into statistical correlations of group behavior; and
ethics becomes little more than an analysis of the probable
instrumental efficacy of certain types of actions as compared
with others. The overriding theme in this reduction of the human
arena to physical explanation is control--the eradication of
disequilibrating tendencies on both the individual and the social
level. In fact, according to Horkheimer, the very possibility of
this control--or, in other words, the operational virtue of both
conceptual models and human activity--becomes the sole criterion
of meaning:

> The more ideas have become automatic, instrumentalized,
> the less does anybody see in them thoughts with a
> meaning of their own. They are considered things,
> machines. Language has been reduced to just another
> tool in the gigantic apparatus of production in modern
> society. Every sentence that is not equivalent to an
> operation in that apparatus appears to the layman just
> as meaningless as it is held to be by contemporary
> semanticists who imply that the purely symbolic and
> operational, that is, the purely senseless sentence,
> makes sense. Meaning is supplanted by function or

effect in the world of things and events.[13]

Finally, the formalized reason which Horkheimer sees as the characteristic feature of neo-positivism and pragmatism, like the conceptual models underlying the modern era's sane society exemplar, is ahistorical and abstract. It denies the possibility that knowledge is contextual, related to historical and cultural conditions. This is just another way of expressing the fact that formalized reason is not concerned with the genesis of knowledge so much as with its operational value in technique and its formal expression in system-building. But Horkheimer, like Mannheim before him, insists that knowledge arises from discrete material conditions, from the "life-process" of a particular cultural milieu. In "Traditionelle und kritische Theorie," for instance, Horkheimer says,

> The world which is given to the individual and which he must accept and take into account is, in its present and continuing form, a product of the activity of society as a whole. The objects we perceive in our surroundings--cities, villages, fields, and words--bear the mark of having been worked on by man.
>
> ...Even the way men see and hear is inseparable from the social life-process as it has evolved over the millennia. The facts which our senses present to us are socially preformed in two ways: through the historical character of the object perceived and through the historical character of the perceiving organ. Both are not simply natural; they are shaped by human activity.[14]

Why this contemporary emphasis upon formalized reason? Horkheimer draws a direct relation between the hegemonic capitalist mode of production and the sway of formalized reason. According to him, capitalism's emphasis upon technique and industrial advancement has led to a progressive disregard for noninstrumental speculation in both methodological and conceptual schemas. The streamlining of productive processes, which claims to provide the maximum in material efficiency, has resulted in an analogous streamlining of knowledge. As such, the formalized reason which characterizes both positivism and pragmatism, far from being in fact "formal" (i.e., abstract) is really a reflection of the contemporary era's socio-economic character. As Horkhemier says,

> Reason has become completely harnessed to the social process. Its operational value, its role in the domination of men and nature, has been made the sole criterion. ...Concepts have become "streamlined," rationalized, labor-saving devices. It is as if thinking itself had been reduced to the level of the industrial processes, subjected to a close schedule--in short, made part and parcel of production.[15]

This "streamlining" of ideas and methodologies, the disregard for their socio-historical foundations, is an example of what Georg Lukacs diagnosed as "reification" in History and Class Consciousness. Reification, according to Lukacs, is the essence of capitalist society. "Its basis is that a relation between people takes on the character of a thing and thus acquires a 'phantom-objectivity', an autonomy that seems so strictly rational and all-embracing as to conceal every trace of its fundamental nature: the relation between people."[16] As such, reification becomes "the central, structural problem of capitalist society in all its aspects."[17] This process of separating forms of knowledge and value structures from their genesis in discrete socio-economic conditions, and, furthermore, of bestowing upon them a life of their own which claims to be both ahistorical and absolute, is, of course, an ideological mechanism. That formalized or instrumental reason became the standard methodological exemplar in the modern era is, for both Lukacs and Horkheimer, directly related to the fact that the commodity structure of capitalism encourages such an assumption.

Horkheimer illustrates the point, for example, by arguing that
the popularity of pragmatism in the late nineteenth and early
twentieth century was influenced by the economic optimism which
permeated the period:

> Both Peirce and James wrote at a period when prosperity
> and harmony between social groups as well as nations
> seemed at hand, and no major catastrophes were
> expected. Their philosophy reflects with an almost
> disarming candor the spirit of the prevailing business
> culture, the very same attitude of "being practical" as
> a counter to which philosophical meditation as such was
> conceived.[18]

Just as materially based capitalist class relations assume
an absolute, independent character through the process of
reification, then, so do the conceptual standards of evaluation
which determine the nature of scientific technique and
philosophical thought. But the reification process does more
than abstract relations and ideas from their historical milieux.
It also imbues them with the same commodity status that
manufactured objects have.

> It is the price paid on the market that determines the
> salability of merchandise and thus the productiveness
> of a specific kind of labor. Activities are branded as
> senseless or superfluous, as luxuries, unless they are
> useful, or, as in wartime, contribute to the main-
> tenance and safe-guarding of the general conditions
> under which industry can flourish. Productive work,
> manual or intellectual, has become respectable, indeed
> the only accepted way of spending one's life, and any
> occupation, the pursuit of any end that eventually
> yields an income, is called productive.[19]

In analyzing the ideological nature of formalized reason,
one of Horkheimer's obvious criticisms is that the latter lacks
self-transparency. Since it is deceived about its own nature,
unable to fathom its own socio-historical roots, the conceptual
and evaluative worldview which it posits is likewise deceptive.

But Horkheimer, like all the thinkers of the Frankfurt School movement, is also concerned with what he sees as the inevitably corrosive effects of an overemphasis upon formalized reason. The consequences are twofold. First, it leads to the increasing solidification of class distinction and privilege within society; second it is ultimately incapable of sustaining the operational efficacy which it posits as its ultimate end.

As we have seen Horkheimer argue, formalized reason transforms knowledge into a commodity. Only those methodologies and intellectual inquiries which have immediate practical value are deemed worthwhile. "Mere" speculation--or, as Horkheimer puts it, "philosophical meditation"--is dismissed as an inutile waste of time and energy unless it leads to operational efficacy. In concrete terms, this valuation of instrumental reason usually means that more and more attention is focused upon technological research, which in turn necessarily leads to increasingly sophisticated (and, presumably, profit-generating) modes of production. Moreover, formalized reason in the intellectual sphere is but a reflection of the larger valuation of utility that gradually informs a capitalist society's values. Individuals immersed within the medium of a total ideology characterized by formalized reason accept the standard of pragmatic instrumentality and apply it to their personal activities as well as techno-industrial processes. Their and their peers' value as human beings comes to be measured in terms of concrete productiveness--with the latter's definition being circumscribed in quite predictable ways. This subjective acceptance of a commodity-based standard of appraisal on the part of society's individuals further augments the solidification of the capitalist mode of production and, of course, the material and intellectual hegemony of the capitalist class. The worldview and normative assumptions of the materially ascendent

capitalist class, in short, become reflected throughout all
levels of society, with the consequence that the members of the
dominant class enjoy increasingly higher levels of prosperity,
power and normative authority. Formalized reason's
"intellectual" justification of this state of affairs, then,
reveals itself to be ideological. As Horkheimer, in one of his
harsher moods, says, "the more the concept of reason becomes
emasculated"--i.e., the more it is formalized--"the more easily
it lends itself to ideological manipulation and to propogation of
even the most blatant lies."[20]

The consolidation of class power which formalized reason
both reflects and encourages is only one consequence of its
ideological nature. In addition, formalized reason is ultimately
incapable of sustaining its drive towards ever higher levels of
technological expertise. Horkheimer describes the situation like
this:

> The neutralization of reason that deprives it of any
> relation to objective content and of its power of
> judging the latter, and that degrades it to an
> executive agency concerned with the how rather than
> with the what, transforms it to an ever-increasing
> extent into a mere dull apparatus for registering
> facts. Formalized reason loses all spontaneity,
> productivity, power to discover and assert new kinds of
> content... Like a too frequently sharpened razor
> blade, this "instrument" becomes too thin and in the
> end is even inadequate for mastering the purely
> formalistic tasks to which it is limited.[21]

Horkheimer's point is that the straitjacketing of reason
into exclusively formalized, instrumental channels retards and
eventually atrophies the ability to speculate in a
nonoperational way. Moreover, it so ossifies already orthodox
canons of procedure as to destroy the likelihood of adaptive
flexibility in the face of future contingencies. This gradual

erosion of formalized reason's instrumental efficacy closely parallels Mannheim's insistence that ideological forms are ultimately incapable of actualizing their social agenda. Recall that Mannheim argued that ideological hegemony inevitably stifles the possibility of meeting new problems which arise in the social milieu and were not foreseen by the original ideological programme. This inability to adapt to changing situations lessens the probability of innovation within the societal matrix. Furthermore, it saps the vitality of the original ideological structure by institutionally discouraging flexibility and far-sightedness within the ranks of its own intelligentsia.

Formalized reason as a methodology, then, carries over into the twentieth century the ideological continuum of the sane society which served as the previous century's outstanding metaphor. In stressing the supremacy of an exclusively instrumentalist approach, it reduces social relations to quantifiable, mechanical terms, thereby desubjectivizing individuals and making them more malleable to the overall ideological programme. Moreover, the stress upon a commodity-based standard of evaluation, and its reification of both economic relations and human activities, encourages a sensibility which is most conducive to the perpetuation of the dominant capitalist mode of production. Concentration upon the means of technique, as Horkheimer says, has replaced a considered reflection upon the desirability of ends. Indeed, the two in effect have collapsed into one another. The production of technique is the end of formalized reason, since it is now identified with individual and societal well-being.

Mills' Critique of Abstracted Empiricism

The American sociologist C. Wright Mills, like Max
Horkheimer, was concerned about the tendency in contemporary
socioanalysis towards purely quantitative, mechanistic
interpretations of individual behavior and social relations.
Unlike Horkheimer, however, Mills never denied that there was a
place for such analysis in sociological studies. For instance,
in a 1953 article entitled "Two Styles of Social Science
Research,"[22] Mills argues that socioanalysis has need of two
different research programmes: the "macroscopic" and the
"molecular." The macroscopic approach deals "with total social
structures in a comparative way." It attempts "to generalize
types of historical phenomena, and in a systematic way to connect
the various institutional spheres of a society, and then relate
them to prevailing types of men and women."[23] The molecular
approach, on the other hand, is "characterized by its usually
smallscale problems and by its generally statistical models of
verification. ...Shying away from social philosophy, it often
appears as technique and little else."[24] When kept in proper
perspective, these two approaches complement one another.
Molecular analysis provides data and methodological criteria,
while macroanalysis attempts to synthesize this data into large
scale conceptual frameworks. Unfortunately, so far as Mills is
concerned, contemporary sociology has tended to "institu-
tionalize"[25] the molecular style at the expense of macroanalysis.
In The Sociological Imagination,[26] Mills calls this trend
"abstracted empiricism."

Abstracted empiricism is that approach to socioanalysis
which claims--and does so proudly--to eschew the assumption of
"substantive propositions or theories."[27] Instead of worrying

about the elaboration of theoretical frameworks, it devotes itself to the more "scientific" enterprise of collecting, correlating and classifying data. It avoids psychological or historical interpretations and exclusively favors statistical analysis. Its "results," according to Mills, "are normally put in the form of statistical assertions."[28] In point of fact, however, this is an understatement. Abstracted empiricism assumes that the only legitimate goals of socioanalysis are the collection of data and the methodological eradication of nonquantifiable variables.[29] It strives always for what might be called the "immaculate perception"--i.e., the observation and description of data unsullied by subjective, historical, normative or conceptual presuppositions.

The school of abstracted empiricism, like Horkheimer's formalized reason, insists that there is no distinction between the methodology and aims of the natural sciences and those of the social sciences. As Mills puts it, "the style of social research I have called abstracted empiricism often seems to consist of efforts to restate and adapt philosophies of natural science in such way as to form a program and a canon for work in social science."[30] Its practitioners "are dominated by concern with their own scientific status; their most cherished professional self-image is that of the natural scientist. In their arguments about various philosophical issues of social science, one of their invariable points is that they are 'natural scientists' or at least that they 'represent the viewpoint of the natural scientist'."[31] Precisely what the advocates of abstracted empiricism take to be the distinctive characteristics of the natural sciences is a bit uncertain; theory, after all, is not one of their strong points. All agree, however, that natural science is generally concerned with methodology rather than interpretations, and collection, correlation and prediction from facts rather than explanation.

The method of abstracted empiricism takes the public survey or opinion poll as its primary source of knowledge about individuals in social groups. Responses from carefully engineered questionnaires, when collected under appropriate controls and statistically analyzed, provide the researcher with the only reliable data about social norms, beliefs, aversions, sympathies, and so on, at his disposal. The ultimate goal of this "scientific" poll-taking is, quite simply, the collection and quantification of behavioral data. Theoretical interpretation of the data is unnecessary; even more to the point, it is distorting. Once again, the abstracted empiricist is not concerned with the "whys" of either social relations and beliefs or of individual activities, but only with the "whats." Pure, mathematically precise description, completely untainted by interpretation, is the ideal.

Advocates of abstracted empiricism claim that this emphasis upon strict quantification has "revolutionized" the arena of public opinion studies in particular, and socioanalysis in general. Mills cites a passage from Bernard Berelson which he believes is descriptive of "most studies in the abstracted empirical manner":

> ...[molecular analysis] spell[s] a revolutionary change in the field of public opinion studies: the field has become technical, specialized and institutionalized, "modernized," "group-ized"--in short, as a characteristic of behavioral science, Americanized. Twenty-five years ago and earlier, prominent writers, as part of their general concern with the nature and functioning of society, learnedly studied public opinion not "for itself" but in broad historical, theoretical, and philosophical terms and wrote treatises. Today, teams of technicians do research projects on specific subjects and report findings.

> Twenty years ago the study of public opinion was part
> of scholarship. Today it is part of science.[32]

Notwithstanding the sarcasm embedded in Berelson's comments, his
point is well taken: abstracted empiricism has streamlined the
explanation of behavioral phenomena by translating it into
exclusively "scientific" terms--with "scientific" here denoting
what Mills would label "molecular quantification."

Abstracted empiricism as a style in social science research
displays several characteristics which we have come to associate
with the ideological sane society exemplar. First and foremost,
it attempts to reduce individual and social behavior to the
mechanistic models of the social sciences. Subjective factors
are dismissed as "uninteresting"--i.e., non-quantifiable--
variables, with the consequence that persons assume the
one-dimensionality of physical objects. This emphasis upon
"objective" description also eschews a taking into account of
historical considerations when examining collected data. Like
Bacon's novum   organum and Horkheimer's formalized reason,
abstracted empiricism remains in the etherial realm of abstract,
ahistorical analysis. Behavior of both individuals and groups is
adequately captured by the simple documentation of responses to
survey questionnaries--questionnaires, by the way, which have
been formulated so as to eliminate the consideration of "merely"
subjective responses such as expressions of purposes or
intentions.

Abstracted empiricism, in short, has as its principle goal
the elaboration of a systematic mathematico-deductive method for
describing human behavior. This method, once fully worked out,
employs identical canons of investigation and procedure in all
areas of human inquiry. The moral, political, economic and
psychological behavior of human beings, just as much as the

motions of solid bodies, the rutting habits of chimpanzees and
the ebb and flow of ocean tides, are susceptible to identical
techniques of observation, correlation and classification. From
these classifications, generalizations about behavior are
derived. Abstracted empiricism's emphasis upon the formulation
of a set of rules suitable for all sciences, both "social" and
"natural," tends, then, to elevate method at the expense of
content. Indeed, the content which is eventually acknowledged as
acceptable is determined by the circumspect boundaries of the
methodological model. As Mills says, "there is a pronounced
tendency [on the part of abstracted empiricism] to confuse
whatever is to be studied with the set of methods suggested for
its study. ...Methodology seems to determine the problems."[33]

This infatuation with a methodology which precludes from
serious consideration nonquantifiable data underscores the
tendency towards desubjectification which abstracted empiricism
inherited from the sane society exemplar. In reducing all human
behavior to mechanistic terms, utterly devoid of "anthropo-
morphic subjectivisms," abstracted empiricism looks at human
beings as automatons whose behavior is, in the final analysis,
exhaustively describable, predictable and manipulative. Clark L.
Hull, the behaviorist psychologist quoted at the beginning of
this chapter, representatively expresses this sentiment in his
Principles of Behavior (1943). He argues that since the
difference between the natural and social sciences is merely "one
not of kind but of degree,"[34] the "scientific" investigation of
behavior, individual and social, moral and immoral, normal and
psychopathic, is generated from the same primary laws.[35] As a
means of training himself to adopt the proper attitude towards
his subject matter, the behavioral scientist is encouraged by
Hull to regard the "behaving organism as a completely
self-maintaining robot, constructed of materials as unlike

ourselves as may be."[36] The ultimate outcome of this method, claims Hull, will be a body of behavioral observations which has the precision of a mathematical science: "as a culmination of the whole, there would finally appear a work consisting chiefly of mathematics and mathematical logic."[37] Once again, the complete quantification of all societal relations and individual activity is clearly seen to be the exemplar towards which abstracted empiricism directs its energies.

It is not unusual that Hull, a behaviorist, should have been so enamored of the abstracted empiricist project. Like Watson before him and Skinner after him, Hull was not only concerned with an exhaustive quantitative description of individual and group behavior. He was also in search of a "scientific" technique of manipulation which would spell out, in precise, mathematical ways, strategies for weaning individuals away from behavioral "irrationalities." The way in which this weeding-out process would take place is through a "re-training" campaign, on a societal level, in which operant conditioning encourages individuals to act and think in ways that are conducive to their and the community's well-being. Spontaneity, whimsy, recalcitrant individualism, over-emotional responses and allegiances to metaphysical worldviews are the behavioral ills that plague the health of society. They inject nonpredictable and hence noncontrollable variables into the overall readout of human behavior, and as such represent loci of uncertainty that the "healthy" society simply cannot tolerate and still maintain its equilibrium. Their eradication will prepare the way for a new code of behavior in which the "scientific nonsense" of earlier moral norms is replaced by "quantitative behavioral symbolic constructs"[38]--i.e., a table of conditioned responses, calculated with mathematical precision, that are most conducive to social stability. When this happens, exults Hull, "the theory of value will cease to be a division of speculative philosophy and will become a <u>bona fide</u> portion of natural science."[39] The enterprise of "rationalizing" individual and social behavior is an immense undertaking, admits Hull, and will undoubtedly take several generations to achieve. But the social engineers who begin the task, even if they won't see its completion, will "have the satisfaction of creating a new and better world, one in which, among other things, there will be a really effective and universal moral education."[40]

Once again, then, we see a key feature of the sane society exemplar in contemporary abstracted empiricism. Human behavior, like the movements of physical bodies, can be described, given sufficient amounts of data, with absolute, mathematical precision. All ambiguity can be eliminated from the analysis because humans, no less than physical objects, are subject to a universally applicable mechanistic schema. Furthermore, just as the quantified formulation of these mechanistic laws allows physical scientists to harness natural phenomena in the service of humankind, so they also enable behaviorists to ultimately control human activity, on the individual and social level, thereby guaranteeing social stability. The quantificational analysis of abstracted empiricism, then, is really a vast "improvement" over the nonmathematical method of Bacon and his modern heirs. The latter were only able to envision the general structure of the future sane society; contemporary analysts, with their computed indices of data correlation and classification, can actually blueprint and construct it.

But the social research style of abstracted empiricism shares another characteristic with the sane society model. It is deceived about its own nature, suffering from the curious blindspot which we have seen to be characteristic of all ideological constructs. The opacity which riddles abstracted empiricism especially permeates its two fundamental claims: that it is a theory- and value-free methodology and that it is ahistorical, in no way reflective of existent socio-material conditions (after all, how can mathematics be contextual?). I shall examine each of these claims in turn.

Recall that abstracted empiricism claims to eschew speculative propositions and theoretical worldviews. Instead, its more pristine approach is that of "pure" description based upon a mathematico-deductive methodology. It allows itself to generalize about behavior only after it has collected and quantitatively analyzed immense amounts of observable data. This procedure of moving from the immaculate perception to general statements supposedly guarantees that both the method and, of course, its ultimate content, are value-free and theory-free. Speculative interpretations and the construction of macroscopic syntheses are left to the less precise (and less scientific) philosophers.

In point of fact, however, it is at least arguable that the objectivity which abstracted empiricism so prides itself upon is illusory. It appears that the methodology which the style endorses, and which in turn tempers the character of its subsequent content, rests upon a prior set of assumptions concerning the nature of reality. The latter is assumed to be such that it is best approached through an exclusively quantitative methodology. Moreover, it is taken for granted that particulars and relations can be subsumed under a mechanistic model which precludes variables such as chance and spontaneity. Reality thus acquires the character of an elaborate machine, an understanding of whose every part and motion is derivable from an analysis of perceived phenomena. Moreover, this machine metaphor is reckoned to be applicable on every level of experience, be it physical, social or psychological. Just as inanimate nature can be compared to a lawlike mechanism, so can social and psychological processes. The only problem is in inferring the general principles that serve as the guides for the translation of this regularity. This hidden set of assumptions about the nature of reality, then, raises doubts as to the "purity" of abstracted empiricism's description. In fact, it can be argued that the immaculate perception which serves as the method's ideal is itself, in fact, interpretative, determining in an a priori way the phenomena it will accept or dismiss.[41] In short, what is believed to be a theory-free foundation in fact reflects a full-blown worldview to which abstracted empiricism is passionately committed.

The theory-ladenness of abstracted empiricism's methodology is accompanied by an equally present set of hidden value assumptions. These values are particularly apparent in the blueprints for the sane society which behaviorists such as Hull formulate. The postulation of certain types of human activity as "irrational" and hence detrimental to psychological and social stability is not simply descriptive; it is also--and perhaps primarily so--evaluative. Social health is defined in terms of equilibrium, of predictable behavior, of the absence of idiosyncracy. The fact that such a definition of stability is interpretative, based upon a set of values which are not self-evident, can hardly be missed. It may indeed be the case that stability as the abstracted empiricists define it is most conducive to individual and social well-being. But within the context of their model it is a stipulation rather than an inferred generalization.

That the method of abstracted empiricism has proven to be

such a popular style in contemporary socioanalysis, notwithstanding the fact that its claims about its own nature are dubious, raises the suspicion that it performs a social function which validates its existence in the eyes of its champions. And, indeed, such seems to be the case. Abstracted empiricism's reduction of human beings to objects which are exhaustively explicable in quantitative terms and thereby manipulatable in the same way that physical phenomena are, is reminiscent of the commodity interpretation of human existence which Horkheimer discusses. The implication of the social agendas of Hull and other abstracted empiricists is that individuals are definitively described in terms of the instrumental efficacy of their actions. Human behavior which lends support to the "stability" of the societal matrix--i.e., behavior which has operational value--is "rational." All other behavior, lacking as it does the saving grace of instrumentality, is irrational, and calls for expungement through institutionalized operant conditioning. Human beings are thereby reduced to the level of social products that perform their functions either adequately or inadequately. And adequate performance, in this context, implies high levels of instrumentality and conformity to statistically-determined standards of achievement, and low levels of "inutile" speculation and individuality. It is precisely this reduction of individuals to the commodity level which is most conducive to the perpetuation of the capitalist economic structure and value system. As Mills point out, abstracted empiricism's emphasis upon statistical analysis and operant conditioning has served as a valuable catalyst in the perfection of administrative and "scientific" management strategies--so much so, in fact, that he wonders if the method is not "propaganda for a philosophy of technique and an admiration for administrative energy, disguised as part of the natural history of science."[42] His point is not that the total ideological structure of

contemporary capitalism has deliberately introduced a putatively
scientific methodology for the sole purpose of bolstering its own
hegemony.   The process, of course, is more subtle than that.
Rather, the thrust of his comment is that the over-emphasis of
"molecular" analysis on the part of contemporary social research
is a   reflection of the   general worldview and normative
assumptions which have arisen from the same material conditions
that serve as the foundations of the capitalist mode of
production.

    Harry Braverman, in his Labor and Monopoly Capitalism,
agrees   with   Mills'   claim   that   abstracted   empiricism's
intoxication with statistical quantification serves as a vehicle
for the perpetuation of the commodity evaluation of human
activity. According to him, the "animating principle" behind
the statistical analysis favored by scientific management
studies is

> the view of human beings in machine terms. Since
> management is not interested in the person of the
> worker, but in the worker as he or she is used in
> office, factory, warehouse, store, or transport
> processes, this view is from the management point of
> view not only eminently rational but the basis of all
> calculation. The human being is here regarded as a
> mechanism articulated by hinges, ball-and-socket
> joints, etc. ...In the system as a whole little is
> left to chance, just as in a machine the motion of the
> components is rigidly governed; results are
> precalculated before the system has been set in
> motion.[43]

Braverman goes on to cite an article in the British Journal of
Psychiatry entitled "Theory of the Human Operator in Control
Systems" which even more strikingly points to the relationship
between the social agenda of abstracted empiricism and the
capitalist production process. According to the article,

> ...as an element in a control system, a man may be
> regarded as a chain consisting of the following items:
> (1) sensory devices... (2) a computing system which
> responds...on the basis of previous experience... (3)
> an amplifying system--the motor--nerve endings and
> muscles... (4) mechanical linkages...whereby the
> muscular work produces externally observable
> effects.[44, 45]

The identification here of humans with production machines, and
of human productive activity with the shifting of mechanical
parts, is obvious. It is only a small step from defining an
individual in the production process as an absolutely
predictable mechanism to defining all individuals in all
processes similarly. And such, is abstracted empiricism's basic
assumption.

III
Technology and the Sane Society

For centuries human beings have dreamt of the ideal society--of
utopia. This almost eschatological vision of a community in
which plenty abounds and misfortune is but a memory from the
archaic past has taken on many guises throughout history.
Probably for as long as humans exist, the yearning for the
perfect society will continue. Whenever there is discontent with
the present, the human spirit will project into the future,
constructing imaginary commonwealths free from the uncertainties
and hardships of real existence.

This utopian propensity, this turning one's back on the
bleak present in search of a brighter future horizon, is both a
healthy and a necessary activity. As we saw in Chapter One, the
bona fide utopian mentality is not a neurotic flight from harsh
reality so much as an imaginative search for a more just and
felicitous way of life. Utopian constructs serve as exemplars to

be striven for, not dream worlds to be retreated into. They provide psychological succor as well as goals to be sought after, ideals to be attained. Frequently, what are today's concrete realities were yesterday's utopian speculations.

Sometimes, however, blueprints of what appear to be the good society are deceptive. Instead of offering visions of normative and socio-economic structures which are truly beneficial for all, they posit ones which in fact are most conducive to the welfare of but one group of individuals. These putative utopias encourage, in a disguised and hence quite effective manner, precisely the unjust and infelicitous institutions they claim to oppose. Instead of providing the catalytic exemplar by which to break with the present, they in effect sustain it; instead of providing outlets for genuine reform and innovation, they subtly reflect and reinforce the classbound status quo whence they originally arose. These putative utopias, moreover, unintentionally promote classbound instead of universal social agendas. They genuinely suppose themselves to be advocates of transcontextual values and social structures which promote the welfare of all men, and consequently are self-deceived as well as deceptive in their claims. They are, in short, ideological constructs.

In this study I have tried to trace the genesis and analyze the characteristics of one of these disguised ideologies--the "sane society" exemplar. This model, one of the most pervasive metaphors of the modern era, accompanied the rise of both the so-called "scientific method" and the capitalist mode of production which characterized the seventeenth, eighteenth and nineteenth centuries. Its fundamental ideal, as we have seen, was a community in which social relations have been "rationalized" by subjecting them to the methods and standards of the natural sciences. This scientization of psychological and social analysis led to the increasing desubjectification of human beings and an exclusive valuation of instrumental reason, both of which furthered the goal of behavioral manipulation in the workplace, the marketplace and the home. The postulation of conformity and instrumentality as the only barometers by which to evaluate human beings and their activities in turn helped to solidify the capitalist worldview's totalizing concentration upon improvement of industrial technique and commodity production. It is, consequently, no accident that the popularity of the sane society motif, as expressed through "utopian" novels such as Looking Backward and Red Star, hit its apogee in the nineteenth century, the era in which industrial expansion and capitalist development surged.

The heyday of popularity enjoyed by the sane society exemplar is over. The vision of transforming all of society into a well-ordered, completely manipulatable and more or less impersonal machine no longer captures the common imagination as it did in the three centuries preceding this one. Indeed, there appears to be a large current of cynical disdain for such a project today. Just one of the indications of this trend is the popularity in the last two generations of the so-called "dystopian" novel, in which the sane society exemplar is depicted in horrific, rather than felicitous, images.[46] Nevertheless, the legacy of the sane society temperament is still with us today. It has become such a part of our way of looking at the world that at least some of its values still find expression in our patterns of thinking as well as in the concrete activities into which we translate those patterns. In the intellectual world, the sane society exemplar has re-emerged, as I have argued in this chapter, in certain branches of philosophy and the social sciences. Pragmatism, positivism and the sociological method of abstracted empiricism are all grandchildren of the nineteenth century's ideal of a scientized society. But there are other indications that the present century has not fully shed the influence of the ideology--indications which, from an historical perspective, are as directly traceable to the sane society's "utopian" worldview as they are, from a concrete political and social perspective, frightening.

One of the more obvious of these is the contemporary era's troubled relationship with technology. I would like to end this study with some brief comments on this strangely mixed marriage. I do not intend these remarks to be definitive. In what follows, I am not so much arguing for a particular thesis as reflecting upon a curious state of affairs, one whose contradictory nature reflects the inconsistencies in its ideological sane society foundation.

The twentieth century has far outstripped the nineteenth in terms of industrial and technological accomplishments (and such a statement of fact is not meant to discount the astonishing revolution in technique that characterized the latter century). In a little over eighty years it has given birth to automation, the automobile, the diesel engine, airplanes, radio, television, computerized space travel and nuclear energy, to mention but some of its more dramatic achievements. The enthusiasm with which the nineteenth century regarded technology has mushroomed to almost unimaginable proportions in the present one. Ordinary language is filled with the jargon of high technology which would have been the exclusive domain of the specialist a bare generation ago. Grammar school children are considered to be less than educated if they have not been introduced to at least the basics of computer science. Financial endowments and grants, whether subsidized by public or private agencies, are increasingly funneled into the sciences at the expense of the humanities. Technology, in the opinion of most, is the wave of the future. It excels in getting things done, in solving concrete problems, instead of merely talking about them.

Furthermore, it can hardly be denied that there is a great deal of truth to this claim. Contemporary technology has created the possibility of eliminating world hunger once and for all and of raising the material standard of living of a major part of the planet's inhabitants to a level unimagined by even the most sanguine of nineteenth-century "utopians." Individuals live longer and healthier lives than their grandparents did. Diseased organs are increasingly replaced with transplanted substitutes, and the possibility of artificial organs eventually taking the place of less reliable organic ones is no longer a science fiction fantasy. Automated commodity production and the high-tech utilization of natural resources as fuel supplies have streamlined both the production and the distribution of goods and services. Communication technology has created and disseminated huge amounts of data and information, and even though the vast majority of it can never be absorbed by an individual in one lifetime, computerized memory banks have increasingly stepped in to process and store the information for convenient human consumption. And the list goes on and on. Entire libraries could be (and have been) filled with the accomplishments of twentieth-century science. The common conclusion is that technology in the contemporary era has changed the face of the world, has increasingly served as the material condition of the good life for all human beings.

But has it? We have paid a high price for the technological sophistication we now possess. Ecological disaster, widespread famine, two world wars, periodic genocide

facilitated by improved techniques of murder, worldwide economic
crises, the threat of nuclear annihilation--contemporary
technology has also given us these and other equally unsavory
gifts. In addition, philosophers, psychologists and sociologists
have created an intellectual industry out of analyzing the
phenomenon of alienation, or anomie, that appears to be such an
intrinsic characteristic of life in heavily technologized
societies. The fear that the individual is being submerged and
eventually drowned by the onslaught of technique is almost as
pervasive as the enthusiasm for technology. Alvin Toffler has
called this phenomenon "future shock." He argues that we have
become so fixated upon the growth of technology in all arenas for
its own sake that we have ignored issues dealing with both the
rate of technological change and the direction of that change.
The consequences of this blindspot are frightening: the more we
concentrate upon technology for its own sake, the faster
technological change accelerates, until we are finally left in a
state of bewildered, numb shock, unable to absorb or comprehend
the spiraling growth of novelty taking place around us. The fact
that this growth is usually pointed towards no goal save its own
acceleration only exacerbates the individual's experience of
being engulfed in a largely incomprehensible and uncontrollable
race towards the future. As Toffler says,

> Millions sense this pathology that pervades the air,
> but fail to understand its roots. These roots lie not
> in this or that political doctrine, still less in some
> mystical core of despair or isolation presumed to
> inhere in the "human condition". Nor do they lie in
> science, technology or legitimate demands for social
> change. They are traceable, instead, to the
> uncontrolled, nonselective nature of our lunge into the
> future. They lie in our failure to direct, consciously
> and imaginatively, the advance toward super-
> industrialism.[47]

The psychological effects of Toffler's future shock are

exacerbated by the ways in which technology has continued the project of desubjectification espoused by the sane society exemplar. The fundamental assumption of the contemporary era seems to be that the possibilities of human survival are enhanced by more technology rather than by less. As we saw earlier, this proposition is obviously true on one level: technique has opened the doors to longer, healthier lives for many individuals in western society. But mere survival is not the only issue at stake; the quality of survival is at least as important a consideration. And even though it can readily be acknowledged that contemporary technique has qualitatively raised standards of existence in some arenas, it is also arguable that it has lowered standards in others.

The commodity standard for evaluating human behavior which has characterized the capitalist ideology has, as we have seen, tended to translate all human activity into economic terms. Behavior which has utility is more valuable than behavior which does not. There is a tendency to reduce individuals to definitions based exclusively upon their instrumental roles in the productive monolith. This reduction, moreover, is gradually internalized by human agents; they accept as necessary society's commodity-based standards of evaluation, and apply them rigorously to both their own lives and the lives of their peers. They take as their own the values and worldview of the total ideology within which they are immersed and thereby consolidate the ideology's hegemony. This occurs in two ways: first, by adapting personae which are most conducive to the economic and political structures of classbound, commodity-based capitalist society; second, by acquiescing to the already sophisticated manipulative techniques which ensure that society's stability.

The alienating consequences of this desubjectification

process, of this transformation of humans into commodities, has
been analyzed by a number of commentators, beginning with Marx in
the nineteenth century.[48] What has not been so thoroughly
examined, however, is the effect that the contemporary era's
increasing emphasis upon technology has upon this already
alienated self-image. Perhaps in no other arena is the sane
society's legacy so disconcerting. Let me point out just one
example of what I mean.

The technologization of the planning, production and
distribution of commodities and services is a characteristic
feature of the present age. Work that traditionally required
human labor-power, either physical or mental, is now performed by
mechanical and computerized contrivances. The general reason for
this move from human to mechanical labor is, of course, the
assumption that when it comes to technology, more is better, with
the ideal of instrumentality being the gauge of "better." More
specifically, mechanical labor is in the process of ousting human
labor because the former is perceived to be more efficient, more
manipulatable and less expensive than the latter. It is
impervious to the subjective foibles that hamper the optimal
performance of human beings. Consequently, it is capable of
finally bringing to fruition the sane society's goal of a
smoothly run, error-free and completely desubjectivized social
structure. The nineteenth century's "utopian" dream of full
automation has become the concrete (and seemingly realizable)
agenda of the twentieth.

The effects of this trend towards total automation upon
commodity-humans is devastating. For generations, individuals
have absorbed the ideological structure's insistence that the
only acceptable standard of evaluation for their activities as
both private and social creatures is instrumentality. With the

advent of increasing automation, however, there are fewer
opportunities to fulfill this function. Moreover, those tasks
which still require human labor are considered to be atavistic
hangovers which will soon be eliminated by the technological
explosion.

The individual caught in this automative revolution has had
the ground swept out from under his feet. The activities by
which he has been taught to evaluate both his own and his peers'
existence have become obsolete. Added to the shock of seeing his
social role usurped by machinery is the knowledge that he can in
no way hope to effectively compete. If instrumentality is the
ultimate barometer for measuring personal worth, human power must
always run a distant second to mechanical power. The former will
simply never be able to match the latter's cost-effectiveness
and efficiency. When coupled with the psychological effects of
commodity-based alienation and future shock, contemporary man's
condition in the technologized West is far from enviable. True,
the chances of his physical survival have doubtlessly been
enhanced by the explosion in technique (although, of course,
there is always the shadow of ecological or nuclear disaster).
But the quality of his existence, robbed as it has been of the
function which he has come to associate with personal worth and
self-esteem (a function, keep in mind, which _itself_ was
alienating), can hardly be said to have improved. He has moved,
in short, from an already alienated existence to one which seems
absolutely gratuitous, completely superfluous. His dream of a
fully rationalized society has finally been achieved; and, to his
horror, there is no place in it for him. The fully actualized
sane society is one which reveals itself to be humanless. The
machine metaphor so valued by Bacon and the nineteenth-century
"utopias" is no longer a heuristic device. It is now reality.

It is a common platitude today to claim that technology is not to be blamed for its less than happy consequences, but rather that the fault lies in the way technology has been misused. It is not clear, however, that this distinction is as limpid as its advocates believe. How is one to separate the normative assumptions which promote the contemporary explosion of technology from the concrete results of the technology itself? The imperial overemphasis upon instrumentality as an end in and of itself, the reduction of all conceptual speculation to problem-solving strategies, and the assumption that no activity is of value unless it leads to an enrichment of technique and profit, are precisely the factors, one might argue, that define technology. It is difficult to imagine how contemporary technology achieved either its happy or its unhappy consequences without the underriding assumption that immediate instrumental efficacy is the ultimate standard of evaluation, valued as an end rather than a means. Moreover, it is equally difficult to understand why technological achievement is accepted as an end if it is not also identified with economic prosperity, psychological health and social stability. The cavalier disregard for both the rate and the direction of technological growth, which has tended to characterize the contemporary sensibility, points to the fact that technology in and of itself is valued as the panacea to societal ills. And this attitude, inseparable from the concrete accomplishments of technique, is a clear legacy from the sane society's goal of "scientizing" human and social relations, of reducing economic, psychological and moral behavior to mechanistic explanations.

Whether or not a "humanized" technology which takes individuals rather than its own proliferation as an end is possible, it seems clear enough that the contemporary era's intoxication with instrumental reason has created a monolith

which, although reckoned to be the vehicle by which the good
society will be inaugurated, is in fact a double-edged sword that
can slay as easily as save. Its contradictory nature is
expressed through the irrationality of its effects: on the one
hand, it facilitates wealth and prosperity for human beings; on
the other, it renders human subjectivity superfluous. These
incommensurate consequences may not be inevitable in a humanized
technology, but they are inseparable from one based on the
mechanistic remnants of the sane society ideology. Until (and
unless) we learn to recognize the deceptive and dangerous
features of that legacy, the actual achievement of the truly good
society--utopia--will remain as distant as the stars.

ENDNOTES

Chapter One

[1] Plato's utopian images are to be found at the beginning (17a-26b) of the _Timaeus_, in the fragment _Critias_ and, of course, in the _Republic_. A fourth dialogue, the so-called _Hermocrates_, supposedly likewise dealt with utopian themes. (In _Critias_ 108a, we find the character Hermocrates promising to discourse at some future date on the ideal "good society.") The _Hermocrates_, if it ever actually existed, is now, at any rate, missing.

[2] Frank E. and Fritzie P. Manuel, _Utopian Thought in the Western World_ (Cambridge, Massachusetts: The Belknap Press of Harvard University Press, 1979), p. 1. See also Elise Boulding, "Utopianism: Problems and Issues in Planning for a Peaceful Society," _Alternatives_ XI (1986), pp. 345-66; Joseph Campbell, _The Masks of God: Primitive Mythology_ (New York: The Viking Press, 1972); A. Dupont Summer, _The Essene Writings from Qumran_, translated by G. Vermes (Oxford: Basil Blackwell, 1961); Sir James Frazier, _The New Golden Bough_, edited by Theodor H. Gastner (New York: Mentor Books, 1964), particularly part viii; C.G. Jung, _The Archetypes and the Collective Unconscious_ (London: Bollingen Press, 1959); Samuel N. Kramer, _Sumerian Mythology_ (New York: Harper and Row, 1961); Margaret Mead, "Toward More Vivid Utopias," _Science_ 126 (November 1957), pp. 957-61; A.R. Radcliffe-Brown, _Structure and Function in Primitive Society_ (New York: The Free Press, 1952), chapter viii; Paul Radin, _Primitive Religion: Its Nature and Origin_ (New York: Dover Publications, Inc., 1957), chapters 1 and 2; and Raymond Ruyer, _L'Utopie et les utopies_ (Paris: Presses Universitaires de France, 1950).

[3] Lewis Mumford, _The Story of Utopias_ (New York: The Viking Press, 1962), chapter 1.

[4] Arthur E. Morgan, _Nowhere Was Somewhere: How History Makes Utopias and Utopias Make History_ (Chapel Hill, North Carolina: University of North Carolina Press, 1946).

[5] David Riesman, "Some Observations on Community Plans and Utopias," in _Selected Essays from Individualism Reconsidered_ (New York: Doubleday Company, 1955).

[6] Ernst Bloch, _Widerstand and Friede: Aufstaze zur Politik_ (Frankfurt, 1968), p. 100. Quoted by Manuel and Manuel, _op. cit._, p. 806.

[7] Harvey Cox, _The Feast of Fools: A Theological Essay on Festivity and Fantasy_ (Cambridge, Massachusetts: Harvard University Press, 1969), especially chapters 4-6; Josef Pieper,

In Tune with the World: A Theory of Festivity, translated by Richard and Clara Winston (Chicago: Franciscan Herald Press, 1973); Alvin Toffler, Future Shock (New York: Random House, 1970), pp. 466-70; Johan Huizinga, Homo Ludens: A Study of the Play Element in Culture (Boston: Beacon Press, 1955), especially chapters I and VIII; Simone de Beauvoir, The Ethics of Ambiguity, translated by Bernard Frechtman (Secaucus, New Jersey: The Citadel Press, 1971), especially part II. Individual citations for Nietzsche on festivity and utopianism are too numerous to list, but for overviews which quote the pertinent primary material, see Lawrence M. Hinman, "Nietzsche's Philosophy of Play," Philosophy Today 18 (1974), pp. 106-24, and my "The Ontological Basis of Nietzsche's Perspectivism," Dialogue 24 (April 1982), pp. 35-46.

[8]Karl Mannheim, Ideology and Utopia: An Introduction to the Sociology of Knowledge, translated by Louis Wirth and Edward Shils (New York: Harcourt, Brace and Co., 1956).

[9]Ibid., p. 208.

[10]Henri Lefevbre, The Sociology of Marx, translated by Norman Guterman (New York: Columbia University Press, 1982), p. 62.

[11]For a discussion of Destutt de Tracy, see George Boas, French Philosophers of the Romantic Period (Baltimore: The Johns Hopkins Press, 1925), chapter 2.

[12]Frederich Engels, Ludwig Feuerbach and the End of Classical Philosophy, no translator cited (Peking: Foreign Language Press, 1975), p. 55.

[13]Karl Marx and Frederich Engels, The German Ideology, edited by R. Pascal (New York: International Publishers, 1965), p. 14.

[14]Engels to Franz Mehring, in Karl Marx and Frederich Engels, Selected Correspondence, edited by S.W. Ryazanskaya (Moscow: Progress Publishers, 1975).

[15]The German Ideology, op. cit., p. 2.

[16]Ibid., p. 14.

[17]"The Method of Political Economy" in the "Introduction" (Notebook M) to the Grundrisse: Foundations of the Critique of Political Economy, translated by Martin Nicolaus (New York: Vintage Books, 1973), pp. 100-108.

[18]Ludwig Feuerbach, op. cit., p. 55.

[19]Selected Correspondence, op. cit.

296

[20]The German Ideology, op. cit., p. 20.

[21]Ibid., pp. 39-40.

[22]Ibid., p. 39.

[23]Karl Marx and Fredrich Engels, Collected Works, II (New York: International Publishers, 1973), pp. 130-31.

[24]Ibid.

[25]The German Ideology, op. cit., pp. 40-41.

[26]See, for instance, Nikolai Bukharin, Historical Materialism: A System of Sociology, no translator cited (Ann Arbor, Michigan: University of Michigan Press, 1978).

[27]Ideology and Utopia, op. cit., p. 55.

[28]Ibid.

[29]Ibid., pp. 55-56.

[30]Ibid., p. 56.

[31]Ibid.

[32]Ibid., p. 87.

[33]Ibid., p. 57.

[34]Ibid., p. 61.

[35]For interesting accounts of antebellum attitudes towards slavery in the South, see Ante-Bellum: Writings of George Fitzhugh and Hinton Rowan Helper on Slavery, edited by Harvey Wish (New York: Capricorn Books, 1960).

[36]Ideology and Utopia, op. cit., p. 57.

[37]Ibid.

[38]Ibid., pp. 59-60.

[39]Ibid., p. 59.

[40]Ibid., p. 57.

[41]Ibid., p. 193.

[42]Ibid., p. 196.

[43]Ibid., p. 40.

297

[44]Ibid., p. 193.

[45]Ibid., p. 95.

[46]Ibid., p. 63.

[47]Ibid., p. 194.

[48]Ibid., p. 196.

[49]Ibid., p. 192.

[50]Ibid.

[51]Ibid., p. 194.

[52]Ibid., p. 195-196.

[53]Ibid., p. 8.

[54]Ibid., pp. 6-7.

[55]Ibid., p. 7.

[56]Ibid., p. 9.

[57]Ibid., p. 10.

[58]Ibid.

[59]Ibid.

[60]Ibid., p. 11.

[61]Ibid.

[62]Ibid., p. 12.

[63]Ibid., p. 207.

[64]Ibid., p. 206.

[65]Ibid., p. 197.

[66]For an excellent short analysis of the ideological elements in nineteenth-century capitalist as well as Marxist "utopias," see Immanuel Wallerstein, "Marxisms as Utopias: Evolving Ideologies," American Council of Sociology 91 (May 1986), pp. 1295-1308.

Chapter Two

[1]Mill was so impressed by the Novum Organum's Tables of Presence, Absence and Degree that he reproduced them in his System of Logic's "Joint Method of Agreement and Difference" (London: Longmans, Green & Co., 1919), pp. 258-59. Herschel expressed his regard for Bacon in the following passage from his Preliminary Discourse on Natural Philosophy: "...by the discoveries of Copernicus, Kepler, Galileo, the errors of the Aristotelian philosophy were effectively overturned on a plain appeal to the facts of nature; but it remained to show on broad and general principles, how and why Aristotle was in the wrong; to set in evidence the peculiar weakness of his method of philosophizing, and to substitute in its place a stronger and better. This important task was executed by Francis Bacon." (London: Longmans, Rees, Orme, Brown and Green, and John Taylor, 1831), pp. 113-14.

[2]William Leiss, The Domination of Nature (Boston: Beacon Press, 1974), pp. 46-47.

[3]Ibid., p. 45.

[4]Ibid., pp. 44-45.

[5]Ibid., p. 47.

[6]E. J. Dijksterhuis, The Mechanization of the World Picture, translated by C. Dikshoorn (Oxford: Oxford University Press, 1969), p. 402.

[7]Benjamin Farrington, The Philosophy of Francis Bacon: An Essay on Its Development from 1603 to 1609 (Chicago: University of Chicago Press, 1966).

[8]Novum Organum I, paragraphs 41-77, in Francis Bacon, Advancement of Learning and Novum Organum, ed. James Edward Creighton (New York: Willey Book Co., 1944).

[9]It is clear that Bacon's schematization of the idola is an early attempt--perhaps one of the first--to work out a theory of ideology. In Mannheimian terms, Bacon's Idols of the Theatre correspond to total ideological structures, while the other three idola, to one degree or another, are analogous to the structure which Mannheim calls particular ideology. One probably shouldn't make too much of the resemblance, but it does exist, at least on a superficial level. In fact, Mannheim himself recognizes the similarity in Ideology and Utopia (pp. 61-62, op. cit.).

[10]Francis Bacon, The Masculine Birth of Time, translated by Benjamin Farrington, in The Philosophy of Francis Bacon, op. cit., p. 63.

[11]Ibid., p. 69.

[12]Francis Bacon, The Refutation of Philosophies, translated by Benjamin Farrington, in The Philosophy of Francis Bacon, op. cit., p. 115.

[13]Birth of Time, op. cit., p. 63.

[14]Refutation, op. cit., p. 112.

[15]Birth of Time, op. cit., p. 64.

[16]Ibid.

[17]Ibid., p. 69.

[18]Refutation, op. cit., p. 118.

[19]Ibid., p. 122.

[20]Birth of Time, op. cit., p. 71.

[21]Refutation, op. cit., p. 121.

[22]Francis Bacon, The Great Instauration, pp. 33-34, in The Works of Francis Bacon, Vol. 1: Philosophical Writings, edited by Spedding, Ellis and Heath (Boston: Houghton, Mifflin & Company, n.d.).

[23]Novum Organum I, op. cit., paragraph 106.

[24]Ibid., paragraph 10.

[25]I am indebted here to John Losee's discussion of Bacon in his A Historical Introduction to the Philosophy of Science (Oxford: Oxford University Press, 1971), pp. 62-64; and to Paolo Rossi's excellent Francis Bacon: From Magic to Science, translated by Sacha Rabinovitch (Chicago: University of Chicago Press, 1968), especially chapters II, IV and VI.

[26]For Bacon's criticism of Aristotelian induction, see Novum Organum I, op. cit., paragraphs 103-14.

[27]Novum Organum I, op. cit., paragraphs 14, 15.

[28]"Preface" to The Great Instauration, op. cit., p. 31.

[29]"Plan of the Work" to The Great Instauration, op. cit., p. 41.

[30]"Proemium" to The Great Instauration, op. cit., p. 18.

[31]Novum Organum I, op. cit., paragraph 3. To my knowledge, Bacon never actually uses the locution, commonly ascribed to him,

that "knowledge is power."

[32]"Plan of the Work," The Great Instauration, op. cit., pp. 40-41.

[33]Ibid., p. 43.

[34]Ibid., p. 42.

[35]Ibid., p. 44.

[36]John Losee, op. cit., p. 65.

[37]Novum Organum II, op. cit., paragraph 10.

[38]Ibid.

[39]Rossi, op. cit., pp. 212-15.

[40]Ibid., p. 214.

[41]Novum Organum II, op. cit., paragraph 36.

[42]Ibid.

[43]"Plan of the Work," The Great Instauration, op. cit., p. 42.

[44]Novum Organum II, op. cit., paragraph 11-35.

[45]Ibid., paragraph 17.

[46]Ibid., paragraph 10.

[47]"Preface," The Great Instauration, op. cit., p. 34.

[48]Losee, op. cit., pp. 63-64.

[49]Rossi, op. cit., pp. 212-31.

[50]Bacon was quite familiar with Ramus' works, as evidenced by the frequent denunciations of him scattered throughout the former's corpus. And indeed, as Rossi argues, it would have been odd if an intellectual of Bacon's time had been ignorant of Ramus, given the rhetorician's pervasive influence in the seventeenth century. Does Bacon protest too much?

[51]For more on the Aristotelian character of Baconian metaphysics, see Losee, op. cit., pp. 67-68.

[52]Abraham Cowley, "Ode to the Royal Society," quoted in Benjamin Farrington, Francis Bacon: Philosopher of Industrial Science (London: Lawrence and Wishart Ltd., 1957), p. 17.

[53]Novum Organum I, op. cit., paragraph 54.

[54]Ibid., paragraph 58.

[55]Thomas More seems to have had a more realistic appreciation of the dangerous consequences of the enclosure of the commons than Bacon. His well-known quip in Utopia that "shepe now eat men," instead of the other way around, is an adequate appraisal of the effect, in Britain at least, of increased international wool competition.

[56]Leiss, op. cit., p. 48.

[57]Keith Thomas, Man and the Natural World: A History of the Modern Sensibility (New York: Pantheon Books, 1983).

[58]Ibid., p. 49.

[59]Novum Organum I, op. cit., paragraph 34.

[60]"Preface," The Great Instauration, op. cit., p. 36.

[61]Novum Organum I, op. cit., paragraph 34.

[62]Francis Bacon, Thoughts and Conclusions, translated by Benjamin Farrington, in The Philosophy of Francis Bacon, op. cit., p. 92.

[63]Quoted by Leiss, op. cit., p. 57.

[64]Ibid., p. 56.

[65]Ibid., p. 57.

[66]Francis Bacon: Philosopher of Industrial Science, op. cit., p. 17.

[67]"Preface," The Great Instauration, op. cit., p. 27.

[68]Francis Bacon: Philosopher of Industrial Science, op. cit., p. 13.

[69]"Preface," The Great Instauration, op. cit., pp. 28-29.

[70]Novum Organum I, op. cit., paragraph 75.

[71]Francis Bacon: Philosopher of Industrial Science, op. cit., p. 13.

[72]For a well-documented, detailed account of the rise of the British middle class as an economic power, see Karl Marx, Capital I, chapters 26-33 (various translations and editions).

[73]Novum Organum I, op. cit., paragraph 129.

[74]Karl Marx, Capital I, p. 897. For descriptions of labor legislation after Edward IV, see pp. 897 ff.

[75]Francis Bacon, "Of the True Greatness of the Kingdom of England," pp. 80-81, in The Works of Francis Bacon, Vol. 1: Philosophical Writings, op. cit.

[76]Francis Bacon, The New Atlantis, p. 372, in The Works of Francis Bacon, Vol. 1: Philosophical Writings, op. cit.

[77]Ibid., p. 412.

[78]Ibid., p. 382.

[79]Ibid., p. 398.

[80]Ibid., pp. 395-96.

[81]Ibid., pp. 396-97.

[82]Ibid., p. 389.

[83]Ibid., p. 387.

[84]Carolyn Merchant, The Death of Nature: Women, Ecology, and the Scientific Revolution (San Francisco: Harper & Row, 1980), especially chapters 7, 8 and 9.

[85]The New Atlantis, op. cit., p. 392.

[86]Ibid., p. 393.

[87]Ibid., p. 394.

[88]Ibid., p. 371.

Chapter Three

[1]By the phrase "nineteenth century" I mean the years between the final defeat of Napoleon at Waterloo in 1815 and the advent of World War I in 1914. Although a strict chronological definition of the nineteenth century falls, of course, between 1800 and 1899, the century of 1815-1914 is characterized by a discernable unity of conceptual and normative thought which has come to be associated with this particular era in Western history. Thus the period 1815-1914 will serve as the logical although not strictly chronological setting for this discussion.

[2]Geoffrey Bruun, Nineteenth Century European Civilization,

1815-1914 (Oxford: Oxford University Press, 1967), p. 138.

[3]Ibid., pp. 138-39.

[4]Ibid., pp. 139-40.

[5]Quoted in Dolf Sternberger, Panorama of the Nineteenth Century, translated by Joachim Neugroschel (New York: Urizen Books, 1977), pp. 21-22.

[6]Quoted by Sternberger, op. cit., p. 32.

[7]Ibid., p. 34.

[8]Quoted in Charles Moraze, The Triumph of the Middle Classes, translated by George Weidenfeld (New York: Anchor Books, 1968), p. 123.

[9]Ibid., p. 124.

[10]See Frank B. Manuel, The New World of Henri Saint-Simon (Cambridge, Massachusetts: Harvard University Press, 1956), p. 119.

[11]Auguste Comte, Positive Philosophy, translated by Harriet Martineau (London: 1893), volume II, p. 61.

[12]For Bentham, a "good" or "bad" disposition is determined by "the nature of the motives [the agent] is apt to be influenced by." But the nature of motives is in turn determined by the subject's perception (be it accurate or inaccurate) of the likely consequences of any action performed in a given social environment. As such, both an individual's specific motives and general disposition are dependent upon those prudential and exhortatory norms which characterize the social milieu in which he finds himself. "Social considerations," then, are the final determining factors in the individual's pursuit of pleasure or the avoidance of pain. See Bentham's An Introduction to the Principles of Morals and Legislation, chapter XI, "Of Human Dispositions in General," in A Bentham Reader, edited by Mary Peter Mach (New York: Pegasus Books, 1969), pp. 113-17. See also the analyses of Bentham's espousal of an artificial harmony of interests based upon social sanctions in Anthony Quinton, Utilitarian Ethics (New York: St. Martin's Press, 1973), pp. 5-11, and Alasdair MacIntyre, A Short History of Ethics (New York: MacMillan Publishing Co., 1966), pp. 232-35. For a discussion of utilitarianism's early "mathematical" morality and its historical relation to later behavioristic psychology, see Floyd W. Matson, The Broken Image: Man, Science and Society (New York: George Braziller, 1964), pp. 31-49.

[13]Richard Hofstadter, Social Darwinism in American Thought (Boston: Beacon Press, 1972), p. 37.

[14]Herbert Spencer, Social Statics (New York: Robert Schalkenback Foundation, 1956), pp. 79-80.

[15]The pervasive influence of the mechanistic worldview upon the nineteenth century is aptly expressed by the following eulogy to Spencer written by one F.A.P. Barnard:

"As it seems to me, we have in Herbert Spencer not only the profoundest thinker of our time, but the most capacious and most powerful intellect of all time. Aristotle and his master were no more beyond the pygmies who preceded them than he is beyond Aristotle. Kant, Hegel, Fichte, and Schelling are gropers in the dark by the side of him. In all the history of science, there is but one name which can be compared to his, and that is Newton's..." (Quoted by Hofstadter, op. cit., p. 31.

Although this passage is a bit florid, it is by no means nonrepresentative.

[16]Moraze, op. cit., p. 107.

[17]Ibid.

[18]Brunn, op. cit., p. 152.

[19]Cambridge Economic History of Europe IV, edited by H.J. Habakkuk and M. Postan (Cambridge: Cambridge University Press, 1965), Part 1, p. 17.

[20]Bruun, op. cit., pp. 153-54.

[21]Ibid., p. 185.

[22]Ibid.

[23]For an account of Bismarck's turbulent relationship with nineteenth-century German socialism, see Edward Crankshaw, Bismarck (London: Penguin Books, 1983), pp. 208-303.

[24]Bruun, op. cit., p. 169.

[25]Ibid.

[26]Ibid.

[27]Glenn Robert Negley, Utopian Literature: A Bibliography (Lawrence, Kansas: The Regents Press of the University of Kansas, 1977), pp. 221-28.

[28]The most famous of these "pastoral utopias"--visions of the future ideal society which eschew technology and call for a

return to a bucolic existence--is William Morris' _News from Nowhere_.

[29]E.A. Burtt, _The Metaphysical Foundations of Modern Science_ (Garden City, New Jersey: Doubleday Anchor Books, 1955), pp. 238-39.

[30]For a fascinating account of the emphasis upon technological success in American utopianism, see Howard P. Segal, _Technological Utopianism in American Culture_ (Chicago: University of Chicago Press, 1985).

[31]Jean Meynard's _Technocracy_, trans. Paul Barnes (New York: The Free Press, 1969) explores the dynamics of a political structure supervised by "experts"--or what Meynard calls "_technicians_."

[32]W.J. Reader, _Life in Victorian England_ (New York: Capricorn Books, 1967), pp. 71-72.

[33]Bruun, _op. cit._, p. 161.

[34]Reader, _op. cit._, p. 74.

[35]_Ibid._, p. 75.

[36]_Ibid._

[37]_Ibid._, p. 72.

[38]For the classic nineteenth-century account of the period's conditions in industrial areas, see Friedrich Engels, _The Condition of the Working Class in England_, no translator cited (Moscow: Progress Publishers, 1973).

[39]Quoted in Reader, _op. cit._, p. 79.

[40]_Ibid._

[41]_Ibid._, p. 80.

[42]_Ibid._, p. 81.

[43]Quoted in _Ibid._, p. 83.

[44]The squalid conditions characteristic of life for the nineteenth-century laboring classes were graphically captured by several novelists of the period. Charles Dickens' _Oliver Twist_, _David Copperfield_ and _Nicholas Nickleby_, George Gissing's _The Nether World_ and _New Grub Street_, Victor Hugo's _Les Miserables_, Robert Tressell's _The Ragged Trousered Philanthropists_ and Emile Zola's _Germinal_ are representative examples.

[45]Quoted in Reader, _op. cit._, p. 86.

[46]Ibid., p. 87.

[47]Quoted in Ibid., pp. 87-88.

[48]Charles Dickens, Oliver Twist, Volume 1, in the Collected Works (New York: Peter Fenelon Collier, Publishers, n.d.), p. 31.

[49]Quoted in Reader, op. cit., p. 88.

[50]Ibid., p. 76.

[51]Harry Braverman, Labor and Monopoly Capitalism: The Degradation of Work in the Twentieth Century (New York: Monthly Review Press, 1974), p. 90.

[52]Frederick W. Taylor, Principles of Scientific Management, in Taylor's Testimony before the Special House Committee (New York: 1947), p. 36.

[53]Frederick W. Taylor, Shop Management, in Taylor's Testimony before the Special House Committee, op. cit., pp.98-99.

[54]Principles of Scientific Management, op. cit., p. 63.

[55]Braverman, op. cit., p. 136.

[56]Quoted in Reader, op. cit., p. 83.

[57]A phrase coined by George Gissing, in his novel of the same title (published 1889), to describe the nineteenth century's working class.

[58]Reader, op. cit., pp.89-90.

[59]Herbert Spencer, The Principles of Sociology II (New York: D. Appleton & Co., 1897), pp. 240-41.

[60]Charles Darwin, The Descent of Man (London: J. Murray, 1874), pp. 151-52. Hofstadter (op. cit., p. 91) argues, however, that this and similar expressions, influential as they might have been upon advocates of Social Darwinism, were "not characteristic of Darwin's moral sentiments, for he went on to say that a ruthless policy of elimination would betray 'the noblest part of our nature', which is itself securely founded in the social instincts. We must therefore bear with the evil effects of the survival and propagation of the weak, and rest our hopes on the fact that 'the weaker and inferior members of society do not marry so freely as the sound'. He also advocated that all who cannot spare their children abject poverty should refrain from marriage; here again he lapsed into Malthusianism with the statement that the prudent should not shirk their duty of

maintaining population, for it is through the pressure of population and the consequent struggles that man has advanced and will continue to advance." All in all, it would appear that Hofstadter's efforts to rehabilitate Darwin's "moral sentiments" are ineffective. John C. Green's Darwin and the Modern World View (Baton Rouge: Louisiana State University Press, 1981), likewise agrees that Darwin accepted natural selection "as the architect and agency of social progress" (98).

Chapter Four

[1] Frank E. and Fritzie P. Manuel, Utopian Thought in the Western World (Cambridge, Massachusetts: The Belknap Press of Harvard University Press, 1979), p. 760.

[2] For discussions of other nineteenth-century utopian novels, see Marie Louise Berneri, Journey through Utopia (Boston: Beacon Press, 1950), chapters V and VI; and Frank E. and Fritzie P. Manuel, op. cit., chapter 32.

[3] Arthur Lipow, Authoritarian Socialism in America: Edward Bellamy and the Nationalist Movement (Berkeley, California: University of California Press, 1982), p. 30.

[4] For Lenin's analysis of state capitalism, see especially his The State and Revolution (New York: International Publishers, 1978).

[5] Lipow, op. cit., pp. 4, 30. According to advertising statistics from the Houghton Mifflin Company, sales figures for Bellamy's novel in the fourteen months are as follows:

November, 1889......175,000

December, 1889......210,000

February, 1890......301,000

March, 1890........310,000

May, 1890..........330,000

July, 1890.........347,000

January, 1891.......371,000

(Cited in Robert L. Shurter, The Utopian Novel in America, 1865-1900, New York: AMS Press, Inc., 1973, p. 138.)

[6]There were, however, hostile reactions to Bellamy's sane society. Most of them were based upon the mistaken notion that Bellamy was anti-capitalist and the less mistaken notion that he was likewise anti-Christian. Richard Michaelis, in his _Looking Further Backward_ (Chicago: Rand McNally, 1890) says (p. iii): "_Looking Backward_ is an effort to improve the lot of mankind and therefore commendable, but its reform proposition, stripped of its fine coloring, is nothing but communism, a state of society, which has proved a failure whenever established without a religious basis and which without such basis is in vogue today only among some barbarous and cannibal tribes." J.W. Roberts, in _Looking Within: The Misleading Tendencies of "Looking Backward" Made Manifest_ (New York: A.S. Barnes, 1893) says (p.iii): "The object of this work is to throw light upon the enigmatical problem [of how it was possible for a people to become willing slaves, to] warn fellow-citizens of the dangers that threaten them from the alluring delusion which, like an _ignis fatuus_, is leading them along the slippery path of ruin, and prevent any such catastrophe from ever overtaking our beloved country in the future." And W.W. Satterlee's _Looking Backward and What I Saw_ (Minneapolis: Harrison & Smith, 1890) agrees with the above estimations (p. vii): "It is the main fault of this as of all other forms of socialism, that it ignores the fact of the natural depravity of the race, provides no adequate remedy for the disease of sin, and in every tenet denies the law of man's being which makes adversity a developing power, and antagonisms the rung in the ladder of human endeavor, which aid in lifting him to the highest possibilities of his manhood."

[7]Edward Bellamy, _Looking Backward, 2000-1887_ (New York: Grosset & Dunlap, 1898), p. 42.

[8]Ibid.

[9]Ibid., pp. 55-56.

[10]Ibid., p. 244.

[11]Ibid., pp. 229-30.

[12]Ibid., p. 181.

[13]Ibid., p. 182.

[14]Ibid., p. 87.

[15]Ibid.

[16]As one of the inhabitants of new Boston tells Julian, "We buy where we please, though naturally most often near home. But I should have gained nothing by visiting other stores [sic]. The assortment in all is exactly the same, representing as it does in each case samples of all the varieties produced or

imported by the United States. That is why one can decide quickly, and never need visit two stores." Ibid., p. 105.

[17]Ibid., p. 187.

[18]Ibid., p. 126.

[19]Ibid., pp. 242-43.

[20]Ibid., p. 41.

[21]Ibid., pp. 118-19.

[22]Ibid., p. 116.

[23]Ibid., p. 90.

[24]Ibid., pp. 60-61.

[25]Ibid., p. 134.

[26]Ibid., p. 268.

[27]Ibid., p. 132.

[28]Ibid., p. 98.

[29]Ibid., p. 177.

[30]Ibid., p. 157.

[31]Ibid., p. 356.

[32]Ibid., p. 257.

[33]Ibid., p. 260.

[34]Ibid., pp. 290,292.

[35]Ibid., p. 49.

[36]Ibid., p. 221.

[37]Ibid., p. 224.

[38]Ibid., p. 79.

[39]Ibid., p. 199.

[40]Ibid., p. 225.

[41]Frank E. and Fritzie Manuel, Utopian Thought in the Western World, op. cit., p. 771.

[42]Glenn Negley, in his admirable <u>Utopian Literature: A Bibliography</u> (Lawrence, Kansas: The Regents Press of Kansas, 1977) defends this date (p. 72).

[43]M. Auburre Hovorre, <u>The Milltillionaire</u>, in <u>American Utopias</u>, edited by Arthur O. Lewis, Jr. (New York: Arno Press & The New York Times, 1971), pp. 1-30.

[44]Perhaps Hovorre calls his society the "Bardic State" to emphasize that it is a work of art, perfectly coordinated and perfectly executed. Unfortunately, however, it is also perfectly lifeless.

[45]<u>The Milltillionaire</u>, <u>op</u>. <u>cit</u>., p. 4.

[46]<u>Ibid</u>.

[47]<u>Ibid</u>., p. 5.

[48]<u>Ibid</u>., p. 8.

[49]<u>Ibid</u>., p. 14.

[50]<u>Ibid</u>., pp. 14, 15.

[51]<u>Ibid</u>.

[52]<u>Ibid</u>., p. 6.

[53]<u>Ibid</u>., p. 19.

[54]<u>Ibid</u>., p. 10.

[55]<u>Ibid</u>.

[56]<u>Ibid</u>., p. 7.

[57]<u>Ibid</u>., p. 8.

[58]<u>Ibid</u>.

[59]<u>Ibid</u>., p. 9.

[60]<u>Ibid</u>., pp. 9, 10.

[61]<u>Ibid</u>., pp. 15, 16.

[62]<u>Ibid</u>., p. 17.

[63]<u>Ibid</u>., p. xviii.

[64]<u>Ibid</u>., p. 6.

[65]<u>Ibid</u>., p. 13.

[66]Ibid., p. 21.

[67]Ibid., p. 12.

[68]Ibid.

[69]Ibid., p. 27.

[70]Ibid., p 10.

[71]See Richard Stites "Introduction" to Alexander Bogdanov, Red Star: The First Bolshevik Utopia, translated by Charles Rougle (Bloomington, Indiana: Indiana University Press, 1984), pp. 1-16.

[72]For a short biography of Malinovski/Bogdanov, see William E. Harkins, Dictionary of Russian Literature (New York: Philosophical Library, 1956), pp. 26-27.

[73]For more on Bogdanov's "Tektology," see Stites, op. cit., pp. 10-13.

[74]Bogdanov, op. cit., p. 34.

[75]Ibid., p. 133.

[76]Ibid., p. 28.

[77]Ibid., p. 29.

[78]Ibid., p. 34.

[79]Ibid., p. 37.

[80]Ibid., p. 79.

[81]Ibid.

[82]Ibid., pp. 79-80.

[83]Ibid., p. 63.

[84]Ibid., p. 67.

[85]Ibid., p. 63.

[86]Ibid., p. 66.

[87]Ibid., p. 70.

[88]Ibid., p. 77.

[89]Ibid., p. 44.

[90]Ibid.

[91]Ibid., p. 74.

[92]Ibid., p. 77.

[93]Ibid., p. 78.

[94]Ibid., p. 77.

Chapter Five

[1]See, for example, D.F. Fleming, The Origins and Legicies of World War I (New York: Doubleday and Company, Inc., 1968), which characterizes the war "as the great turning point of modern history, the catastrophic collapse which opened the way for others, perhaps the final one." (p. v); Reginald Pound, The Lost Generation (London: Constable and Co., Ltd., 1964), which argues that the "biological health" of Britain was shattered by the conflict (pp. 272-76); Rene Albrect-Carrie, "Economic Consequences" in The First World War: Causes, Conduct, Consequences, edited by Joachim Remak (New York: John Wiley and Sons, Inc., 1971) claims that "the single word that sums up best the economic effects of the war is dislocation, and there was no reason to assume that the scattered fragments would be put back together in their old pattern" (p. 81); and Jack J. Roth, "The First World War as a Turning Point" in World War I: A Turning Point in History, edited by Jack J. Roth (New York: Alfred A. Knopf, 1967), which claims that the conflict led to the "decline of the European system" (p. 94). For a more personal account which agrees that the first world war represented a cultural watershed, see Robert Graves, Good-Bye to All That (New York: Blue Ribbon Books, 1930).

[2]For general overviews of Weimar cultural history, see Peter Gay, Weimar Culture: The Outsider as Insider (New York: Harper Torchbooks, 1968) and Walter Laqueur, Weimar: A Cultural History (New York: Capricorn Books, 1974).

[3]In fact, most of the futuristic novels written during this period are "dystopian" rather than "utopian"--i.e., they present the sane society image as horrific rather than desirable. For a general overview of this genre, see Chad Walsh, From Utopia to Nightmare (New York: Harper and Row, 1962).

[4]For general accounts of the Frankfurt School, see Tom Bottomore, The Frankfurt School (London: Tavistock Publications, 1984), Martin Jay, The Dialectical Imagination: A

[25]Ibid., p. 555.

[26]C. Wright Mills, The Sociological Imagination (New York: Oxford University Press, 1959).

[27]Ibid., p. 55.

[28]Ibid., p. 50.

[29]Ibid., pp. 55-58.

[30]Ibid., p. 57.

[31]Ibid., p. 56.

[32]Bernard Berelson, "The Study of Public Opinion" in The State of the Social Sciences, edited by Leonard D. White (Chicago: University of Chicago Press, 1956), pp. 304-5; Mills, op. cit., p. 54.

[33]Ibid., pp. 51, 57.

[34]Clark L. Hull, Principles of Behavior: An Introduction to Behavior Theory (New York: Appleton-Century, 1943), p. 28.

[35]Ibid., p. v.

[36]Ibid., p. 27.

[37]Ibid., p. 399.

[38]Clark L. Hull, A Behavior System: An Introduction to Behavior Theory Concerning the Individual Organism (New York: Yale University Press, 1952), p. 345.

[39]Ibid.

[40]Principles of Behavior, op. cit., p. 401.

[41]Compare Norwood Russell Hanson's arguments against the doctrine of the immaculate perception in his Patterns of Discovery (Cambridge University Press, 1958).

[42]The Sociological Imagination, op. cit., p. 64.

[43]Harry Braverman, Labor and Monopoly Capitalism: The Degradation of Work in the Twentieth Century (New York: Monthly Review Press, 1974), pp. 179-80.

[44]K.J.W. Kraik, "Theory of the Human Operator in Control Systems," British Journal of Psychiatry XXXVIII, pp. 56-61, 142-48; Braverman, op. cit., p. 179.

314

[45]For a recent criticism of this type of psychological mechanism, see David Faust and Richard A. Miner's "The Empiricist and the New Clothes: DSM-III in Perspective," _American Journal of Psychiatry_ 143 (1986), pp. 962-67.

[46]Of course there are explicit exceptions to this general trend. B.F. Skinner's _Walden Two_, a twentieth-century self-proclaimed utopia, appears to display many sane society characteristics. Moreover, the novel has enjoyed immense popularity.

[47]Alvin Toffler, _Future Shock_ (New York: Random House, 1970), p. 384.

[48]A particularly intriguing recent analysis may be found in Ashley Montagu and Floyd Matson, _The Dehumanization of Man_ (New York: McGraw-Hill, 1983).

BIBLIOGRAPHY

Bacon, Francis. Advancement of Learning and Novum Organum, edited by James Edward Creighton. New York: Willey Book Co., 1944.

_____. The Works of Francis Bacon. Volume I: Philosophical Writings, edited by Spedding, Ellis and Heath. Boston: Houghton, Mifflin & Company, n.d.

Beauvoir, Simone de. The Ethics of Ambiguity, translated by Bernard Frechtman. Secaucus, New Jersey: The Citadel Press. 1971.

Bellamy, Edward. Looking Backward, 2000-1887. New York: Crosset & Dunlap, 1898.

Bentham, Jeremy. An Introduction to the Principles of Morals and Legislation, edited by Mary Peter Mach. New York: Pegasus Books, 1969.

Berneri, Marie Louise. Journey through Utopia. Boston: Beacon Press, 1950.

Boas, George. French Philosophers of the Romantic Period. Baltimore: The Johns Hopkins Press, 1925.

Bogdanov, Alexander. Red Star: The First Bolshevik Utopia, translated by Charles Rougle. Bloomington, Indiana: Indiana University Press, 1984.

Bottomore, Tom. The Frankfurt School. London: Tavistock Publications, 1984.

Boulding, Elise. "Utopianism: Problems and Issues in Planning for a Peaceful Society," Alternatives XI (1986), pp. 345-66.

Braverman, Harry. Labor and Monopoly Capitalism: The Degradation of Work in the Twentieth Century. New York: Monthly Review Press, 1974.

Bruun, Geoffrey. Nineteenth Century European Civilization, 1815-1914. Oxford: Oxford University Press, 1967.

Bukharin, Nikolai. Historical Materialism: A System of Sociology, no translator cited. Ann Arbor, Michigan: University of Michigan Press, 1978.

Burtt, E.A. The Metaphysical Foundations of Modern Science. Garden City, New Jersey: Doubleday Anchor Books, 1955.

Cambridge Economic History of Europe. Volume IV, edited by H.J.
Habakkuk and M. Poston. Cambridge: Cambridge University
Press, 1965.

Campbell, Joseph. The Masks of God: Primitive Mythology. New
York: The Viking Press, 1972.

Comte, Auguste, Positive Philosophy. Volume II, translated by
Harriet Martineau. London, 1893.

Cox, Harvey. The Feast of Fools: A Theological Essay on
Festivity and Fantasy. Cambridge, Massachusetts: Harvard
University Press, 1969.

Crankshaw, Edward. Bismarck. London: Penguin Books, 1983.

Darwin, Charles. The Descent of Man. London: J. Murray, 1874.

Dickens, Charles. The Works of Charles Dickens. Volume I:
Oliver Twist. New York: Peter Fenelon Collier, Publishers,
n.d.

Dijksterhuis, E.J. The Mechanization of the World Picture,
translated by C. Dikshoorn. Oxford: Oxford University
Press, 1969.

Dupont-Summer, A. The Essene Writings from Qumran, translated by
G. Vermes. Oxford: Basil Blackwell, 1961.

Engels, Friedrich. The Conditions of the Working Class in
England, no translator cited. Moscow: Progress Publishers,
1973.

_____. Ludwig Feuerback and the End of Classical Philosophy, no
translator cited. Peking: Foreign Language Press, 1976.

Farrington, Benjamin. Francis Bacon: Philosopher of Industrial
Science. London: Lawrence and Wishart Ltd., 1957.

_____. The Philosophy of Francis Bacon: An Essay on Its
Development from 1603 to 1609. Chicago: University of
Chicago Press, 1966.

Faust, David and Richard A. Miner. "The Empiricist and the New
Clothes: DSM-III in Perspective." American Journal of
Psychology 143 (1986), pp. 962-67.

Fleming, D.F. The Origins and Legacies of World War I. New
York: Doubleday & Company, Inc., 1968.

Frazier, Sir James. The New Golden Bough, edited by Theodor H.
Gastner. New York: Mentor Books, 1964.

Gay, Peter. Weimar Culture: The Outsider as Insider. New York:

Harper Torchbooks, 1968.

Graves, Robert. Good-Bye to All That. New York: Blue Ribbon Books, 1930.

Greene, John C. Darwin and the Modern World View. Baton Rouge: Louisiana State University Press, 1981.

Hanson, Norwood Russell. Patterns of Discovery. Cambridge: Cambridge University Press, 1958.

Harkins, William E. Dictionary of Russian Literature. New York: Philosophical Library, 1956.

Herschel, John. Preliminary Discourse on Natural Philosophy. London: Longmans, Rees, Orme, Brown and Green, and John Taylor, 1831.

Hinman, Lawrence M. "Nietzsche's Philosophy of Play," Philosophy Today 18 (1974), pp. 106-24.

Hofstadter, Richard. Social Darwinism in American Thought. Boston: Deacon Press, 1972.

Horkheimer, Max. Eclipse of Reason. New York: The Seabury Press, 1974.

Hovorre, M. Auburre. The Milltillionaire. In American Utopias, edited by Arthur O. Lewis, Jr. New York: Arno Press, 1971.

Huizinga, Johan. Homo Ludens: A Study of the Play Element in Culture. Boston: Beacon Press, 1955.

Hull, Clark L. A Behavior System: An Introduction to Behavior Theory Concerning the Individual Organism. New York: Yale University Press, 1952.

_____. Principles of Behavior: An Introduction to Behavior Theory. New York: Appleton-Century, 1943.

Jay, Martin. The Dialectical Imagination: A History of the Frankfurt Institute of Social Research, 1923-1950. Boston: Little, Brown & Company, 1973.

Jung, C.G. Collected Works. Volume IX. The Archetypes and the Collective Unconscious. London: Bollingen Press, 1959.

Kramer, Samuel N. Sumerian Mythology. New York: Harper and Row, 1961.

Laqueur, Walter. Weimar: A Cultural History. New York: Capricorn Books, 1974.

318

Lefevbre, Henry. The Sociology of Marx, translated by Norman Guterman. New York: Columbia University Press, 1982.

Leiss, William. The Domination of Nature. Boston: Beacon Press, 1974.

Lenin, Vladimir. The State and Revolution, no translator cited. New York: International Publishers, 1978.

Lewis, Arthur O., Jr. (editor) American Utopias. New York: Arne Press, 1971.

Lipow, Arthur. Authoritarian Socialism in America: Edward Bellamy and the Nationalist Movement. Berkeley, California: University of California Press, 1982.

Losee, John. A Historical Introduction to the Philosophy of Science. Oxford: Oxford University Press, 1971.

Lukacs, Georg. History and Class Consciousness: Studies in Marxist Dialectics, translated by Rodney Livingstone. Cambridge, Massachusetts: The MIT Press, 1979.

MacIntyre, Alasdair. A Short History of Ethics. New York: MacMillan Publishing Co., 1966.

Mannheim, Karl. Ideology and Utopia: An Introduction to the Sociology of Knowledge, translated by Louis Wirth and Edward Shils. New York: Harcourt, Brace and Co., 1956.

Manuel, Frank E. The New World of Henri Saint-Simon. Cambridge, Massachusetts: Harvard University Press, 1956.

_____ and Fritzie E. Utopian Thought in the Western World. Cambridge, Massachusetts: The Belknap Press of Harvard University Press, 1979.

Marx, Karl. Capital. Volume 1, translated by Ben Fowkes. New York: Vintage Books, 1977.

_____. Grundrisse: Foundations of the Critique of Political Economy, translated by Martin Nicolaus. New York: Vintage Books, 1973.

_____ and Engels, Friedrich. Collected Works. Volume II, no translator cited. New York: International Publishers, 1973.

_____. The German Ideology, edited by R. Pascal. New York: International Publishers, 1965.

_____. Selected Correspondence, edited by S.W. Ryazanskaya. Moscow: Progress Publishers, 1975.

Matson, Floyd W. The Broken Image: Man, Science and Society. New York: George Braziller, 1964.

Meade, Margaret. "Toward More Vivid Utopias," Science 126 (November 1957), pp. 957-61.

Merchant, Carolyn. The Death of Nature: Women, Ecology and the Scientific Revolution. San Francisco: Harper & Row, 1980.

Meynard, Jean. Technology, translated by Paul Barnes. New York: The Free Press, 1969.

Michaelis, Richard. Looking Further Backward. Chicago: Rand McNally, 1890.

Mill, John Stuart. System of Logic. London: Longmans, Green & Co., 1919.

Mills, C. Wright. Power, Politics and People: The Collected Essays of C. Wright Mills, edited by Irving Louis Horowitz. New York: Oxford University Press, 1963.

_____. The Sociological Imagination. New York: Oxford University Press, 1959.

Montagu, Ashley and Floyd Matson. The Dehumanization of Man. New York: McGraw-Hill, 1983.

Moraze, Charles. The Triumph of the Middle Class, translated by George Weidenfeld. New York: Anchor Books, 1968.

Morgan, Arthur E. Nowhere Was Somewhere: How History Makes Utopias and Utopias Make History. Chapel Hill, North Carolina: University of North Carolina Press, 1946.

Mumford, Lew. The Story of Utopias. New York: The Viking Press, 1962.

Negley, Glenn Robert. Utopian Literature: A Bibliography. Lawrence, Kansas: The Regents Press of the University of Kansas, 1977.

Pieper, Josef. In Tune with the World: A Theory of Festivity, translated by Richard and Clara Winston. Chicago: Franciscan Herald Press, 1973.

Plato. Collected Dialogues, edited by Edith Hamilton and Huntington Cairns. Princeton: Princeton University Press, 1973.

Pound, Reginald. The Lost Generation. London: Constable and Co., Ltd., 1964.

Quinton, Anthony. Utilitarian Ethics. New York: St. Martin's

Press, 1973.

Radcliffe-Brown, A.R. Structure and Function in Primitive Society. New York: The Free Press, 1952.

Radin, Paul. Primitive Religion: Its Nature and Origin. New York: Dover Publications, Inc., 1957.

Reader, W.J. Life in Victorian England. New York: Capricorn Books, 1967.

Remak, Joachim (editor). The First World War: Causes, Conduct, Consequences. New York: John Wiley & Sons, Inc., 1971.

Riesman, David. Selected Essays from Individualism Reconsidered. New York: Doubleday Company, 1955.

Roberts, J.W. Looking Within: The Misleading Tendencies of "Looking Backward" Made Manifest. New York: A.S. Barnes, 1893.

Rossi, Paolo. Francis Bacon: From Magic to Science, translated by Sacha Rabinovitch. Chicago: University of Chicago Press, 1968.

Roth, Jack J. (editor) World War I: A Turning Point in History. New York: Alfred A. Knopf, 1967.

Ruyer, Raymond. L'Utopie et les utopies. Paris: Presses Universitaires de France, 1950.

Satterlee, W.W. Looking Backward and What I Saw. Minneapolis: Harrison and Smith, 1890.

Segal, Howard P. Technological Utopianism in American Culture. Chicago: University of Chicago Press, 1985.

Shurter, Robert L. The Utopian Novel in America, 1865-1900. New York: AMS Press, Inc., 1973.

Spencer, Herbert. The Principles of Sociology. Volume II. New York: D. Appleton & Co., 1897.

_____. Social Statics. New York: Robert Schalkenback Foundation, 1956.

Sternberger, Dolf. Panorama of the Nineteenth Century, translated by Joachim Neugroschel. New York: Urizen Books, 1977.

Tar, Zoltan. The Frankfurt School: The Critical Theories of Max Horkheimer and Theodor Adorno. New York: Schocken Books, 1985.

Taylor, Frederick W. Testimony before the Special House Committee. New York, 1947.

Thomas, Keith. Man and the Natural World: A History of the Modern Sensibility. New York: Pantheon Books, 1983.

Toffler, Alvin. Future Shock. New York: Random House, 1970.

Wallerstein, Immanuel. "Marxisms as Utopias: Evolving Ideologies." American Journal of Sociology 91 (May 1986), pp. 1295-1308.

Walsh, Chad. From Utopia to Nightmare. New York: Harper and Row, 1967.

Walters, Kerry S. "The Ontological Basis of Nietzsche's Perspectivism," Dialogue 24 (April 1982), pp. 35-46.

Wish, Harvey (editor). Writings of George Fitzhugh and Hinton Rowan Helper on Slavery. New York: Capricorn Books, 1960. (1986), pp. 962-67.

INDEX

PROBLEMS IN CONTEMPORARY PHILOSOPHY